ASSEMBLY LANGUAGE PROGRAMMING MADE CLEAR

A SYSTEMATIC APPROACH

80X86 ASSEMBLY LANGUAGE COMPUTER ARCHITECTURE

Howard Dachslager, PhD

cognella® | ACADEMIC PUBLISHING

Bassim Hamadeh, CEO and Publisher
Kassie Graves, Director of Acquisitions and Sales
Jamie Giganti, Senior Managing Editor
Jess Estrella, Senior Graphic Designer
Mieka Portier, Senior Acquisitions Editor
Sean Adams, Project Editor
Alisa Munoz, Licensing Coordinator
Christian Berk, Associate Production Editor
Bryan Mok, Interior Designer

Cover image copyright © iStockphoto LP/BlackJack3D.

Printed in the United States of America.

ISBN: 978-1-5165-1422-9 (pbk) / 978-1-5165-1423-6 (br)

To the faculty of the Computer Science Department, Irvine College:

Seth Hochwald, Albert Murtz, and Chan Loke

TABLE OF CONTENTS

ABOUT THE AUTHOR

Howard Dachslager received a PhD in mathematics from the University of California, Berkeley, where he specialized in real analysis and probability theory. Prior to beginning his doctoral studies at UC Berkeley, he earned a master's degree in economics from the University of Wisconsin.

After graduating from the University of Wisconsin in 1956, he went to work for Remington Rand Co. as a machine language programmer. For the next two years he worked on various mathematical applications, such as missile guidance systems and tracking systems of naval sea vessels. In 1958 he was admitted as a graduate student to the department of mathematics at UC Berkeley. To finance his education, he worked for the first year as a programmer and programming consultant for the astronomy department at UC Berkeley. During that year he also worked during the summer as a machine language programmer for Lockheed Corporation in Palo Alto, California. His main duty was to find and correct errors in existing programs. Starting his second year at UC Berkeley, he received a teaching assistantship in the mathematics department. His main duty was to teach courses in numerical analysis and programming. He also worked with several professors in this field.

Since completing his PhD in mathematics, he has taught mathematics and programming to a diverse student population on many levels. As a faculty member of the Department of Mathematics at the University of Toronto, he prepared and presented undergraduate-level courses in mathematics. Later he returned to the mathematics and computer science department at UC Berkeley, where he taught undergraduate mathematics and programming courses for several years.

While working in the State Department's Alliance for Progress program, he taught advanced mathematics courses at a statistics institute in Santiago, Chile. Other teaching experience includes presenting undergraduate and community college mathematics courses.

Throughout his teaching career in mathematics and computer science, he has always attempted to find and use the most effective teaching methodologies to communicate an understanding of mathematics and programming. Unable to find an appropriate text for use in his courses in assembly language programming, and drawing on his own extensive teaching experience, education, and training, he developed an assembly language text that has significantly improved the understanding and performance of students in this language.

"Everything should be made as simple as possible, but not simpler."

—Albert Einstein

I. WORKING WITH INTEGER NUMBERS

CHAPTER ONE

NUMBER BASES FOR INTEGERS

INTRODUCTION

In order to become a proficient assembly language programmer, one needs to have a good understanding of how numbers are represented in the assembler. To accomplish this, we start with the basic ideas of integer numbers. In later chapters we will expand these numbers to the various forms that are needed. We will also later study decimal numbers as floating point numbers.

1.1   DEFINITION OF INTEGERS

There are three types of integer numbers: positive, negative, and zero.

Definition: The positive integer numbers are represented by the following symbols: 1, 2, 3, 4, ...

Definition: The negative integer numbers are represented by the following symbols:

−1, −2, −3, −4, ...

Definition: The integer number zero is represented by the symbol 0.

Definition: Integers are therefore defined as the following numbers: 0, 1, −1, 2, −2.

Examples:

1. 123

2. −143

3. 44

4. 3333333333333

5. −72

Although the study of these numbers will give us a greater understanding of the types of numbers we are going to be concerned with when writing assembler language program, the reality is that the only kind of numbers the assembler can handle are integers and finite decimals numbers. Further, we need to understand that the assembler cannot work within our decimal number system. The assembler must convert all numbers to the base 2. The number system that we normally work with is in the base 10, and numbers will then be converted by the assembler to the base 2. This chapter will define and examine the various number bases, including those we need to use when programming.

Numbers in the base 10

Definition: The set of all numbers whose digits are 0, 1, 2, 3, 4, 5, 6, 7, 8, 9 are said to be of the base 10.

Representing positive integers in the base 10 in expanded form

Definition: Decimal integers in expanded form:

$$a_n a_{n-1} \cdots a_1 a_0 = a_n \times 10^n + a_{n-1} \times 10^{n-1} + \ldots + a_1 \times 10 + a_0$$

where $a_k = 0, 1, 2, 3, 4, 5, 6, 7, 8, 9$.

Examples:

1. $235 = 2*10^2 + 3*10 + 5$

2. $56{,}768 = 5*10^4 + 6*10^3 + 7*10^2 + 6*10 + 8$

Exercises:

Write the following integers in expanded form:

(a) 56

(b) 26,578

(c) 23,556,891,010

The number system that we use is in the base 10. This because we only use the 10 digits listed above to build our decimal number system. For the following discussion, all numbers will be integers and nonnegative. The following table shows how starting with 0, we systematically create numbers from these 10 digits:

0	1	2	3	4	5	6	7	8	9
10	11	12	13	14	15	16	17	18	19
20	21	22	23	24	25	26	27	28	29
30	31	32	33	34	35	36	37	38	39

::::::::	::::::::	::::::::	::::::::	::::::::	::::::::	::::::::	::::::::	::::::::	::::::::
90	91	92	93	94	95	96	97	98	99
100	101	102	103	104	105	106	107	108	109
::::::::	::::::::	::::::::	::::::::	::::::::	::::::::	::::::::	::::::::	::::::::	::::::::

The way to think about creating these numbers is best described as follows: First we list the 10 digits 0 to 9 (row 1):

0, 1, 2, 3, 4, 5, 6, 7, 8, 9.

At this points we have run out of digits. To continue, we start over again by first writing the digit 1 and to the right placing the digits 0 to 9: (row 2):

10, 11, 12, 13, 14, 15, 16, 17, 18, 19.

Again we have run out of digits. To continue, we start over again by first writing the digit 2 and to the right placing the digits 0 to 9 (row 3):

20, 21, 22, 23, 24, 25, 26, 27, 28, 29.

Continuing this way, we can create the positive integers as shown in the above table.

1.2   NUMBERS IN OTHER BASES

From below, we observe that the numbers 0, 1, 10 are in all bases. Therefore, we have the following expanded forms:

Base 8 (N_8)

Definition: Octal integers in expanded form:

$$a_n a_{n-1} \ldots a_1 a_0 = a_n * 10_8^n + a_{n-1} * 10_8^{n-1} + \ldots + a_1 * 10_8 + a_0$$

where $a_k = 0, 1, 2, 3, 4, 5, 6, 7$.

Examples:

1. $56761 = 5*10_8^4 + 6*10_8^3 + 7*10_8^2 + 6*10_8 + 1$

2. $235 = 2 \times 10_8^2 + 3 \times 10_8 + 5$

This number system is called the octal number system. In the early development of computers, the octal number system was extensively used. How do we develop the octal number system? In the same way we showed how we developed the decimal system; by using only 8 digits:

0, 1, 2, 3, 4, 5, 6, 7.

Note: Integer numbers that are in a base other than 10 will distinguished by a subscript N.

0_8	1_8	2_8	3_8	4_8	5_8	6_8	7_8
10_8	11_8	12_8	13_8	14_8	15_8	16_8	17_8
20_8	21_8	22_8	23_8	24_8	25_8	26_8	27_8
30_8	31_8	32_8	33_8	34_8	35_8	36_8	37_8
::::::::	::::::	::::::::	::::::::	::::::::::	:::::::::	:::::::	:::::::::
70_8	71_8	72_8	73_8	74_8	75_8	76_8	77_8
100_8	101_8	102_8	103_8	104_8	105_8	106_8	107_8
::::::::::	::::::::::	::::::::::	::::::::::	::::::::::	::::::::::	::::::::::	::::::::::

First, we list the eight digits 0 to 7 (row 1):

0, 1, 2, 3, 4, 5, 6, 7.

At this point we have run out of digits. To continue, we start over again by first writing the digit 1 and to the right placing the digits 0 to 7 (row 2):

10, 11, 12, 13, 14, 15, 16, 17.

Again we have run out of digits. To continue, we start over again by first writing the digit 2 and to the right placing the digits 0 to 7 (row 3):

20, 21, 22, 23, 24, 25, 26, 27.

Continuing this way, we can create the positive integers as shown in the above table. We can easily compare the development of the decimal and octal number systems:

DECIMAL NUMBERS	OCTAL NUMBERS (Base 8)
0	0_8
1	1_8
2	2_8
3	3_8
4	4_8
5	5_8
6	6_8
7	7_8
8	10_8
9	11_8
10	12_8
11	13_8
12	14_8
13	15_8
14	16_8
15	17_8
16	20_8
17	21_8
18	22_8
19	23_8
20	24_8
....	....

Exercises:

1. Write the octal number $2,370,123_8$ in expanded form.

2. Write an example of a five-digit octal integer number.

3. In the octal number system, simplify the following expressions:

   (a) $2361_8 + 4_8$

   (b) $33_8 - 2_8$

   (c) $777_8 + 3_8$

4. What is the largest 10-digit octal number?

5. Add on 10 more rows to the above table.

6. We wish to create a number system in the base 5 (N_5). What digits would make up these numbers?

7. Create a 2-column, 21-row table, where the first column contains the decimal numbers 0 to 20 and the second column consists of the corresponding numbers in the base 5, starting with the digit 0.

8. Write out the largest seven-digit number in the base 5.

9. In the base 5 number system, simplify the following expressions:

   $n_5 =$

   (a) $22,212_5 + 3_5$

   (b) $23,333_5 + 2_5$

   (c) $12,011_5 - 2_5$

Base 2 (N_2)

Definition: Binary integers in expanded form:

$$a_n a_{n-1} \dots a_1 a_0 = a_n * 10_2{}^n + a_{n-1} * 10_2{}^{n-1} + \dots + a_1 * 10_2 + a_0$$

where $a_k = 0, 1$.

Examples:

(a) $101 = 1*10_2^2 + 0*10_2 + 1$

(b) $11011 = 1*10_2^4 + 1*10_2^3 + 0*10_2^2 + 1*10_2 + 1$

This number system is called the binary number system. Binary numbers are the most important numbers, since all numbers stored in the assembler are in the base 2. The digits that make these numbers are 0 and 1, and they are called bits. Numbers made from these bits are called the binary numbers.

How do we develop the binary number system? In the same way we showed how to develop the decimal and the octal number system; by using only the two bits: 0 and 1:

DECIMAL NUMBERS	BINARY NUMBERS
0	0_2
1	1_2
2	10_2
3	11_2
4	100_2
5	101_2
6	110_2
7	111_2
8	1000_2
9	1001_2
10	1010_2
11	1011_2
12	1100_2
13	1101_2
14	1110_2
15	1111_2

16	10000_2
17	10001_2
18	10010_2
19	10011_2
20	10100_2
::::::::::::::::::::::	::::::::::::::::::::::

Exercises:

1. Write the binary number 110110101_2 in expanded form.

2. Extend the above table for the integer numbers 21 to 30.

3. Simplify the following:

   (a) $10011_2 + 1_2$

   (b) $1011_2 + 11_2$

   (c) $10111_2 + 111_2$

4. Complete the following table.

OCTAL NUMBERS	BINARY NUMBERS
0_8	
1_8	
2_8	
3_8	
:::::::::	:::::::::::::
16_8	

5. What does the above table tell us about the relationship of the digits of the octal system and the binary numbers?

Base 16 (N_{16})

Definition: Hexadecimal integers in expanded form:

$$a_n\, a_{n-1} \ldots a_1\, a_0 = a_n*10_{16}{}^n + a_{n-1}*10_{16}{}^{n-1} + \ldots + a_1*10_{16} + a_0$$

where $a_k = 0, 1, 2, 3, 4, 5, 6, 7, 8, 9, A, B, C, D, E, F$.

Examples:

1. $2E5 = 2 \times 10_{16}{}^2 + E \times 10_{16} + 5$
2. $56ADF = 5 \times 10_{16}{}^4 + 6 \times 10_{16}{}^3 + A \times 10_{16}{}^2 + D \times 10_{16} + F$

The number system in the base 16 is called the hexadecimal number system. Next to the binary number system, hexadecimal numbers are very important in that these numbers are used extensively to help the programmer interpret the binary numeric values computed by the assembler. Many assemblers will display the numbers only in hexadecimal.

We can easily compare the development of the decimal and hexadecimal number systems:

DECIMAL NUMBERS	HEXADECIMAL NUMBERS
0	0_{16}
1	1_{16}
2	2_{16}
3	3_{16}
4	4_{16}
5	5_{16}
6	6_{16}
7	7_{16}
8	8_{16}
9	9_{16}
10	A_{16}

11	B_{16}
12	C_{16}
13	D_{16}
14	E_{16}
15	F_{16}
16	10_{16}
17	11_{16}
18	12_{16}
19	13_{16}
20	14_{16}
21	15_{16}
22	16_{16}
23	17_{16}
24	18_{16}
25	19_{16}
26	$1A_{16}$
27	$1B_{16}$
28	$1C_{16}$
29	$1D_{16}$
30	$1E_{16}$
31	$1F_{16}$
32	20_{16}
::::::::::	::::::::::::::

Exercises:

1. Write the hexadecimal number $4E0AC1_{16}$ in expanded form.

2. Extend the above table for the decimal integer numbers 33 to 50

3. Simplify $n_{16} =$

    (a) $A_{16} + 6_{16}$

    (b) $FFFF_{16} + 1_{16}$

    (c) $100_{16} + E_{16}$

4. Complete the following table.

OCTAL NUMBERS	HEXADECIMAL NUMBERS
0_8	
1_8	
2_8	
3_8	
....	....
26_8	

5. Complete the following table.

HEXADECIMAL NUMBERS	BINARY NUMBERS
0_{16}	
1_{16}	
2_{16}	
3_{16}	
....	....
$2F_{16}$	

6. What does the above table tell you about the relationship of the binary and hexadecimal numbers?

PROJECT

In assembly language the basic binary numbers are made up of eight bits. A binary number of this type is called a byte. Therefore, a byte is an eight-bit number. For example, the decimal number 5 can be represented as the binary number 00000101.

Complete the following table.

OCTAL BYTE	HEXADECIMAL BYTE	BINARY BYTE	DECIMAL BYTE
00 000 000	0000 0000	00000000	0
00 000 001	0000 0001	00000001	1
:::::::::::::::	::::::::::::	:::::::::::	:::::::::
3 7 7	F F	11111111	255

CHAPTER TWO

RELATIONSHIPS BETWEEN NUMBER BASES

INTRODUCTION

This chapter will examine the one-to-one correspondence that exists between the various number bases. To accomplish this, we approach these number systems as sets.

2.1 SETS

Definition of a set:

A set is a well-defined collection of items where

1. each item in the set is unique

   and

2. the items can be listed in any order.

Examples:

1. $S = \{a, b, c, d\}$

2. $A = \{23, -8, 23.3 \}$

3. $N_{10} = \{0, 1, 2, 3, 4, 5, ...\}$ (base 10)

4. $N_8 = \{0, 1, 2, 3, 4, 5, 6, 7, 10, 11, 12, 13, 14, 15, 16, 17, 20, ...\}$ (base 8)

5. $N_2 = \{0, 1, 10, 11, 100, 101, 110, 111, 1000, ...\}$ (base 2)

6. $N_{16} = \{0, 1, 2, 3, 4, 5, 6, 7, 8, 9, A, B, C, D, E, F, 10, 11, ... 19, 1A, ... 1F, 20 ...\}$ (BASE 16)

Exercises:

1. For the following bases, write out the first 10 numbers as a set in natural order:

   (a) N_3

   (b) N_4

   (c) N_5

   (d) N_6

   (e) N_7

2. Assume we need to define a number system in the base 20 (N_{20}). Create N_{20} by using digits and capital letters. Write out the first 40 numbers in their natural order.

2.2 ONE-TO-ONE CORRESPONDENCE BETWEEN SETS

Assume we have two sets: D and R. The set D is called the domain, and the set R is called the range.

Definition of a one-to-one correspondence between sets:

We say there is a one-to-one correspondence between sets if the following rules hold:

Rule 1: There exists function f : D => R: for every x contained in D, there exists a value y such that y = f(x).

Rule 2: The function f is one-to-one

Rule 3: The function f is onto

Definition of a one to one function:

A function is said to be one-to-one if the following is true:

$$\text{if } f(x_1) = f(x_2) \text{ then } x_1 = x_2 \text{ where } x_1, x_2 \text{ are contained in D.}$$

Definition of an onto function:

A function is said to be onto if the following is true:

$$\text{if for every y in R, there exists a element x in D where f(x) = y.}$$

Change in notation

For such functions, we will use the notation:

D => R

and x => y

If D => R, we write

D => R,

meaning the two sets D and R are in one-to-one correspondence.

Examples:

1. Let D = {1, 2, 3, 4, 5, ...} and R = {2, 4, 6, 8, 10, 12, ...}.

Show there is a one-to-one correspondence between these two sets.

Solution:

k => 2k, where

k = 1, 2, 3, ...

2. D = {1, 2, 3, 4, 5, ...} and R = {1, –1, 2, –2, 3, –3, ...}

Show there is a one-to-one correspondence between these two sets.

Solution:

For the odd numbers of D:

2k + 1 => k + 1

where k = 0, 1, 2, 3, ...

For the even numbers of D:

2k =>–k

k = 1, 2, 3, ...

Combining these into one function gives:

1 => 1

2 => –1

3 => 2

4 => –2

5 => 3

6 => –3

7 => 4

8 => –4

::::::::::

Exercises:

If D = {2, 4, 6, 8, 10, ...} and R = {1, 3, 5, 7, 9, ...}, show that D => R.

2.3   EXPANDING NUMBERS IN THE BASE B (N_B)

In the base 10 system (N_{10}),

$$a_n a_{n-1} \ldots a_1 a_0 = a_n * 10^n + a_{n-1} * 10^{n-1} + \ldots + a_1 * 10 + a_0$$

Does such an expansion hold for all numbers in the base b (N_b) ? The answer is yes, and the expansion can be written as:

$$(a_n a_{n-1} \ldots a_1 a_0)_b = a_n \times 10_b^{\ n} + a_{n-1} \times 10_b^{\ n-1} + \ldots + a_1 \times 10_b + a_0$$

The following explains the validity of this expansion.

First note that the digits of any number in a given base is:

$$0, 1, 2, \ldots b{-}1.$$

Following these digits is the number 10:

$$0, 1, 2, \ldots b{-}1, 10_b.$$

Now in the base b, the following arithmetic holds:

$$0 + 0 = 0, 0 \times 0 = 0, 1 + 0 = 1, 1 \times 1 = 1, a_k \times 0 = 0, a_k \times 1 = a_k, a_k \times 10 = a_k 0.$$

Therefore, the following rules holds for any given base:

$$10_b \times 10_b^{\ n} = 10_b^{\ n+1}$$

and

$$a_n 10_b^{\ n} + a_{n-1} \, 10_b^{\ n-1} + \ldots + a_1 10_b + a_0 = a_n 100\ldots0_b + \ldots + a_1 10_b + a_0 =$$

$$a_n 00\ldots0_b + \ldots + a_1 0_b + a_0.$$

Examples

1. $2562_8 : 2 \times 1000_8 + 5 \times 100_8 + 6 \times 10_8 + 2_8 =$

    $2000_8 + 500_8 + 60_8 + 2_8 = 2562_8$

2. $10111_2 : 1 \times 10000_2 + 0 \times 1000_2 + 1 \times 100_2 + 1 \times 10_2 + 1 =$

    $10000_2 + 000_2 + 100_2 + 10_2 + 1 = 10111_2$

3. $97FA_{16} : 9 \times 1000_{16} + 7 \times 100_{16} + F \times 10_{16} + A_{16} =$

    $9000_{16} + 700_{16} + F0_{16} + A_{16} = 97FA_{16}$

Exercises:

1. Find the expansions for the following numbers in their given bases:

   (a) 4312322_5

   (b) $ABCDEF_{16}$

   (c) 12322_4

   (d) 111101101_2

Finding the one-to-one correspondence between number bases

It is important to be able to find the functions that establish one-to-one correspondence between number bases.

To assist us, we establish the following laws about one-to-one correspondence:

1. If D => R then R => D (reflexive law)

2. If A => B and B => C then A => C (transitive law)

We begin by finding the formula that gives a one-to-one correspondence:

$$N_b => N_{10.}$$

2.4   CONVERTING A NUMBER IN ANY BASE B TO ITS CORRESPONDING NUMBER IN THE BASE 10

We will consider two cases: b < 10 and b = 16.

Case 1: b < 10

Let n_b be an arbitrary number in the base b and n_{10} be an arbitrary number in the base 10.

In chapter 1, we wrote the expanded form of n_b as

$$n_b = a_n\, a_{n-1} \ldots a_1\, a_0 = a_n \times 10_b{}^n + a_{n-1} \times 10_b{}^{n-1} + \ldots + a_1 \times 10_b + a_0$$

where a_k are digits of the base b.

Now we begin by defining the mapping :

$$10_b{}^k => b_{10}{}^k \text{ where } k = 0, ..., n$$

and

10_b is a number in the base b

and

b is a number in the base 10.

Since b < 10, b and all the numbers a_k are in the base b, and they are also in the base 10.

Therefore, we define the mapping:

$$a_n \times 10_b{}^n + a_{n-1} \times 10_b{}^{n-1} + ... + a_1 \times 10_b + a_0 \Rightarrow a_n b^n + a_{n-1} b^{n-1} + ... + a_1 b + a_0$$

which is a number in the base 10.

We can write this as:

$$n_b = a_n a_{n-1} ... a_1 a_0 => a_n b^n + a_{n-1} b^{n-1} + ... + a_1 b + a_0 = n_{10}$$

This give us a one-to-one mapping $N_b => N_{10}$ where

N_b is the set of numbers of the base b

and

N_{10} is the set of numbers of the base 10.

Important: All computations are performed in the base 10.

Note: The above expansion is from right to left.

Examples:

1. $n_5 = 32412_5 = 3_5 \times 10_5{}^4 + 2_5 \times 10_5{}^3 + 4_5 \times 10_5{}^2 + 1_5 \times 10_5{}^1 + 2_5 =>$

   $3_{10} \times 5_{10}{}^4 + 2_{10} \times 5_{10}{}^3 + 4_{10} \times 5_{10}{}^2 + 1_{10} \times 5_{10}{}^1 + 2_{10} =$

   $3(625) + 2(125) + 4(25) + 1(5) + 2 = 2232_{10}$

   Therefore, $32412_5 => 2232_{10}$

2. $n_2 = 1110101_2 =>$

   $1_{10} \times 2_{10}{}^6 + 1_{10} \times 2_{10}{}^5 +$

   $1_{10} \times 2_{10}{}^4 + 0_{10} \times 2_{10}{}^3 +$

   $1_{10} \times 2_{10}{}^2 + 0_{10} \times 2_{10}{}^1 + 1_{10}$

$$= 64 + 32 + 16 + 4 + 1 = 117_{10}$$

Therefore, $1110101_2 => 117_{10}$.

3. $n_8 = 73106_8 => 7_{10} \times 8_{10}{}^4 + 3_{10} \times 8_{10}{}^3 + 1_{10} \times 8_{10}{}^2 + 0_{10} \times 16_{10}{}^1 + 6_{10} = 30278_{10}$

Therefore,

$$73106_8 => 30278_{10}$$

Case 2: b = 16

$(N_{16} => N_{10})$:

For b = 16, we needed to replace the hexadecimal digits which are greater than 9 with the decimal numbers 10, through decimal number 15. The reason we are able to make a correspondence is that we can show there a one to one correspondence between the hexadecimal digits and the corresponding numbers of the decimal system (base 10) as shown in the following table:

BASE 16

0	1	2	3	4	5	6	7	8	9	A	B	C	D	E	F

BASE 10

0	1	2	3	4	5	6	7	8	9	10	11	12	13	14	15

$$n_{16} = a_n a_{n-1} \ldots a_1 a_0 = a_n \times 10_{16}{}^n + a_{n-1} \times 10_{16}{}^{n-1} + \ldots + a_1 \times 10_{16} + a_0$$

Now we begin by defining the mapping:

$$10_{16}{}^k => 16_{10}{}^k \text{ where } k = 0, \ldots, n$$

Therefore, we define the mapping:

$$a_n \times 10_b{}^n + a_{n-1} \times 10_b{}^{n-1} + \ldots + a_1 \times 10_b + a_0 => (a_n)_{10} 16^n + (a_{n-1})_{10} 16^{n-1} + \ldots + (a_1)_{10} 16 + (a_0)_{10}$$

where 16 is a number in the base 10 and

a_n =>	0	1	2	3	4	5	6	7	8	9	10	11	12	13	14	15

We can write this as:

$$n_{16} = a_n a_{n-1} \ldots a_1 a_0 \text{ (base 16)} \underset{n}{=>} (a_n)_{10} 16^n + (a_{n-1})_{10} 16^{n-1} + \ldots + (a_1)_{10} 16 + a_0 = n_{10}$$

This give us a one-to-one mapping $N_b => N_{10}$.

Example:

Convert the number $2E0FA6_{16}$ to the base 10.

Solution:

$$2E0FA6_{16} => 2 \times 16^5 + 14 \times 16^4 + 0 \times 16^3 + 15 \times 16^2 + 10 \times 16^1 + 6 \times 16^0 = 3018662_{10}$$

Exercises:

1. Convert the following numbers to the base 10.

   (a) 2022301_6

   (b) 66061_9

   (c) 11101101_2

   (d) 756402_8

   (e) $A0CD8_{16}$

2.5 CONVERTING A NUMBER IN THE BASE 10 TO ITS CORRESPONDING NUMBER IN ANY BASE B

When we converted a number from the base b to the base 10, we arrived at:

$$n_b = a_n a_{n-1} \ldots a_1 a_0 \text{ (base b)} => n_{10} = (a_n)_{10} b^n + (a_{n-1})_{10} b^{n-1} + \ldots + (a_1)_{10} b + (a_0)_{10}$$

To convert a number in the base 10 to its corresponding number in any base b, we use the famous Euclidean division theorem, which will reverse this correspondence:

Euclidean division theorem: Assume N and b are nonnegative integers. There exist unique integers Q and R where

$$N_{10} = Qb + R, \text{ where } 0 \leq R < b.$$

To compute Q and R, we use the following algorithm:

Step 1: Divide N by b, which will result in a decimal value in the form *integer. fraction*.

Step 2: From Step 1, Q = *integer*.

Step 3: R = N–Qb.

Example:

N_{10} = 3451, b = 34

Step 1: 3451/34 = 101.5

Step 2: Q = 101

Step 3: R = 3451–101 × 34 = 17

Step 4: Therefore, N = Qb + R = 101 × 34 + 17.

Using the Euclidean division theorem, we now show how to convert a number in the base 10 to its corresponding number in the base b.

We want to write N_{10} in the form: $N_{10} = a_n b^n + a_{n-1} b^{n-1} + \ldots + a_1 b + a_0$

Step 1: Factor out the number b: $N_{10} = (a_n b^{n-1} + a_{n-1} b^{n-2} + \ldots + a_1)b + a_0 = Qb + R$ where

$Q = a_n b^{n-1} + a_{n-1} b^{n-2} + \ldots + a_2 b + a_1$

$R = a_0$

Step 2: Set $N = Q = a_n b^{n-1} + a_{n-1} b^{n-2} + \ldots + a_2 b + a_1$

$Q = Q_1 b + R_1 = (a_n b^{n-2} + a_{n-1} b^{n-3} + \ldots + a_2)b + a_1$ where

$Q_1 = a_n b^{n-2} + a_{n-1} b^{n-3} + \ldots + a_2$,

$R_1 = a_1$.

Step 3: Continue in this manner until $Q_n = 0$.

$N_{10} \Leftrightarrow (a_n \, a_{n-1} \ldots a_1 \, a_0)_b$

Examples:

Convert the following decimal numbers to the specified base.

1. $1625_{10} <=> N_8$

Step 1: 1625/8 = 203.125

$$a_0 = 1625 - 203 \times 8 = 1$$

Step 2: $203/8 = 25.375$

$$a_1 = 203 - 25 \times 8 = 3$$

Step 3: $25/8 = 3.125$

$$a_2 = 25 - 3 \times 8 = 1$$

Step 4: $3/8 = 0.375$

$$a_3 = 3 - 0 \times 8 = 3$$

Since $Q = 0$, the algorithm is completed.

$$1625_{10} <=> (a_3 a_2 a_1 a_0)_8 = 3131_8$$

2. $89629_{10} <=> N_{16}$

Step 1: $89629/16 = 5601.8125$

$$a_0 = 89629 - 5601 \times 16 = 13 <=> D$$

Step 2: $5601/16 = 350.0625$

$$a_1 = 5601 - 350 \times 16 = 1$$

Step 3: $350/16 = 21.875$

$$a_3 = 350 - 21 \times 16 = 14 <=> E$$

Step 4: $21/16 = 1.3125$

$$a_4 = 21 - 1 \times 16 = 5$$

Step 5: $1/16 = 0.0625$

$$a_5 = 1 - 0 \times 16 = 1$$

Therefore, $89629 <=> (a_4 a_3 a_2 a_1 a_0)_{16} = 15E1D_{16}$.

Exercises:

1. Convert the following:

   (a) $2545601_{10} <=>$ base 2

   (b) $16523823_{10} <=>$ base 16

(c) 5321_{10} <=> base 3

(d) 81401_{10} <=> base 8

2. Convert the number 2245_6 <=> N_4 (Hint: first convert 2245_6 to a decimal).

2.6   A QUICK METHOD OF CONVERTING BETWEEN BINARY AND HEXADECIMAL NUMBERS

Of primary concern is to develop an easy conversion between binary and hexadecimal numbers without multiplication and division. Later we will see that the ability to convert quickly between binary and hexadecimal decimal will be critical in learning to program in assembly language.

To perform this conversion, we first construct a table comparing the 16 digits of the hexadecimal number system and the corresponding binary numbers:

HEXADECIMAL DIGITS	CORRESPONDING BINARY NUMBERS
0	0000_2
1	0001_2
2	0010_2
3	0011_2
4	0100_2
5	0101_2
6	0110_2
7	0111_2
8	1000_2
9	1001_2
A	1010_2
B	1011_2

C	1100_2
D	1101_2
E	1110_2
F	1111_2

Note: Each digit of the hexadecimal system corresponds to a number of 4 bits in the binary number system.

Now we can convert between any binary number and hexadecimal number directly by the following rules:

Converting a binary number to its corresponding hexadecimal number

Given any binary number, the following steps will convert the number to a hexadecimal number:

Step 1: Group the binary number from right to left into 4 binary bit groups.

Step 2: From the table above, match the hexadecimal digit with each of the 4 binary bit group.

Example:

$$11011011010101101_2 = \frac{011}{3} \frac{0110}{6} \frac{1101}{D} \frac{0101}{5} \frac{1101_2}{D} \iff 36D5D_{16}$$

Converting a hexadecimal number to its corresponding binary number

Given any hexadecimal number, the following steps will convert the number to a binary number:

From the table above, match each of digits of the hexadecimal number with the corresponding 4 bit binary number.

Example:

$34ABC02DE0F_{16}$ = 3   4   A   B   C   0   2   D   E   0 F_{16}

<=> 0011 0100 1010 1011 1100 0000 0010 1101 1110 0000 1111_2

= $00110100101010111100000000101101111000001111_2$

Exercises:

1. Complete the table below by matching each digit of the octal number system with its corresponding binary number.

OCTAL DIGITS	CORRESPONDING BINARY NUMBERS
0	000
1	001

2. From the tables above, convert quickly the following numbers:

   (a) $11101101110001101010 11_2$ <=> n_8

   (b) $675741120 14_8$ <=> n_2

   (c) 235621103_8 <=> n_{16}

   (d) $A2B3C4D5E6D7F_{16}$ <=> n_2

   (e) 11011010110111001_2 <=> n_{16}

3. Create a similar table to convert numbers of the base 4 to the base 2.

4. Using the tables, convert the following:

   (a) 121301_4 <=> n_2

(b) $121301_8 <=> n_4$

(c) $10011100110_2 <=> n_4$

2.7 PERFORMING CONVERSIONS AND ARITHMETIC FOR DIFFERENT NUMBER BASES

Definition $n_b => n_c$: Assume $n_b => n_{10}$ and $n_{10} => n_c$ then $n_b => n_c$

Example:

Convert $5762_8 => n_5$

Solution:

$$5762_8 => n_{10} = 3058_{10} => n_5 = 44213_5$$

Given any number base, one can develop arithmetic operations so that we can perform addition, subtraction, and multiplication between integers. For example, $ABC23_{16} + 5_{16} = ABC28_{16}$. Performing operations such as addition, subtraction, and multiplication within the given number system can be very confusing and prone to errors. The best way to do such computations is to convert the numbers to the base 10 and then perform arithmetic operations only in the base 10. Finally, convert the resulting computed number back to the original base. The following theorem assures us that there is a consistency in arithmetic operations when we convert any number to the base 10.

Theorem: Invariant properties of arithmetic operations between bases:

1. Invariant property of addition: If $N_b <=> N_c$ and $M_b <=> M_c$ then $N_b + M_b <=> N_c + M_c$

2. Invariant property of subtraction: If $N_b <=> N_c$ and $M_b <=> M_c$ then $N_b - M_b <=> N_c - M_c$

3. Invariant property of multiplication: If $N_b <=> N_c$ and $M_b <=> M_c$ then $N_b \times M_b <=> N_c \times M_c$

The following algorithm will allow us to perform arithmetic operations using the above theorem.

Step 1: Convert each number to the base 10: $n_b => n_{10}$; $m_b => m_{10}$

Step 2: Perform the arithmetic operation on the converted numbers:

(a) $n_b + m_b => n_{10} + m_{10} => n_c + m_c$

(b) $n_b - m_b \Rightarrow n_{10} - m_{10} \Rightarrow n_c - m_c$

(c) $n_b \times m_b \Rightarrow n_{10} \times m_{10} \Rightarrow n_c \times m_c$

Step 3: Convert the resulting number from step 2 back to the original base.

Examples:

1. Perform $2367_8 + 471123_8$

Step 1: $2367_8 \Rightarrow 2 \times 8^3 + 3 \times 8^2 + 6 \times 8 + 7 = 1271_{10}$

$471123_8 \Rightarrow 4 \times 8^5 + 7 \times 8^4 + 1 \times 8^3 + 1 \times 8^2 + 2 \times 8 + 3 = 160339_{10}$

Step 2: $1271_{10} + 160339_{10} = 161610_{10}$

Step 3: Through long division,

$161610_{10} \Rightarrow 473512_8$

Step 4: Therefore,

$2367_8 + 471123_8 = 473512_8$

2. Perform $56AF02_{16} \times 682FA_{16}$

Step 1: $56AF02_{16} \Rightarrow 5 \times 16^5 + 6 \times 16^4 + 10 \times 16^3 + 15 \times 16^2 + 0 \times 16^1 + 2 = 5680898_{10}$

$682FA_{16} \Rightarrow 426746_{10}$

Step 2: $5680898_{10} \times 426746_{10} = 2{,}424{,}300{,}497{,}908_{10}$

Step 3: Through long division,

$2{,}424{,}300{,}497{,}908_{10} \Rightarrow 2347391EBF4_{16}$

Step 4: Therefore,

$56AF02_{16} \times 682FA_{16} = 2347391EBF4_{16}$

3. Perform $1011101101_2 - 10101011_2$

Step 1:

$1011101101_2 \Rightarrow 749_{10}$

$10101011 \Rightarrow 171_{10}$

Step 2: $749_{10} - 171_{10} = 578_{10}$

Step 3: Through long division,

$$578_{10} => 1001000010_2$$

Step 4: Therefore,

$$1011101101_2 - 10101011_2 = 1001000010_2$$

Note: Since we are only working with integer numbers, we will postpone division for later chapters.

Exercises:

1. Perform the following:

   (a) $(212_3 + 2222_3) \times 101_3$

   (b) $(101101_2 - 1101_2) \times 11101_2$

   (c) $AB2F_{16} \times 23D_{16} + 2F5_{16}$

   (d) $2_{16}A_{16}$

   (e) $EF156_{16} \Rightarrow N_5$

   (f) $(212_3 \times 2222_3) - 101_3 \Rightarrow N_{16}$

2. For each of the above examples, verify the result in step 3.

3. Using the laws of arithmetic, show that for any number in the base b, N_b = $a_n a_{n-1} \ldots a_1 a_0$, $a_k < b$ can be written in the expanded form:

   $$N_b = a_n \times 10_b{}^n + a_{n-1} \times 10_b{}^{n-1} + \ldots + a_1 \times 10_b + a_0$$

4. Show that $10^n{}_b \Rightarrow b^n{}_{10}$

PROJECT

Show that the one-to-one function $f^{-1} : N_{10} \Rightarrow N_b$ is the inverse of $f : N_b => N_{10}$

(Hint: Show $f^{-1}(f(n_b)) = n_b$)

CHAPTER THREE

PSEUDOCODE AND WRITING ALGORITHMS

INTRODUCTION

This chapter will explain the basics of computer programming. This involves defining a set of instructions, called pseudocode, that when written in a specific order will perform desired tasks. When completed, such a sequence of instructions is call a computer program. The word *pseudocode* indicates that the codes are independent of any specific computer language. We use this code as a guide to writing the desired programs in assembly language.

The form of the assignment statement is:

VARIABLE := VALUE

where

VARIABLE is a name that begins with a letter and can be letters or digits.

VALUE is any numeric value of the base 10, variable or mathematical expressions.

3.1   THE ASSIGNMENT STATEMENT

Note: Frequently, instructions are referred to as statements.

The assignment statement is used to assign a numeric value to a variable.

Rules of assignment statements

R1: The left-hand side of an assignment statement **must** be a variable.

R2: The assignment statement will evaluate the right-hand side of the statement first and will place the result in the variable name specified on the left-side of the assignment statement. The quantities on the right-hand side are unchanged; only the variable on the left-hand side is changed. Always read the assignment statement from right to left.

Examples:

ASSIGNMENT STATEMENTS	X	X2	XYZ	SAM	TURNS
X2 := 3		3			
XYZ := 23		3	23		
TURNS := XYZ		3	23		23
X2 := 5		5	23		23

Exercises:

1. Complete the following table.

ASSIGNMENT STATEMENTS	T	YZ2	TABLE	FORM	TAB
YZ2 := 3					
TABLE :=YZ2					
YZ2 := 1123					
FORM :=TABLE					
YZ2 := FORM					

2. Which of the following are illegal assignment statements? State the reason.

(a) XYZ := XYZ

(b) 23 := S1

(c) 2ZX := XZ

(d) MARY MARRIED := JOHN

Exchanging the contents of two variables

An important task is swapping or exchanging the contents of two variable. The following example shows how this is done:

Example:

ASSIGNMENT STATEMENTS	X	Y	TEMP
X := 4	4		
Y :=12	4	12	
TEMP := X	4	12	4
X :=Y	12	12	4
Y := TEMP	12	4	4

Note: To perform the swap, we needed to create an additional variable TEMP.

Exercises:

1. Assume we have the following assignments:

A	B	C	D
10	20	30	40

Write a series of assignment statements that will rotate the values of A, B, C, and D as shown in the table below:

A	B	C	D
40	10	20	30

Only use 1 temporary variable.

2. The following instructions

   S := R

   R :=T

   T := S

   will exchange the contents of the variables R and T.   a. True   b. False

3. The following instructions

   A := 2

   B := 3

   Z := A

   A := B

   B := Z

   will exchange the contents of the variables A and B.   (a).True   (b). False

4.

X := 5

Y := 10

Z := 2

Z := X

X := Y

Y := Z

The above sequence of commands will exchange the values in the variables _____ and _____.

3.2   MATHEMATICAL EXPRESSIONS

Our system has the following mathematical operators that can be used to evaluate mathematical expressions:

MATHEMATICAL OPERATOR	SYMBOL	EXAMPLE	RESTRICTIONS
Multiplication	X*Y	3*5 = 15	none
Integer Division	X%Y	7%2 = 3	$y \neq 0$
Modulo n	$r = y$ mod n $y = qn + r$	$1 = 7$ mod 2 $7 = 3*2 + 1$	$0 < r < n$
Addition	x + y	2 + 4 = 6	none
Subtraction	x–y	5–9 =–4	none

IMPORTANT: All numbers are of type integer.

Order of operations

The following are the order of operations:

- parenthesis, multiplication, integral division, modulo n, addition, and subtraction

- when in doubt, make use of parenthesis.

Examples:

ASSIGNMENT STATEMENTS	X	Y
X := 4	4	
Y :=5	4	5
X := 2*X + 3*Y + X	27	5

ASSIGNMENT STATEMENTS	X	Y
X := 4	4	
Y :=5	4	5
X := 2*(X +Y)*(X + Y) + X	166	5

Important: Remember to *always* evaluate assignment statements from right to left.

Iterative addition

Addition of several numbers can be computed using repetitive addition:

S := S + X

Examples:

1. Add, using repetitive addition, the numbers 2, 4, 6, 8.

ASSIGNMENT STATEMENTS	S	X
S := 0	0	
X := 2	0	2
S := S + X	2	2
X := 4	2	4
S := S + X	6	4
X := 6	6	6
S := S + X	12	6
X := 8	12	8
S := S + X	20	8

2. Add the digits of 268: 2 + 6 + 8

INSTRUCTIONS	N	R	SUM
N:= 268	268		
SUM := 0	268		0
R := N MOD 10	268	8	0
SUM := SUM + R	268	8	8
N := N – R	260	8	8
N := N ÷ 10	26	8	8
R := N MOD 10	26	6	8
SUM := SUM + R	26	6	14

N := N − R	20	6	14
N := N ÷ 10	2	6	14
R := N MOD 10	2	2	14
SUM := SUM + R	2	2	16
N := N − R	0	2	16
N := N ÷ 10	0	2	16

Exercises:

1. Complete the table below.

ASSIGNMENT STATEMENTS	X
X := 2	
X := X*X	
X := X + X	
X := X*X	

2. Complete the table below.

ASSIGNMENT STATEMENTS	X	U	W
X:=5			
W:= 2			
U := 4			
W := W*(W + U ÷ W)*(W + U ÷ W)			
X := X*X + U			

3. Complete the table below.

ASSIGNMENT STATEMENTS	X	T1	Z
X:=3			
Z := 15			
T1:=10			
X:=Z + X*X			
Z:=X + Z + 1			
T1:=T1 + Z ÷ T1 + T1			

4. Evaluate the following expressions:

(a) 2 + 3*4

(b) 2 + 2*2*2 ÷ 4–3

(c) 2 + 2*2*2 ÷ (7–3)

(d) 17 ÷ 2

(e) 17 ÷ 2

(f) 16 ÷ 2

(g) 3 + 9 ÷ 3

(h) 3 + 8 ÷ 3

(i) 3 + 79 ÷ 3

(j) 3 + 2*2*2 ÷ 8*2–5

(k) 3 + 2*2*2 ÷ (8*2–5)

5. Set up a table for evaluating the following sequence of instructions:

NUM1 := 0

NUM2 := 20

NUM3 := 30

SUM1 := NUM1 + NUM2

SUM2 := NUM2 + NUM3

TOTAL := NUM1 + NUM2 + NUM3

AVG1 := SUM1 ÷ 2

AVG2 := SUM2 ÷ 2

AVG := TOTAL ÷ 3

6. Set up a table for evaluating the following sequence of instructions:

X := 2

X := 2*X + X

X := 2*X + X

X := 2*X + X

X := 2*X + X

X := 2*X + X

X := 2*X + X

3.3 ALGORITHMS AND PROGRAMS

Definition of an algorithm:

An algorithm is a sequence of instructions that solves a given problem.

Definition of a program:

A program is a sequence of instructions and algorithms.

Examples

1. Assume N and P are positive integers. We can write

N = QP + R where R < P.

The following algorithm and program will demonstrate how to compute and store Q and R.

Algorithm

ASSIGNMENT STATEMENTS	EXPLANATION
Q := N ÷ P	COMPUTES AND STORES THE INTEGRAL
R := N MOD P	COMPUTES AND STORES THE REMAINDER R

Task 1: Store the number 957.

Task 2: Store the number 35.

Task 3: Find Q and R for 957 = Q*35 + R.

Program

ASSIGNMENT STATEMENTS	N	P	Q	R
N := 957	**957**			
P := 35	957	**35**		
Q := N ÷ P	957	35	**27**	
R := N MOD P	957	35	27	**12**

2. We define n- factorial:

$$N! = N*(N-1)*(N-2) \ldots *(1)$$

for N, a positive integer.

The following algorithm uses the repetitive multiplication statement to compute N!

Algorithm

ASSIGNMENT STATEMENTS	EXPLANATION
NFACTORIAL := N	SET THE INITIAL VALUE
N:= N – 1	REDUCES N BY 1
NFACTORIAL:= NFACTORIAL*N	
N:= N – 1	
NFACTORIAL:= NFACTORIAL*N	
N:= N – 1	
NFACTORIAL:= NFACTORIAL*N	
::::::::::::::::::::::	
N:= N – 1	
NFACTORIAL:= NFACTORIAL*N	TERMINATES WHEN N = 1

The following program computes 5!

Program

ASSIGNMENT STATEMENTS	N	NFACTORIAL
N:= 5	5	
NFACTORIAL := N	5	5
N:= N – 1	4	5
NFACTORIAL:= NFACTORIAL*N	4	20
N:= N – 1	3	20

NFACTORIAL:= NFACTORIAL*N	3	**60**
N:= N – 1	**2**	60
NFACTORIAL:= NFACTORIAL*N	2	**120**
N:= N – 1	1	120
NFACTORIAL:= NFACTORIAL*N	1	120

3. The Fibonacci sequence

To create a Fibonacci sequence, we begin with the numbers 0 and 1.

Step 1: Add the above two numbers (0 + 1 = 1) and insert the number in the above sequence:

0, 1, 1

Step 2: Add the last two numbers (1 + 1 = 2) of the above sequence and insert the number in the above sequence:

0, 1, 1, 2

Step 3: Add the last two numbers (1 + 2 = 3) of the above sequence and insert the number in the above sequence:

0, 1, 1, 2, 3

Continue as often as desired.

The following algorithm uses the above steps to compute the Fibonacci sequence to a desired number of members of the sequence.

Algorithm

ASSIGNMENT STATEMENTS	EXPLANATION
FIBON_NUM1 := 0	FIRST VALUE OF THE SEQUENCE
FIBON_NUM2 : = 1	SECOND VALUE OF THE SEQUENCE
SUM := FIBON_NUM1 + FIBON_NUM2	SUM OF THE LAST TWO VALUES OF THE SEQUENCE

FIBON_NUM1:= FIB_NUM2	PLACE THE NUMBER IN THE SEQUENCE
FIBON_NUM2 := SUM	PLACE THE NUMBER IN THE SEQUENCE
SUM := FIBON_NUM1 + FIBON_NUM2	SUM OF THE LAST TWO VALUES OF THE SEQUENCE
FIBON_NUM1:= FIB_NUM2	PLACE THE NUMBER IN THE SEQUENCE
FIBON_NUM2 := SUM	PLACE THE NUMBER IN THE SEQUENCE
:::::::::::::::::::::::::::::::;	::::::::::::::::::::::::::::
SUM := FIBON_NUM1 + FIBON_NUM2	SUM OF THE LAST TWO VALUES OF THE SEQUENCE
FIBON_NUM1:= FIB_NUM2	PLACE THE NUMBER IN THE SEQUENCE
FIBON_NUM2 := SUM	PLACE THE NUMBER IN THE SEQUENCE

The following program will generate the first six numbers of the Fibonacci sequence:

0, 1, 1, 2, 3, 5, 8

Program

ASSIGNMENT STATEMENT	FIBON_NUM1	FIBON_NUM2	SUM
FIBON_NUM1 := 0	0		
FIBON_NUM2 := 1	0	1	
SUM := FIBON_NUM1 + FIBON_NUM2	0	1	1

FIBON_NUM1:= FIB_NUM2	1	1	1
FIBON_NUM2 := SUM	1	1	1
SUM := FIBON_NUM1 + FIBON_NUM2	1	1	2
FIBON_NUM1:= FIB_NUM2	1	1	2
FIBON_NUM2 := SUM	1	2	2
SUM := FIBON_NUM1 + FIBON_NUM2	1	2	3
FIBON_NUM1:= FIB_NUM2	2	2	3
FIBON_NUM2 := SUM	2	3	3
SUM := FIBON_NUM1 + FIBON_NUM2	2	3	5
FIBON_NUM1:= FIB_NUM2	3	3	5
FIBON_NUM2 := SUM	3	5	5
SUM := FIBON_NUM1 + FIBON_NUM2	3	5	8
FIBON_NUM1:= FIB_NUM2	5	5	8
FIBON_NUM2 := SUM	5	8	8

Exercises:

1. Write a program that computes 10!

2. Write a program that will compute a Fibonacci sequence where each number in the sequence is less than 50.

3.4 NONEXECUTABLE STATEMENTS

All assignment statements are executable statements: When the assembler encounters the statement, it will be executed.

There are however, nonexecutable statements. The first one we will here introduce is the REM statement.

Definition of the REM statement:

The form of the REM statement is:

REM: comment; where comment can be any words made up of alphanumeric characters.

Example:

STATEMENTS	X	Y	SUM
REM: The following program will assign numbers to X and Y and then add them			
X := 34	34		
Y := 100	34	100	
SUM := X + Y	34	100	134

PROJECT

Assume the numbers $n_1, n_2, \ldots n_m$

1. Write an algorithm that will perform iterative multiplication.

2. Using this algorithm, write a program to compute n = 34*226*12*44*5

3. Define a^N = a^N

   Write an algorithm to perform a^N.

CHAPTER FOUR

SIMPLE ALGORITHMS FOR CONVERTING BETWEEN A NUMBER BASE AND THE BASE 10

INTRODUCTION

This chapter will show how to write algorithms to convert a number in the base b (b <10) to its corresponding number in the base 10 and from a number in the base 10 to its corresponding number in the base b (b <10). These algorithms are based on the conversion methods developed in chapter 2. To help us write these algorithms, we first create a sample program from a specific example. Once the program is written, we will use it as a guide to create the algorithm. Later chapters will generalize these algorithms.

4.1   AN ALGORITHM TO CONVERT ANY POSITIVE INTEGER NUMBER IN ANY BASE B < 10 TO ITS CORRESPONDING NUMBER IN THE BASE 10

To convert between an integer number in any base b to its corresponding number in the base 10, we recall from chapter 2 the following formula:

$$n_b = a_n a_{n-1} \ldots a_1 a_0 <=> a_n b^n + a_{n-1} b^{n-1} \ldots + a_1 b + a_0 \text{ base } 10$$

.

Example

The following program will convert the number 267_8 to its corresponding number in the base 10:

$$n_8 = 267_8 <=> 2 \times 8^2 + 6 \times 8^1 + 7 \times 8^0 = 2(64) + 6(8) + 7 = 183_{10}$$

.

Program

PSEUDOCODE INSTRUCTIONS	N8	P	A	N10	BASE
N10:= 0				**0**	
N8 := 267	**267**			0	
BASE := 8	267			0	**8**
P := 1	267	1		0	8
A := N8 MOD 10	267	1	7	0	8

N10 := N10 + A*P	267	1	7	7	8
N8 := N8 ÷ 10	**26**	1	7	7	8
P := P*BASE	26	8	7	7	8
A := N8 MOD 10	26	8	6	7	8
N10 := N10 + A*P	26	8	6	**55**	8
N8 := N8 ÷ 10	**2**	8	6	55	8
P := P*BASE	2	**64**	6	55	8
A := N8 MOD 10	2	64	**2**	55	8
N10 := N10 + A*P	2	64	2	**183**	8
N8 := N8 ÷ 10	0	64	2	183	8

Therefore, $267_8 \Rightarrow 183_{10}$

Using the above program as a model, the following algorithm will convert any positive integer number in the base b < 10 to its corresponding number in the base 10:

Algorithm

PSEUDOCODE INSTRUCTIONS
$N_{10} := 0$
$P := 1$
$A := N_b \text{ MOD } 10$
$N_{10} := N_{10} + A*P$
$N_b := N_b \div 10$
$P := P*BASE$
....

Exercises:

1. Modify the above program to convert the number 5632_8 to the corresponding number in the base 10.

2. Modify the above program to convert the number 1101_2 to the corresponding number in the base 10.

4.2 AN ALGORITHM TO CONVERT ANY INTEGER NUMBER IN THE BASE 10 TO A CORRESPONDING NUMBER IN THE BASE B < 10

Using the Euclidean division theorem explained in chapter 2, we now review how to convert numbers in the base 10 to any in the base b < 10.

Step 1: We want to write n in the form: $n = a_n b^n + a_{n-1} b^{n-1} + ... + a_1 b + a_0$

Step 2: $N = Qb + R = (a_n b^{n-1} + a_{n-1} b^{n-2} ... + a_1)b + a_0$

Here, $Q = a_n b^{n-1} + a_{n-1} b^{n-2} + ... + a_2 b + a_1 = (a_n b^{n-2} + a_{n-1} b^{n-3} ... + a_2)b + a_1$

and $R = a_0$

Step 3: Set N = Q.

$Q = Q_1 b + R_1 = (a_n b^{n-2} + a_{n-1} b^{n-3} ... + a_2)b + a_1$ where

$Q_1 = a_n b^{n-2} + a_{n-1} b^{n-3} ... + a_2$

and $R_1 = a_1$

Step 4: Continue in this manner, until $Q_n = 0$.

Example

Convert the following decimal numbers to the specified base:

1. $1625 => n_8$

   Step 1: $1625 = 203*8 + 1$

   $a_0 = 1$

   Step 2: $203 = 25*8 + 3$

   $a_1 = 3$

Step 3: 25 = 3*8 + 1

$a_2 = 1$

Step 4: 3 = 0*8 + 3

$a_3 = 3$

Therefore, n = $3*8^3 + 1*8^2 + 3*8 + 1 \Leftrightarrow n_g = 3131$.

Program

Task: Convert the integer number 1625 to the base 8.

PSEUDOCODE	N10	Q	N8	R	BA	P	TEN
N10 := 1625	**1625**						
BASE := 8	1625				**8**		
TEN := 10	1625				8		**10**
P := 10	1625				8	**10**	10
N8 := 0	1625		**0**		8	10	10
R := N10 MOD BASE	1625		0	**1**	8	10	10
Q:= (N10–R) ÷ BASE	1625	**203**	0	1	8	10	10
N8:= N8 + R	1625	203	**1**	1	8	10	10
N10 := Q	203	203	1	1	8	10	10
R := N10 MOD BASE	203	203	1	3	8	10	10
Q:= (N10–R) ÷ BASE	203	25	1	3	8	10	10
N8 := N8 + R*P	203	25	**31**	3	8	10	10
P := P*TEN	203	25	31	3	8	**100**	10
N10 := Q	25	25	31	3	8	100	10
R := N10 MOD BASE	25	25	31	1	8	100	10

Q:= (N10–R) ÷ BASE	25	3	31	1	8	100	10
N8 := N8 + R*P	25	3	**131**	1	8	100	10
P := P*TEN	25	3	131	1	8	**1000**	10
N10 := Q	**3**	3	131	1	8	1000	10
R := N10 MOD BASE	3	3	131	3	8	1000	10
Q:= (N10–R) ÷ BASE	3	**0**	131	3	8	1000	10
N8:= N8 + R*P	3	0	3131	3	8	1000	10
N10 := Q	0	0	3131	3	8	1000	10

$1625 \Rightarrow 3131_8$

Algorithm

PSEUDOCODE INSTRUCTIONS
P := 10
N_b := 0
R := N_{10} MOD BASE
Q:= (N_{10}–R) ÷ BASE
N_b:=N_b + R
N10 := Q
R := N_{10} MOD BASE
Q:= (N10–R) ÷ BASE
N_b := N_b + R*P
P := P*10
N10 := Q
::

Exercises:

1. Use the above algorithm to write a program to convert the decimal number 2543_{10} to octal.

2. Write an algorithm to convert any decimal number a_1a_0 to the base 2.

PROJECT

(a) Write a program that will convert the number $2356_7 => n_b$ where $b = 9$.

(b) Write an algorithm that will convert a number n_b to n_c where b, c < 10.

CHAPTER FIVE

THE IF-THEN CONDITIONAL STATEMENT

INTRODUCTION

The statements used so far are called unconditional statements. Each statement performs its task without any conditions placed on it. This chapter will discuss conditional statements. The manner in which these instructions are carried out will depend on various conditions in the programs and algorithms. We begin by defining and explaining conditional expressions.

5.1   CONDITIONAL EXPRESSIONS

We begin with the definition of conditional values.

Definition of conditional values:

Conditional values take on the value *TRUE* or *FALSE*. Each conditional value is determined by six relational operators preceded and followed by numeric values or variables.

Definition of six relational operators

The six relational operators are:	
Operator	**Interpretation**
1. =	Equality
2. <>	Inequality
3. <	Less than
4. >	Greater than
5. <=	Less than or equal to
6. >=	Greater than or equal to

Examples	**Values**
5 = 2 + 3	*TRUE*
9 <> 3*3	*FALSE*
4 <= 4	*TRUE*

Exercises

1. Evaluate the following conditional expressions:

    (a) 3 + 3 = 6

    (b) 8 >= 10

    (c) 7 <> 7

Definition of conditional expressions:

Conditional expressions are conditional values connected by three logical operators.

Definition of the three logical operators

Logical operators connect conditional expressions and return a value of TRUE or False. The three logical operators are:

Operator	Interpretation
NOT	NOT conditional expression (*TRUE* if the conditional expression is *FALSE*; *FALSE* if the if the conditional expression is *TRUE*).
AND	Conditional expression AND conditional expression (*TRUE* if all the conditional expressions are true).
OR	Conditional expression OR conditional expression (*TRUE* if one or more of the conditional expressions are *TRUE*).

Values returned by operators

NOT *TRUE*	*FALSE*
NOT *FALSE TRUE*	*TRUE*
AND *TRUE*	*TRUE*
TRUE AND *FALSE*	*FALSE*
FALSE AND *FALSE*	*FALSE*
TRUE OR *TRUE*	*TRUE*
TRUE OR *FALSE*	*TRUE*
FALSE OR *FALSE*	*FALSE*

Examples:

Conditional expressions	Value
(2 < 3) OR (5 = 7)	*TRUE*
NOT (2 <= 2)	*FALSE*
NOT ((2 > 0) AND (3 <> 2 + 1))	*TRUE*

5.2 THE IF-THEN STATEMENT

Definition of the if-then statement:

The form of the if-then statement is:

> IF *conditional expression* THEN
>
> BEGIN
>
> *statements*
>
> END

If the conditional expression is *TRUE*, then the

> BEGIN
>
> *statements*
>
> END

will be carried out.

If the conditional expression is *FALSE*, then the

> BEGIN
>
> *statements*
>
> END

will NOT be carried, out and the program will go to the instruction following the END.

The BEGIN and END statements are nonexecutable statements.

The

BEGIN

statements

END

is called a compound statement.

Examples:

Program

PSEUDOCODE INSTRUCTIONS	X	Y
X := 5	5	

IF X = 5 THEN
 	
BEGIN
 	
X := 2*X
 	
END
	10	

Y := 2	10	2

IF X = Y THEN
 	
BEGIN
 	
X := 2*X
 	
END
	10	2

X := 100	100	2

The following program will perform the following tasks:

Task 1: Assign three numbers.

Task 2: Count the number of negative numbers.

Program

PSEUDOCODE	X1	X2	X3	COUNT
X1 := 6	6			
X2 := -5	6	-5		
X3 := -25	6	-5	-25	
COUNT := 0	6	-5	-25	0

IF X1 < 0 THEN
BEGIN
COUNT := COUNT + 1
END
	6	-5	-25	0

IF X2 < 0 THEN
BEGIN
COUNT := COUNT + 1
END
	6	-5	-25	1

IF X3 < 0 THEN
BEGIN
COUNT := COUNT + 1
END
	6	-5	-25	2

Exercises:

1. Modify the above program so that it performs the following tasks:

   Task 1: Assign four numbers.

   Task 2: Count the number of positive numbers entered.

   Task 3: Add the positive numbers.

2. Modify the above program so that it performs the following tasks:

   Task 1: Assign four numbers.

   Task 2: Multiply the negative numbers.

Examples:

   1. The following algorithm will perform the following task:

      Task 1: Find the largest of three numbers.

Algorithm

PSEUDOCODE INSTRUCTIONS	EXPLANATION
LARGEST := X1	We start by assuming X1 is the largest

IF X2 > LARGEST THEN
 	
BEGIN
 	
LARGEST := X2
 	
END
	If the contents of X2 is larger than the contents of LARGEST replace LARGEST with the contents of X2.

IF X3 > LARGEST THEN
 	
BEGIN
 	
LARGEST := X3
 	
END
	If the contents of X3 is larger than the contents of LARGEST replace LARGEST with the contents of X3,

   2. The following program will perform the following tasks:

      Task 1: Assign three numbers.

      Task 2: Find the largest of these three numbers.

Program

PSEUDOCODE INSTRUCTIONS	X1	X2	X3	LARGEST
X1 := 5	5			
X2 := 6	5	6		
X3 := 10	5	6	10	
LARGEST := X1	5	6	10	5

IF X2 > LARGEST THEN
 	
BEGIN
 	
LARGEST := X2
 	
END
	5	6	10	6

IF X3 > LARGEST THEN
 	
BEGIN
 	
LARGEST := X3
 	
END
	5	6	10	10

3. The following program will perform the following tasks:

Task 1: Assign two numbers to variables.

Task 2: If the number is negative, change it to its absolute value.

Program

PSEUDOCODE INSTRUCTIONS	X	Y
X := 23	23	
Y := -17	23	-17

IF X < 0 THEN
 	
BEGIN
 	
X := -1*X
 	
END
	23	-17

IF Y < 0 THEN
 	
BEGIN
 	
Y := -1*Y
 	
END
	23	17

Exercises:

1. Complete the table below.

PSEUDOCODE INSTRUCTIONS	X	Y	Z
X := 2			
Y := 5			
Z := -4			
IF (X + Y + Z) <> X*Y THEN			
BEGIN			
X : = (X - Y)÷X			
Y := X + 2*Y			
Z : = X - 2			
END			
IF (X - Y + Z) <> X +Y THEN			
BEGIN			
X : = 2*(X - Y)÷X			
Y := X - 3*Z			
Z : = X + 2			
END			

2. Assume X is an integer. Explain what the following algorithm does:

IF 2*(X ÷ 2) = X THEN

BEGIN

X : = 3*X–1

END

IF 2*(X ÷ 2) <> X THEN

BEGIN

X := 2*X + 1

END

3. Write an algorithm to find the second-largest number among four numbers.

5.3   THE IF-THEN-ELSE STATEMENT

Definition of the if-then-else statement:

The form of the if-then-else statement is:

IF *conditional expression* THEN

BEGIN

statements 1

END

ELSE

BEGIN

statements 2

END

If the conditional expression is *TRUE,* statements 1 following the THEN will be carried out, and the program will skip statements 2.

If the conditional expression is *FALSE,* statements 1 following the THEN will not be carried out, and the program will execute statements 2.

Examples:

1. The following program will perform the following tasks:

   Task 1: Assign two positive integer numbers to variables.

   Task 2: If the number is even, add 1 to the number.

   Task 3: If the number is odd, subtract 1 from the number.

Program

PSEUDOCODE INSTRUCTIONS	X	Y
X := 23	23	
Y := 44	23	44

IF 2*(X÷2) = X THEN
BEGIN
X := X + 1
	22	44

END ELSE X := X - 1 END		

IF 2*(Y÷2) = Y THEN
BEGIN
Y := Y + 1
	22	45

END ELSE Y := Y - 1 END		

2. The following program will perform the following tasks:

Task 1: Assign two numbers.

Task 2: Find the smaller of the two numbers.

Program

PSEUDOCODE INSTRUCTIONS	X	Y	SMALLEST
X := 723	723		
Y := 54	723	54	
IF X < Y THEN	723	54	
BEGIN	723	54	
SMALLEST := X	723	54	
END	723	54	
ELSE	723	54	
BEGIN	723	54	
SMALLEST : = Y	723	54	54
END	723	54	54

PROJECT

The bubble sort algorithm

Perhaps the most important application of computers is the ability to sort data. Data is either sorted in ascending or descending order. For the following four numbers, we will state the tasks that show how the bubble sort algorithm is applied using the if-then statement to move the highest remaining numbers to the right.

List of numbers (unsorted)

X1	X2	X3	X4
W	x	y	z

Task 1: Move the highest number to variable X4.

Task 2: Move the next-highest number to variable X3.

Task 3: Move the next-highest number to variable X2.

Write a program using the bubble sort tasks to sort the numbers below in ascending order.

X1	X2	X3	X4
23	17	3	1

CHAPTER SIX

THE WHILE CONDITIONAL STATEMENT

INTRODUCTION

So far in our programs, we have not had the ability to perform repetitive operations. This chapter will define the WHILE statement, which will allow us to make such repetitive operations.

6.1 THE WHILE STATEMENT

Definition of the WHILE statement:

The form of the while statement is:

WHILE *conditional statement*

BEGIN

statements

END

where the statements enclosed in the BEGIN–END are repeated as long as the conditional expression is true.

If the conditional statement is false, then the statement following the END will be executed.

Examples:

1. The following is an algorithm that will compute the sum of the numbers 1 to R.

Algorithm

PSEUDOCODE INSTRUCTIONS	EXPLANATION
N := 1	N<= 1
SUM := 0	SUM <= 0
WHILE N ≤ R	
BEGIN	
SUM := SUM + N	SUM ⇐ SUM + N
N := N + 1	N <= N + 1
END	

Program

The following program will compute the sum of the numbers 1 to 5.

PSEUDOCODE INSTRUCTIONS	CYCLE OF INSTRUCTIONS	SUM	N
N := 1	N := 1		1
SUM := 0	SUM := 0	0	1
WHILE N <= 5	WHILE N <= 5	0	1
BEGIN	BEGIN	0	1
SUM := SUM + N	SUM := SUM + N	1	1
N := N + 1	N := N + 1	1	2
	SUM := SUM + N	3	2
	N := N + 1	3	3
	SUM := SUM + N	6	3
	N := N + 1	6	4
	SUM := SUM + N	10	4
	N := N + 1	10	5
	SUM := SUM + N	15	5
	N := N + 1	15	6
END	END	15	6

2. The following algorithm will sum all the proper divisors of a positive integer number

N > 1. A proper divisor d of an integer number N is a number where $1 < d < N$ and

N MOD d = 0. To find all the proper divisors, we only need to check all values of $d \leq N \div 2$

Algorithm

PSEUDOCODE INSTRUCTIONS	EXPLANATION
SUM := 0	
D := 2	A DIVISOR
WHILE D <= N ÷ 2	
BEGIN	
IF N MOD D = 0	CHECK TO SEE IF D DIVIDES N
BEGIN	
SUM := SUM + D	IF D DIVIDES N ADD D TO SUM
END	
D := D + I	
END	

Program

The following program will find and add the sum of all proper divisors of 18.

PSEUDOCODE INSTRUCTIONS	CYCLE OF INSTRUCTIONS	N	SUM	D
N := 18	N := 18	18		
SUM := 0	SUM := 0	18	0	
D := 2	D := 2	18	0	2
WHILE D <= N ÷ 2	WHILE D <= N ÷ 2	18	0	2
BEGIN	BEGIN	18	0	2

IF N MOD D = 0	IF N MOD D = 0	18	0	2
BEGIN	BEGIN	18	0	2
SUM := SUM + D	SUM := SUM + D	18	2	2
END	END	18	2	2
D := D + I	D := D + I	18	2	**3**
	IF N MOD D = 0	18	2	3
	BEGIN	18	2	3
	SUM := SUM + D	18	**5**	3
	END	18	5	3
	D := D + I	18	5	**4**
	IF N MOD D = 0	18	5	4
	BEGIN	18	5	4
	SUM := SUM + D	18	5	4
	END	18	5	4
	D := D + I	18	5	**5**
	IF N MOD D = 0	18	5	5
	BEGIN	18	5	5
	SUM := SUM + D	18	5	5
	END	18	5	5
	D := D + I	18	5	**6**
	IF N MOD D = 0	18	5	6
	BEGIN	18	5	6

	SUM := SUM + D	18	11	6
	END	18	11	6
	D := D + 1	18	11	7
	IF N MOD D = 0	18	11	7
	BEGIN	18	11	7
	SUM := SUM + D	18	11	7
	END	18	11	7
	D := D + 1	18	11	8
	IF N MOD D = 0	18	11	8
	BEGIN	18	11	8
	SUM := SUM + D	18	11	8
	END	18	11	8
	D := D + 1	18	11	9
	IF N MOD D = 0	18	11	9
	BEGIN	18	11	9
	SUM := SUM + D	18	20	9
	END	18	20	9
	D := D + 1	18	20	10
END	END	18	20	10

3. Length of numbers:

Definition of the length of a number:

The length of a number is the number of digits that define the number.

Example:

2654 is of length 4.

Algorithm

The following algorithm computes the length of any positive integer.

PSEUDOCODE INSTRUCTIONS	EXPLANATION
COUNT := 0	WILL COUNT # OF DIGITS
WHILE N <> 0	N IS THE POSITIVE INTEGER
BEGIN	
COUNT := COUNT + 1	WILL COUNT # OF DIGITS
N := N ÷ 10	REDUCES THE LENGTH OF N
END	

Program

The following program will compute the length of the number 431.

PSEUDOCODE	CYCLE OF INSTRUCTIONS	N	COUNT
N: = 431	N := 431	431	
COUNT := 0	COUNT := 0	431	0
WHILE N <> 0	WHILE N <>0	431	0
BEGIN	BEGIN	431	0
COUNT := COUNT + 1	COUNT := COUNT + 1	431	1

N := N ÷ 10	N := N ÷ 10	43	1
	COUNT := COUNT + 1	43	2
	N := N ÷ 10	4	2
	COUNT := COUNT + 1	4	3
	N := N ÷ 10	0	3
END	END	0	3

4. Adding digits

Algorithm

The following algorithm will sum the digits of an integer $a_n a_{n-1} \ldots a_0 : a_n + a_{n-1} + \ldots + a_0$.

PSEUDOCODE INSTRUCTIONS	EXPLANATION
SUM := 0	USED TO ADD THE DIGITS
WHILE N <>0	
BEGIN	
R := N MOD 10	$R \Leftarrow a_k$
SUM := SUM + R	$SUM \Leftarrow a_n + a_{n-1} + \ldots + a_k$
N := N–R	$NUMBER \Leftarrow a_n \ldots a_0$
N := N ÷ 10	
END	

Program

The following program will add the digits of the number 579.

PSEUDOCODE INSTRUCTIONS	CYCLE OF INSTRUCTIONS	N	R	SUM
N := 579	N := 579	**579**		
SUM := 0	SUM := 0	579		**0**
WHILE N <>0	WHILE N <>0	579		0
BEGIN	**BEGIN**	579		0
R := N MOD10	R := N MOD 10	579	9	0
SUM := SUM + R	SUM := SUM + R	579	9	**9**
N := N–R	N := N – R	570	9	9
N := N ÷ 10	N := N ÷ 10	**57**	9	9
	R := N MOD10	57	7	9
	SUM := SUM + R	57	7	**16**
	N := N – R	**50**	7	16
	N := N ÷ 10	**5**	7	16
	R := N MOD10	5	5	16
	SUM := SUM + R	5	5	**21**
	N := N – R	**0**	5	21
END	**END**	0	5	21

Exercises:

1. Write an algorithm that performs the following tasks:

   Task 1: Find the proper divisors of a positive integer N.

   Task 2: Sum the proper divisors.

2. Write an algorithm that will multiply all the proper divisors of a positive integer number N > 1.

3. A factorial number, written as N!, is defined as N! = N(N–1)(N–2) ... (2)(1), where N is a positive integer > 1.

   Write a program that will perform the following tasks:

   Task 1: Enter a positive integer number N > 1.

   Task 2: Compute N!.

4. For the following program, what is the final value assigned to S?

   K := 2

   S := 0

   WHILE K < 10

   BEGIN

   S := S + 2*K + 1

   K := K + 1

   END

5. A positive integer greater than 1 is prime if it has no proper divisors. Write a program that will find all prime numbers less than 25.

6. Find the final value R computed in the following program:

   K := 0

   R := 2258–K*55

   WHILE R > 0

   BEGIN

   K := K +1

```
R :=2258 -K*55

END

R := R + 55
```

7. For the following program, what is the final value X?

```
K := I

X : = 2

WHILE K <= 6

BEGIN

X := X + 3

K : = K + I

END
```

8. For the following program, what is the final value X?

```
K := I

X : = 2

WHILE K <= 6

BEGIN

X := X* 3

K : = K + I

END
```

PROJECT

1. A polynomial is defined as $P_n(x) = a_n x^n + a_{n-1} x^{n-1} + \ldots + a_1 x + a_0$ where x is any number.

One way of evaluating $P(x)$ without using exponents is to write

$$P_n(x) = (\ldots (((a_n x + a_{n-1})x + a_{n-2}) x + a_{n-2}) x + \ldots + a_1)x + a_0$$

Example:

$$P_3(x) = ((a_3x + a_2)x + a_1)x + a_0$$

$$P_6(x) = (((((a_6x + a_5)x + a_4)x + a_3)x + a_2)x + a_1)x + a_0$$

Write an algorithm that will perform $P_n(x)$ using the evaluation of $P(x)$ without using exponents with the following restrictions:

a_k are integers and $0 \leq a_k \leq 9$.

CHAPTER SEVEN

COMPUTING NUMBER BASIS WITH ALGORITHMS

INTRODUCTION

This chapter will show how to write algorithms and programs that will convert numbers from one base to another. The methods used are based on the conversion formulas that have been developed in several of the previous chapters.

7.1 WRITING A PROGRAM AND ALGORITHM TO CONVERT NUMBERS IN THE BASE B < 10 TO THE BASE 10

In chapter 2 we saw that to convert numbers in any base b to its corresponding number in the base 10, we use the following formula:

$$N_b = a_n a_{n-1} \ldots a_1 a_0 => a_n b^n + a_{n-1} b^{n-1} + \ldots + a_1 b + a_0$$

Example:

$$N_8 = 4671 => 4*8^3 + 6*8^2 + 7*8 + 1 = 2048 + 384 + 56 + 1 = 2489_{10}$$

Program

The following program will convert the number 4671_8 to the base 10.

INSTRUCTIONS	CYCLE OF INSTRUCTIONS	N8	N10	R	P
N8 := 4671	N8 := 4671	**4671**			
P := 1	P := 1	4671			1
N10 := 0	N10 := 0	4671	**0**		1
WHILE N8 <> 0	WHILE N8 <> 0	4671	0		1
BEGIN	**BEGIN**	4671	0		1
R := N8 MOD 10	R := N8 MOD 10	4671	0	1	1
N8 := N8–R	N8 := N8–R	4670	0	1	1
N8:= N8 ÷ 10	N8:= N8 ÷ 10	**467**	0	1	1

N10 := N10 + R*P	N10 := N10 + R* P	467	I	I	I
P := 8*P	P := 8*P	467	I	I	8
	R := N8 MOD 10	467	I	7	8
	N8 := N8–R	460	I	7	8
	N8:= N8 ÷ 10	46	I	7	8
	N10 := N10 + R*P	46	57	7	8
	P := 8*P	46	57	7	64
	R := N8 MOD 10	46	57	6	64
	N8:= N8–R	40	57	6	64
	N8:= N8 ÷ 10	4	57	6	64
	N10 := N10 + R*P	4	441	6	64
	P := 8*P	4	441	6	512
	R := N8 MOD 10	4	441	4	512
	N8:= N8–R	0	441	4	512
	N8:= N8 ÷ 10	0	441	4	512
	N10 := N10 + R*P	0	2489	4	512
	P := 8*P	0	2489	4	4096
END	END	0	2489	4	4096

Algorithm

The following algorithm will convert a number in the base b < 10 to the base 10.

INSTRUCTIONS
P := 1
N10 := 0
WHILE N8 <> 0
BEGIN
R := N8 MOD 10
N8 := N8 – R
N8:= N8 ÷ 10
N10 := N10 + R*P
P := 8*P
END

Exercise:

1. Write a program that will convert the number 231_4 to the base 10 and complete a table as above.

7.2   WRITING AN ALGORITHM TO CONVERT A NUMBER IN THE BASE 10 TO ITS CORRESPONDING NUMBER IN THE BASE B < 10

Example:

The following method will convert the number 523 to the base 8:

$a_0 = 523 \bmod 8 = 3$

$523 \div 8 = 65$

$a_1 = 65 \bmod 8 = 1$

$65 \div 8 = 8$

$a_2 = 8 \bmod 8 = 0$

$8 \div 8 = 1$

$a_3 = 1 \bmod 8 = 1$

$1 \div 8 = 0$

$523 \rightarrow 1013_8$

Algorithm

The following algorithm will convert any positive integer to any number in the base b < 10.

INSTRUCTIONS	EXPLANATION
K := 1	
SUM := 0	
WHILE N <> 0	
BEGIN	
A := N MOD BASE	THE REMAINDER WHICH IS TO BE ADDED
SUM := SUM + A*K	$a_n b^n + a_{n-1} b^{n-1} \ldots + a_1 b + a_0$
N := N ÷ B	B is the base
K := 10*K	
END	

Program:

The following program will convert the number 523 to the base 8.

INSTRUCTIONS	CYCLE OF INSTRUCTIONS	N10	A	N8	K
N10 := 523	N10 := 523	**523**			
K := 1	K := 1	523			1
N8 := 0	N8 := 0	523		0	1
WHILE N10 <> 0	WHILE N10 <> 0	523		0	1
BEGIN	**BEGIN**	523		0	1
A := N10 MOD 8	A := N10 MOD 8	523	**3**	0	1
N8 := N8 + A*K	N8 := N8 + A*K	523	3	3	1
N10 := N10 ÷ 8	N10 := N10 ÷ 8	**65**	3	3	1
K := 10*K	K := 10*K	65	3	3	**10**
	A := N10 MOD 8	65	1	3	10
	N8 := N8 + A*K	65	1	**13**	10
	N10 := N10 ÷ 8	**8**	1	13	10
	K := 10*K	8	1	13	**100**
	A := N10 MOD 8	8	0	13	100
	N8 := N8 + A*K	8	0	13	100
	N10 := N10 ÷ 8	1	0	13	100
	K := 10*K	1	0	13	**1000**

	A := N10 MOD 8	1	1	13	1000
	N8 := N8 + A*K	1	1	**1013**	1000
	N10 := N10 ÷ 8	0	1	1013	1000
	K := 10*K	0	1	1013	**10000**
END	**END**	0	1	1013	10000

Exercises:

1. Write a program and complete the table that converts the decimal number 25 to base 2.

2. Write a program and complete the table that will print the first 100 numbers in the base 8.

PROJECT

Write a program that will convert the number 23_8 to the base 5.

CHAPTER EIGHT

RINGS AND MODULAR ARITHMETIC

INTRODUCTION

Modular arithmetic plays a major role when doing arithmetic in assembly language. We will see in the next chapter that the number systems we will be working with are not infinite in number. To perform arithmetic on finite systems, we need to use modular arithmetic. We start with the definition of rings.

8.1   RINGS

Definition of a ring:

A ring R is a set of numbers having two binary operations: addition $\oplus$ and multiplication $\otimes$ with the following rules:

Rule 1: Closure under addition.

Rule 2: Closure under multiplication.

Rule 3: Contains an additive identity.

Rule 4: Contains a multiplicative identity.

Rule 5: For every number n there is an additive inverse ~n.

Definition of the above rules:

Rule 1: If n, m are numbers in R, then $c = n \oplus m$ is in R.

Rule 2: If n, m are numbers in R, then $c = n \otimes m$ is in R.

Rule 3: Contains a number $\odot$ in R, where for every number n in R, $n \oplus \odot = n$.

Rule 4: Contains a number 1 in R, where for every number n in R, $n \otimes 1 = n$.

Rule 5: For every number n in R, there is a number $-n$ in R where $n \oplus -n = 0$.

There are two general type of rings: infinite and finite.

Example of an infinite ring

1. All integers: R = {0, 1, -1, 2, -2, 3, -3, ... }

    Rule 1: Let $\oplus$ = +. The sum of two integer numbers is an integer number.

    Rule 2: Let $\otimes$ = *. The product of two integer numbers is an integer number.

Rule 3: Let Θ = 0. If n is an integer number, then n + 0 = n.

Rule 4: The number 1 is an integer and n*1 = n.

Rule 5: Assume n is in R . Let ~n = -n. Therefore, n + ~n = 0.

Important: For rings, there is no subtraction operation.

Example of a finite ring

One well-known finite ring is the hourly clock time:

R = {1, 2, 3, 4, 5, 6, 7, 8, 9, 10, 11, 12}

For addition or multiplication, we use the traditional system.

For example: $1 \oplus 5 = 6, 2 \oplus 11 = 1, 3 \oplus 12 = 3, 5 \otimes 2 = 10, 6 \otimes 3 = 6$, etc.

Now we show that the R is a ring, by verifying the five rules:

Rule 1: If n, m are numbers in R, then $c = n \oplus m$ is in R.

Rule 2: If n, m are numbers in R, then $c = n \otimes m$ is in R.

Rule 3: Contains a number ⊙ = 12 where for every number n in R, $n \oplus 12 = n$.

Rule 4: Contains a number 1 where for every number n in R, $n \otimes 1 = n$.

Rule 5: For every number n in R, there is a number ~n where $n \oplus$ ~n = 12.

To verify this rule, we use the following table, which shows that every number of R has an additive inverse: $n \oplus$ ~n = 12.

Hour	1	2	3	4	5	6	7	8	9	10	11	12
~ hour	11	10	9	8	7	6	5	4	3	2	1	12
hour ⊕ ~ hour	12	12	12	12	12	12	12	12	12	12	12	12

Exercises:

1. Assume R is clock time. Simplify the following:

   (a) $7 \oplus 8 \oplus$ ~7 $\oplus 11 \oplus$ ~ 4

   (b) $2 \otimes (6 \oplus$ ~10)

   (c) ~ $11 \otimes [(2 \otimes$ ~11$) \otimes (11 \oplus$ ~9$)]$

2. Assume R is military time: R = {1, 2, 3, ..., 24}

   (a) 7 ⊕ 18 ⊕ (~7 ⊕ 21) ⊕ (~23)

   (b) 22⊗(16 ⊕ (~10))

   (c) ~ 21⊗[(2⊗~21) ⊗ (11 ⊕ ~19)]

3. Show that the set R = {0, 1, -1, 2, -2, 4, -4, 6, -6, ... ± 2n, ...} is not a ring.

4. Show that the set R = {0, 1, 3, -3, 5,–7, ..., ± 2n + 1} is not a ring.

5. Assume R = {0, 1, -1, 2, -2, 3, -3, 4, -4, ...}. Define ⊕ and ⊗ are defined under the following rules:

   Rule 1: n ⊕ m = n + m + 2

   Rule 2: n⊗ m = n *m

   (a) Find ⊙.

   (b) For n in R, find ~ n, the additive inverse of n.

   (c) Show R is a ring.

8.2   THE FINITE RING R

For assembly language, the most important set of numbers are R = {0, 1, 2, 3, ..., N–1},

where N > 1.

We want R to be a ring. To do this, we need to define operations of addition and multiplication:

Definition of addition a ⊕ b: If a and b are members of R, then a⊕b = (a + b)mod N.

Definition of multiplication a⊗b: If a and b are members of R, then a⊗b = (a*b)mod N.

Note: The mod operator is defined in chapter 3.

Examples

R_8 = {0, 1, 2, 3, 4, 5, 6, 7} then

5 ⊕ 7 = (5 + 7)mod(8) = 12mod(8) = 4

5 ⊗ 6 = (5*6)mod(8) = 30mod(8) = 6

2 ⊕ 5 = (2 + 5) mod(8) = 7mod(8) = 7

$(6 \otimes 7) \oplus 6 = [(42)\mod(8)] \oplus 6 = 2 \oplus 6 = 8 \mod 8 = 0$

$R_2 = \{000, 001, 010, 011, 100, 101, 110, 111\}$

$(101 + 011)\mod 1000 = (1000)\mod 1000 = 0$

Exercises:

1. For $R_5 = \{0, 1, 2, 3, 4\}$, simplify:

   (a) $4 \otimes 4$

   (b) $[(4 \oplus 2) \otimes 4 \oplus 4] \otimes 3$

   (c) $3 \otimes (3 \oplus 4)$

2. For $R_8 = \{0, 1, 2, ..., 7\}$, verify if the following are true:

   (a) $6 \otimes (7 \oplus 5) = (6 \otimes 7) \oplus (6 \otimes 5)$

   (b) $(4 \otimes 3) \otimes 7 = 4 \otimes (3 \otimes 7)$

   (c) $(4 \oplus 3) \oplus 7 = 4 \oplus (3 \oplus 7)$

3. For the following finite rings, find the additive inverse of each number in the ring.

   (a) R_{10}

n	0	1	2	3	4	5	6	7	8	9
~n										

   (b) R_2

n	0	1
~n		

   (c) R_8

n	0	1	2	3	4	5	6	7
~n								

(d) R_{16}

n	0	1	2	3	4	5	6	7	8	9	10	11	12	13	14	15
~n																

(e) R_{Hex}

n	0	1	2	3	4	5	6	7	8	9	A	B	C	D	E	F
~n																

4. For R_N = {0, 1, 2, ..., N–1}, what is the additive identity? What is the multiplicative identity?

8.3   SUBTRACTION FOR R

How do we subtract two numbers in R? We accomplish this using the following definition:

Definition of subtraction a–b for a and b in R:

$a \ominus b = (a + \sim b)\text{mod}(N)$, where

a and ~b are values in the ring R_N = {0, 1, 2, ..., N–1}

Examples:

Assume ring R_8 = {0, 1, 2, 3, 4, 5, 6, 7}, then

$6 \ominus 3 = (6 + \sim3)\text{mod}(8) = (6 + 5)\text{mod}(8) = 11 \text{ mod}(8) = 3$

$5 \ominus 7 = (5 + \sim 7)\text{mod}(8) = (5 + 1)\text{mod}(8) = 6 \text{ mod}(8) = 6$

$\sim4 \ominus 3 = (\sim4 + \sim3)\text{mod}(8) = (4 + 5) \text{ mod}(8) = 9 \text{ mod}(8) = 1$

Exercises:

1. Assume a byte ring. If n < 256, and ~n = n, find all solutions.

2. Are the following true or false for numbers in R_n? Show examples of each.

   (a) $\sim\sim a = a$?

   (b) $\sim(a \sim b) = b \sim a$

   (c) $\sim a + \sim b = \sim(a + b)$

8.4   RINGS IN DIFFERENT BASES

So far we have built our finite rings in the decimal number system. We will now define binary and hexadecimal rings, which play an important role in the assembly language.

Definition of a binary finite ring:

Assume we are in a binary number system.

We define $R_2 = \{0, 1, 10, 11, 100, ..., N\}$

Examples

1. $R_2 = \{000, 001, 010, 011, 100, 101, 110, 111\}$

2. $R_2 = \{0000, 0001, 0010, 0011, 0100, 0101, 0110, 0111, 1000, 1001, 1010, 1011, 1100, 1101, 1110, 1111\}$

Definition of a hexadecimal finite ring:

Assume we are in a hexadecimal number system. We define

$R_{16} = \{0, 1, 2, 3, 4, 5, 6, 7, 8, 9, A, B, C, D, E, F, 10, 11, ..., N\}$

Examples:

1. $R_{16} = \{0, 1, 2, 3, 4, 5, 6, 7, 8, 9, A, B, C, D, E, F\}$

2. $R_{16} = \{0, 1, 2, 3, 4, 5, 6, 7, 8, 9, A, B, C, D, E, F, 10, 11, 12, 13, 14, 15, 16, 17, 18, 19, 1A, 1B, 1C, 1D, 1E, 1F\}$

Exercises:

1. For the finite ring $R_{16} = \{0, 1, 2, 3, 4, 5, 6, 7, 8, 9, A, B, C, D, E, F\}$, find:

   (a) $9 \oplus 8$

   (b) $5 \otimes B$

2. For the finite ring $R_2 = \{00000000, 00000001, ..., 11111111\}$, find:

   (a) $10010110 \oplus 01010111$

   (b) $11010111 \ominus 10101010$

   (c) $11010111 \otimes 10101010$

Modular arithmetic in the base b

As in the decimal number system, we define

$$r_b = a_b \bmod (n_b) = \text{where}$$

$$a_b = q_b * n_b + r_b$$

and

$$r_b < n_b$$

To easily perform such modular arithmetic, we will use the following results:

$$r_b = (a_b) \bmod n_b \iff r_{10} = (a_{10}) \bmod n_{10}.$$

Similarly, we have

$$a_b \oplus c_b = (a_b + c_b) \bmod n_b \iff (a_{10} + c_{10}) \bmod n_{10}$$

$$a_b \otimes c_b = (a_b * c_b) \bmod n_b \iff (a_{10} * c_{10}) \bmod n_{10}.$$

Examples:

1. Octal numbers: $\{0, 1, 2, 3, 4, 5, 6, 7, 10, 11, 12, 13, 14, 15, 16, 17, 20, ...\}$

   (a) $762_8 \bmod (52_8) \iff 498_{10} \bmod (42_{10}) = 36_{10} \iff 44_8$

   Therefore, $762_8 \bmod (52_8) = 44_8$

   (b) $(771_8 + 236_8) \bmod (106_8) \iff (505_{10} + 158_{10}) \bmod (70_{10}) = (663_{10}) \bmod (70_{10}) = 33_{10} \iff 41_8$

   Therefore, $(771_8 + 236_8) \bmod (106_8) = 41_8$

   (c) $(771_8 * 236_8) \bmod (106_8) \iff (505_{10} * 158_{10}) \bmod (70_{10}) = (79790_{10}) \bmod (70_{10}) = 60_{10} \iff 74_8$

   Therefore, $(771_8 * 236_8) \bmod (106_8) = 74_8$

2. Binary numbers:

(a) $100110_2 \bmod (1101_2)$ <=> $38_{10} \bmod (13_{10}) = 12_{10}$ <=> 1100_2

Therefore, $100110_2 \bmod (1101_2) = 1100_2$

(b) $(110111_2 + 11011_2) \bmod (1111_2)$ <=> $(55_{10} + 27_{10}) \bmod (15_{10}) = (82_{10}) \bmod (15_{10}) = 7_{10}$ <=> 111_2

Therefore, $(110111_2 + 11011_2) \bmod (1111_2) = 111_2$

(c) $(110111_2 * 11011_2) \bmod (1111_2)$ <=> $(55_{10} * 27_{10}) \bmod (15_{10}) = (1485_{10}) \bmod (15_{10}) = 0_{10}$ <=> 0_2

Therefore, $(110111_2 * 11011_2) \bmod (1111_2) = 0$

3. Hexadecimal numbers:

(a) $9A23F_{16} \bmod (AD_{16})$ <=> $631359_{10} \bmod (173_{10}) = 82_{10}$ <=> 52_{16}

Therefore, $9A23F_{16} \bmod (AD_{16}) = 52_{16}$

(b) $(AC2301F_{16} + 27DD1_{16}) \bmod (AD_{16})$ <=> $(180498463_{10} + 163281_{10}) \bmod (173_{10}) = (180661744_{10}) \bmod (173_{10})$ 93_{10} <=> $5D_{16}$

Therefore, $(AC2301F_{16} + 27DD1_{16}) \bmod (AD_{16}) = 5D_{16}$

(c) $(AC2301F_{16} * 27DD1_{16}) \bmod (AD_{16})$ <=> $(180498463_{10} * 163281_{10}) \bmod (173_{10}) = (29471969537103_{10}) \bmod (173_{10}) = 135_{10}$ <=> 87_{16}

Therefore, $(AC2301F_{16} * 27DD1_{16}) \bmod (AD_{16}) = 87_{16}$

Exercises:

1. Assume a byte ring. If $a \oplus b = 0$, does $b = {\sim}a$ and $a = {\sim}b$?

2. Simplify the following:

(a) $251_6 \bmod (301F_6)$

(b) $(235432 + 251_6) \bmod (301F_6)$

(c) $(235432 * 251_6) \bmod (301F_6)$

The additive inverse of a number

Recall the definition of an additive inverse:

Definition of an additive inverse:

Assume a is a number in a ring. The additive inverse is a number

~ a in the ring where ~a + a = 0.

Example:

1. Assume we have the following bytering:

$R_8 = \{0, 1, 2, 3, 4, 5, 6, 7\}$

If a = 5, then ~ a = 3

since

$(5_8 + 3_8) \bmod 8_8 = 8_8 \bmod 8_8 = 0$

8.5 THE ADDITIVE INVERSE OF NUMBERS FOR THE RINGS $R_b = \{0 \dots 0, 0 \dots 1, 0 \dots 2, \dots, \beta_1\beta_2 \dots, \beta_N\}$

Definition of $\beta_1\beta_2 \dots, \beta_n$:

The number is a positive integer $\beta_1\beta_2 \dots \beta_n$ where the digits are all equal and $\beta_k = b-1$.

Examples

1. $R_{10} = \{0000, 0001, 0002, 0003, 0004, \dots, 9999\}$

2. $R_2 = \{0000, 0001, 00010, 0011, 0100, \dots, 1111\}$

3. $R_8 = \{000, 001, 002, 003, 004, \dots, 777\}$

4. $R_{16} = \{00, 01, 02, 03, 04, \dots, FF\}$

For these types of rings, we can easily compute the additive inverse of a number by taking the complement of a number. The following is the definition of a complement of a number:

Definition of a complement of a number $a' = a_1a_2a_3 \dots a_n'$ in R:

Let R = $\{0 \dots 0, 0 \dots 1, 0 \dots 2, \dots, \beta\beta\beta \dots \beta\}$. The complement of a number a = $a_1a_2a_3 \dots a_n$ in R is a' = $a_1'a_2'a_3' \dots a_n'$

where $a_k' = \beta-a_k$

The following tables give the digit complements of important number systems for the assembly language.

Binary

a_k	0	1
a_k'	1	0
$a_k + a_k'$	1	1

Decimal

a_k	0	1	2	3	4	5	6	7	8	9
a_k'	9	8	7	6	5	4	3	2	1	0
$a_k + a_k'$	9	9	9	9	9	9	9	9	9	9

Octal

a_k	0	1	2	3	4	5	6	7
a_k'	7	6	5	4	3	2	1	0
$a_k + a_k'$	7	7	7	7	7	7	7	7

Hexadecimal

a_k	0	1	2	3	4	5	6	7	8	9	A	B	C	D	E	F
a_k'	F	E	D	C	B	A	9	8	7	6	5	4	3	2	1	0
$a_k + a_k'$	F	F	F	F	F	F	F	F	F	F	F	F	F	F	F	F

Examples:

1. $R_{10} = \{00, 01, 02, 03, ..., 99\}$

   $25\,' = 74$

2. $R_8 = \{00, 01, 02, 03, ..., 77\}$

   $42\,' = 35$

3. $R_{16} = \{000, 001, 002, 003, ..., FFF\}$

   $0C4' = F3B$

4. $R_2 = \{000, 001, 010, 011, 100, 101, 110, 111\}$

   $101' = 010$

The following rule, can be useful to compute the inverse of a number:

Rule: $\sim a = a\,' + 1$

Examples:

1. $R_2 = \{000000, 000001, ..., 111111\}$

   $a = 100101_2$

   $a\,' = 011010_2$

   $\sim 100101_2 = 011010_2 + 1 = 011011_2$

   $a \oplus \sim a = (100101 + 011010 + 1) \bmod (1000000) = (111111 + 1) \bmod (1000000) = (1000000) \bmod (1000000) = 0$

2. $R_{16} = \{00, 01, 02, 03, ..., FF\}$

   $a = 9C$

   $9C\,' = 63$

   $\sim 9C = 63 + 1 = 64$

   $9C \oplus 64 = (9C + 63 + 1) \bmod 100 = (FF + 1) \bmod 100 = 0$

Question: Why doesn't the assembly language allow us to do normal subtraction? It is not the assembly language that prevents this, it is the way the computer circuitry is designed. To allow subtraction would require doubling the circuitry. Since subtraction can be accomplished by adding the additive inverse, the design of computers is simpler and faster. Also, since only binary numbers are used to represent numbers, the complement of a binary number is simply changing the 0s to 1s and the 1s to 0s. Therefore, the additive inverse of a binary number is the complement plus 1.

Exercises:

1. Assume a word ring. For each of the following binary numbers, find their additive inverses.

    (a) 10011100110   (b) 11011011   (c) 10101010

2. For the octal ring $R_8 = \{0, 1, 2, 3, 4, 5, 6, 7, 10, \ldots, 77\}$, compute the following:

    (a) $43\ominus56$ (b) $55\ominus55$ (c) $\sim\!10\ominus56$ (d) $\sim\!43\text{-}\ominus56$

3. Assume we have the hexadecimal ring: $R_{16} = \{0, 1, 2, 3, 4, 5, 6, 7, 8, 9, A, B, C, D, E, F, 10, \ldots, FF\}$. Find the following:

    (a) $\sim\!AC$ (b) $A9\ominus\!\sim\!55$ (c) $\sim\!10\ominus5E$ (d) $(\sim\!10)\ominus(\sim\!5E)$

Modular arithmetic for rings $R_b = \{0 \ldots 0, 0 \ldots 1, 0 \ldots 2, \ldots, \beta_1\beta_2\ldots\beta_n\}$, $\beta_k = b\text{--}1$

In this section, we will study the modular arithmetic $a_b \bmod(\beta_1\beta_2 \ldots \beta_n + 1)$.

First observe that $\beta_1\beta_2 \ldots \beta_n + 1 = 10_b^{\,n}$.

Examples:

1. $77_8 + 1 = 100_8 = 10_8^{\,2}$

2. $FFFFF_{16} + 1 = 100000_{16} = 10_{16}^{\,5}$

3. $11111111_2 + 1 = 100000000_2 = 10_2^{\,8}$

Therefore, for R_b, the following examples will show how to evaluate

$$a_b \bmod(\beta_1\beta_2 \ldots \beta_n + 1) = a_b \bmod(10_b^{\,n}).$$

Examples:

1. $253_8 \bmod(77 + 1) = 253_8 \bmod(10_8^2) = 253_8 \bmod(100_8)$

    Solution:

    $253_8 = 2*100_8 + 53_8$

Therefore,

$$253_8 \bmod (77_8 + 1) = 53_8$$

2. $AC23D_{16} \bmod (FFF + 1) = AC23D_{16} \bmod (1000_{16})$

Solution:

$$AC23D_{16} = AC_{16} * 1000_{16} + 23D_{16}$$

Therefore,

$$AC23D_{16} \bmod (FFF_{16} + 1) = 23D_{16}$$

3. $111001101_2 \bmod (1111_2 + 1) = 111000101_2 \bmod (10000_2)$

Solution:

$$111001101_2 = 11100_2 * 10000_2 + 1101_2$$

Therefore, $111001101_2 \bmod (1111_2 + 1) = 1101_2$

From these examples, the following formula evolves:

$$(a_n a_{n-1} a_{n-2} \dots a_1 a_0)_b = (a_n a_{n-1} \dots a_{k+1}) 10^k + (a_k a_{k-1-1} \dots a_1 a_0)_b$$

Therefore, $(a_n a_{n-1} a_{n-2} \dots a_1 a_0)_b \bmod (10^k) = (a_k a_{k-1-1} \dots a_1 a_0)_b$

8.6   SPECIAL BINARY RINGS FOR ASSEMBLY LANGUAGE

In assembly language we will need to be concerned about following three special binary rings, which will be used throughout the assembly language.

THE BYTE RING (8 bits)	THE WORD RING (16 bits)	THE DWORD (32 bits)
00000000	0000000000000000	00000000000000000000000000000000
00000001	0000000000000001	00000000000000000000000000000001
00000010	0000000000000010	00000000000000000000000000000010
00000011	0000000000000011	00000000000000000000000000000011

00000100	0000000000000100	00000000000000000000000000000100
00000101	0000000000000101	00000000000000000000000000000101
00000110	0000000000000110	00000000000000000000000000000110
00000111	0000000000000111	00000000000000000000000000000111
00001000	0000000000001000	00000000000000000000000000001000
::::::::::::::	::::::::::::::::::::::::	:::
IIIIIIII	IIIIIIIIIIIIIIII	IIIIIIIIIIIIIIIIIIIIIIIIIIIIIIII

To better understand these three rings, we will now study them as equivalent rings in the base 10.

THE BYTE RING (8 bits)	THE WORD RING (16 bits)	THE DWORD (32 bits)
0	0	0
I	I	I
2	2	2
3	3	3
4	4	4
5	5	5
6	6	6
7	7	7
8	8	8
9	9	9
::::::::::::::::	::::::::::::::::	::::::::::::::::
255	65,535	4,294,967,295

Exercises

1. Convert the above each of the binary table to hexadecimal.

2. Assume we have a binary number $n_2 = a_1 a_2 a_3 \ldots a_n = 111 \ldots 1$, consisting of n 1 bits.

   Show $n_2 \Rightarrow N_{10} = 2^n - 1$

   Hint: Show $(2^{n-1} + 2^{n-2} + 2^{n-3} + \ldots 2 + 1)(2-1) = 2^n - 1$.

3. Using exercise 2, show the following:

   (a) The largest decimal number in the byte ring is 255.

   (b) The largest decimal number in the word ring is 65,535.

   (c) The largest decimal number in the dword ring is 4,294,967,295.

Modular arithmetic for the byte ring (in decimal)

The modulus formula is r = m mod (256).

Examples:

1. $5 \oplus 254 = (5 + 254) \mod(256) = 259 \mod(256) = 3$

2. $164 \otimes 21 = (164*21) \mod(256) = 5,442,444 \mod(256) = 140$

   $100 \ominus 253 = (100 - 253) \mod(256) = -153 \mod(256) = 103 \mod(256) = 103$

Exercises

1. Compute:

   (a) $122 \oplus 122$ (c) $175 \otimes 222 \otimes 13$

   (b) $162 \otimes 31$ (d) $(175 \oplus 222) \otimes 13$

2. Find the additive inverse for the following:

   (a) 214   (b) 0   (c) 128

Modular arithmetic for the word ring (in decimal)

The modulus formula is r = m mod (65,536).

1. $5 \oplus 254 = (5 + 254) \bmod(65,536) = 259 \bmod(65,536) = 259$

2. $23,641 \otimes 500 = (23,641 * 500) \bmod(65,536) = 11,820,500 \bmod(65,536)$
   $= 24,020$

Exercises:

1. Find the additive inverse for the following:

   (a) 214   (b) 0   (c) 60000

2. Compute:

   (a) $122 \oplus 122$ (b) $162 \otimes 31$ (c) $175 \otimes 222 \otimes 13$ (d) $(175 \oplus 222) \otimes 13$

Modular arithmetic for the dword ring (in decimal)

The modulus formula is $r = m \bmod (4,294,967,296)$.

1. $3,000,000,000 \oplus 4,254,256,111 = (7,254,256,111) \bmod(4,294,967,296)$
   $= 2,959,288,815$

2. $2,323,641 \otimes 3,200,241,001 = (2,323,641 \otimes 3,200,241,001) \bmod(4,294,967,296) = 465,288,199,804,641 \bmod(4,294,967,296) = 1,507,727,073$

Exercises:

1. Find the additive inverse for the following:

   (a) 214   (b) 0   (c) 60000

2. Compute:

   (a) $127,567,222 \oplus 2,123,567,222$ (b) $127,567,222 \otimes 2,123,567,222$

   (c) $175 \otimes 222 \otimes 13,000$ (d) $(175 \oplus 222) \otimes 13$

3. Convert the decimal number ~ 202 to a binary number in a

   (a) byte ring   (b) word ring   (c) dword ring

8.7   ORDERED RELATIONS OF RINGS

Definition of an ordered relationship of a ring:

Assume we have the following ring $R_{10} = \{0, 1, 2, \ldots, N-1\}$ containing N numbers. A set of ordered pairs of these numbers is defined as $\{(a,b)\}$, where a and b are numbers in R and the order is defined by some given rule. Such a set of ordered pairs of numbers is defined as an ordered relationship of the ring R_{10}.

Examples:

R = {0, 1, 2, 3, 4}

A natural set of ordered pairs

Definition: A natural set of ordered pairs is where the numbers (a, b) are defined in their order of magnitude: A natural set of ordered pairs for ring R_{10} would be

{(0, 0), (0, 1), (0, 2), (0, 3), (0, 4), (1, 1), (1, 2), (1, 3), (1, 4), (2, 2), (2, 3), (2, 4), (3, 3), (3, 4), (4, 4)}.

Note: In this example, the ordered pair is defined as (a, b), where b is greater than a or b is equal to a.

For all ordered pairs of this type, we will use the following symbols:

a equals to b: a = b, where

b is greater than a or a is less than b: a < b

These symbols will be used to describe the ordered pair relationships of the number in the ring:

The pair (a, a) will be written as a = a.

If a ≠ b, the pair (a, b) will be written as a< b.

For example, the pair (2, 2) will be written as 2 = 2, but the pair (3, 4) will be written as 3 < 4. Therefore, we have 0 < 1 < 2 < 3 < 4.

Other sets of ordered pairs

The following is another example of a set of ordered pairs of the ring R:

{(4, 0), (4, 1), (4, 2), (4, 3), (4, 4), (3 ,0), (3, 1), (3, 2), (3, 3), (2, 0), (2, 1), (2, 2), (1, 0), (1, 1), (0, 0)}.

Using our special symbols

=, <

we will still have (a, b) where a = a, and a < b where a ≠ b.

Therefore, for our ordered pair the following will hold true:

4 < 0, 4 < 1, 4 < 2, 4 < 3, 4 = 4, 3 < 0, 3 < 1, 3 < 2, 3 = 3, 2 < 0, 2 < 1, 2 = 2, 1 < 0, 1 < 1, 1 = 1, 0 = 0.

Laws of ordered relations

For the above special sets of ordered pairs, the following two laws apply:

1. *Reflexive law:* For each number a in the ring, a = a.

2. *Transitive law:* If a < b and b < c, then a < c.

Exercises:

1. For the ring R = {0, 1, 2, 3, 4}, using the special symbols, write out the relations of the ordered pair:

{(0, 0), (1, 1), (1, 0), (2, 2), (2, 1), (2, 0), (3, 3), (3, 2), (3, 1), (3, 0), (4, 4), (4, 3), (4, 2), (4, 1), (4, 0)}.

2. Show for the ring R = {0, 1, 2, 3, 4} that the above two laws hold for both the natural and the ordered pairs:

{(0, 0), (1, 1), (1, 0), (2, 2), (2, 1), (2, 0), (3, 3), (3, 2), (3, 1), (3, 0), (4, 4), (4, 3), (4, 2), (4, 1), (4,0)}.

8.8   SPECIAL ORDERING OF RINGS FOR ASSEMBLY LANGUAGE

In assembly language, we will need to be concerned about following three special binary rings: bytes, words, and dwords. For each of these rings, the assembly language will recognize two types of ordered pairs:

1. The natural order pairs

2. The signed order pairs

For demonstration purposes, all the rings will be represented as decimal integer numbers.

Ordered pairs for the byte ring

In decimal, we will write the byte ring as R = {0, 1, 2, 3, ..., 255}.

The natural order

The natural order for R is:

{(0, 0), (0, 1), ..., (0, 255), (1, 1), (1, 2), ..., (1, 255), (2, 2), (2 ,3) ..., (2, 255), ..., (255, 255)},

which can be written as

0	1	2	3	4	5	6	...	251	252	253	254	255

where the ordered pairs can be seen as a list of numbers in their increasing order:

0 < 1 < 2 < 3 < ... < 254 < 255.

For an example, we can write 5 < 214, 211 < 244, 255 = 255.

The signed order

128	129	...	253	254	255	0	1	2	3	...	126	127

where the ordered pairs can be seen as a list of numbers in their increasing order:

128 < 129 < 130 < ... < 255 < 0 < 1 < 2 < ... < 126 < 127.

In the following table, the second row gives the "traditional" representation of additive inverse of the numbers

0, 1, 2, 3, ..., 126, 127.

128	129	...	253	254	255	0	1	2	3	...	126	127
-128	-127	...	-3	-2	-1	0	1	2	3	...	126	127

The next table gives the binary representation.

128	129	...	254	255	0	1	2	---	... ...	126	127
1000	1000	...	1111	1111	0000	0000	0000	---	...	0111	0111

Therefore, sticking to our rules on ordered relationships, we have, for example:

251 = 251,

251 < 0

5 < 122

254 < 15.

Therefore, in decimal we have

128 < 129 < 130 < ... < 254 < 255 < 0 < 1 < 2 < 3 < ... < 126 < 127 .

Exercises:

1. Construct a natural order table for the values the word ring.

2. Construct a signed order table for the values of the word ring.

3. Construct a natural order table for the values the dword ring.

4. Construct a signed order table for the values of the dword ring.

PROJECT

We defined a mod(n) as

$r = a \bmod(n) =$ where

$a = q * n + r$

and $r < n$.

Write an algorithm, without using the mod instruction, that given a and n (base 10), it will calculate r.

CHAPTER NINE

ASSEMBLY LANGUAGE BASICS

INTRODUCTION

A close examination of our pseudolanguage programs reveals that such programs are made up of four major components: numbers, arithmetic expressions, variables, and instructions. This chapter will demonstrate at an elementary level how these four components are defined and used in the assembly language. Also for this chapter, as well as several subsequent chapters, all numbers will be integers.

9.1   DATA TYPES OF INTEGER BINARY NUMBERS

First we must understand that when programming in assembly language, all numbers are converted by the assembler into binary numbers of a well-defined data type. Most assemblers will only recognize the following three data types of binary integer numbers:

1. 8-bit binary numbers

2. 16-it binary numbers

3. 32-bit binary numbers

Special names are given to each of these data types: bytes, words, and dwords.

Definition: A byte is an 8-bit binary number.

Definition: A word is a 16-bit binary number.

Definition: A dword (i.e., double word) is a 32-bit binary number.

Important: All numbers must be defined as a given data type by the programmer in order for the assembler to process the program.

Examples:

1. byte (8 bits)

    (a)

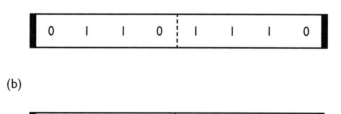

    (b)

2. word (16 bits)

   (a)

   | 1 | 0 | 0 | 1 | 1 | 1 | 1 | 0 | 0 | 0 | 0 | 1 | 0 | 1 | 0 | 1 | 0 |

   (b)

   | 0 | 0 | 1 | 1 | 0 | 0 | 1 | 1 | 1 | 0 | 0 | 1 | 0 | 1 | 0 | 1 |

3. dword (32 bits)

   (a)

   | 1 0 0 1 | 1 0 1 0 | 1 1 1 0 | 0 1 1 1 | 1 1 1 0 | 1 0 1 1 | 0 1 1 1 | 1 0 0 1 1 |

   (b)

   | 0 0 0 0 | 0 0 0 0 | 0 0 0 0 | 0 0 0 0 | 0 0 0 0 | 0 0 0 0 | 1 0 1 1 | 0 1 1 0 |

Exercises

For the examples above of bytes:

   1. Find the binary complements.

   2. Find the binary additive inverses.

   3. Find the equivalent numbers in the hexadecimal base.

9.2   OTHER INTEGERS

Besides binary numbers, the assembler recognize three other number bases: decimal, octal, and hexadecimal. Except for the decimal numbers, all numbers must be followed by the following suffixes.

NUMBER SYSTEM	BASE	SUFFIX
Hexadecimal	16	h
Binary	2	b
Octal	8	o
Decimal	10	none (or d)

Examples

(a) e239ch   (b) 101101b   (c) 23771o   (d) 3499h

Exercises

1. For the examples above, convert each to decimal.

2. Which of the following are valid numbers?

(a) 2397h   (b) 1011011o   c) 01101101h

9.3   VARIABLES

As in the pseudo language code, variables are names that will contain numbers. The following rules are required when defining a variable name in assembly language.

1. The first character of the variable name must begin with either a letter

   (A, B, ..., Z, a, b, ..., z), an underscore (_), or a symbol (@, ?, or $).

   The other characters can also be digits.

2. They are not case sensitive.

3. The maximum number of characters in the name is 247.

Examples

    (a) apple_of_my_eye   (f) X

    (b) S23x   (g) y

    (c) $money2   (h) $124

    (d) hdachslager@ivc   (i) _ @yahoo

    (e) X1_or_X2   (j) z2

Variable types

As in binary numbers, variables are of three data types: byte, word, and dword. We will identify the data types as follows:

    variable name   byte

    variable name   word

    variable name   dword

Examples:

1. x byte

2. Number word

3. Large_Number_dword

Exercise:

1. Which of the following are legal variable names?

    (a) _apple_of_my_eye

    (b) S_23x

    (c) $money2&

    (d) hdachslager@ivc.edu

    (e) 1XorX2

9.4   ASSIGNING INTEGERS TO VARIABLES

There are two ways to assign an integer to a variable:

- By initialing the variable when the variable's data type is defined

- By using the *mov* assignment instruction

Initialing the variable

To initialize the variable, we use the form:

    variable name   *data type*   *integer*

Examples

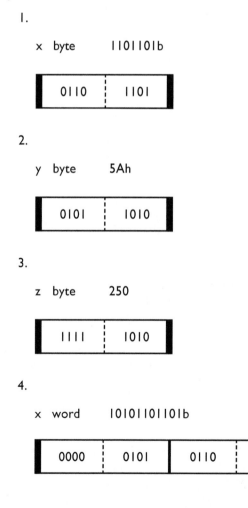

1.

    x byte   1101101b

    | 0110 | 1101 |

2.

    y byte   5Ah

    | 0101 | 1010 |

3.

    z byte   250

    | 1111 | 1010 |

4.

    x word   10101101101b

    | 0000 | 0101 | 0110 | 1101 |

5.

y   word   1D5Ah

0001	1101	0101	1010

6.

z   word   65500

1111	1111	1101	1100

7.

x   dword   11010111101010100011010110110 1b

0011	0101	1110	1010	1000	1101	0110	1101

8.

y   dword   2ABC1D5Ah

0010	1010	1011	1100	0001	1101	0101	1010

9.

z   dword   4294967216

1111	1111	1111	1111	1111	1111	1011	0000

Exercises:

1. Verify that the conversions to binary are correct for examples 1 to 9 above.

2. For examples 1 to 9 above, convert each data type to its hexadecimal value.

Defining a variable without initialization

If you do not wish to initialize the variable, use the symbol ? in place of the integer.

Examples:

x byte ?

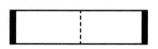

y word ?

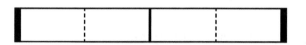

z dword ?

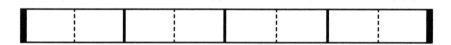

Using the *mov* assignment instruction

The *mov* instruction is of the general form: mov *destination, source* where the destination must be a variable or register (discussed below) and the source can be an integer, variable, or register.

The mov instruction can be used in five ways:

MOVE INSTRUCTION	ORDER OF ASSIGNMENT
mov register1, register2	*register1 <= register2*
mov register, variable	*register <= variable*
mov variable, register	*variable <= register*
mov register, integer	*register <= integer*
mov variable, integer	*variable <= integer*

Note: The definition of registers is given in the next section.

Important: You **cannot** use the mov instruction to move data contained in one variable directly into another variable: mov *variable, variable* **is not a legal statement**.

The following rules apply:

> **Rule 1:** The destination and the source <u>cannot</u> both be variables.
>
> **Rule 2:** If the source is a variable, then both the destination and the source must be of the <u>same</u> <u>data type</u>.
>
> **Rule 3:** All hexadecimal numbers must begin with a digit (0 to 9)

Examples:

1.

x byte ?

mov x, 1011010b

0101	1010

2.

z byte ?

mov z, 8Fh

1000	1111

3.

y byte ?

mov y, 252

1111	1100

4.

x word ?

mov x, 1001100101101010b

| 0010 | 0110 | 0101 | 1010 |

5.

z word ?

mov z, 1D8Fh

| 0001 | 1101 | 1000 | 1111 |

6.

y byte ?

mov y, 65010

| 1111 | 1101 | 1111 | 0010 |

7.

x dword ?

mov x, 10101110101010011001011010b

| 0000 | 0010 | 1011 | 1010 | 1010 | 0110 | 0101 | 1010 |

8.

z dword ?

mov z, 0ACEF1D8Fh

| 1010 | 1100 | 1110 | 1111 | 0001 | 1101 | 1000 | 1111 |

9.

y dword ?

mov y, 4194967096

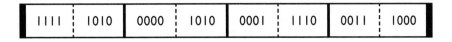

| 1111 | 1010 | 0000 | 1010 | 0001 | 1110 | 0011 | 1000 |

Note

1. mov x, A23F h is not valid by rule 3. However mov x, 0A23F h is valid.

2. mov x,y is not valid by Rule 1.

Exercises:

1. Verify that the conversions to binary are correct for examples 1 to 9 above.

2. For examples 1 to 9 above, convert each data type to its hexadecimal value.

9.5   REGISTERS

Registers are used by the programmer for storing data and performing arithmetic operations.

There are three types of registers that are used for arithmetic operations and storage: 32 bit, 16 bit, and 8 bit.

Important: All three types of registers are rings.

The 32-bit registers

The 32-bit registers that we have are EAX, EBX, ECX, EDX.

These four registers are used to store 32-bit binary numbers. They all can be used to perform arithmetic operations. However, the recommended convention is to use only the EAX for arithmetic operations and the other three 32-bit registers for temporary storage. These registers will be broken into four bytes sections:

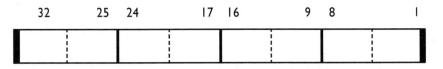

where each byte is divided into two 4 bits.

Examples

1.

mov eax, 5

EAX

| 0000 | 0000 | 0000 | 0000 | 0000 | 0000 | 0000 | 0101 |

2.

mov ebx, 10101010010b

EBX

| 0000 | 0000 | 0000 | 0000 | 0000 | 0101 | 0101 | 0010 |

3.

mov ecx, 0A93F2CAh

ECX

| 0000 | 1010 | 1001 | 0011 | 1111 | 0010 | 1100 | 1010 |

4.

mov edx, 345771110

EDX

| 0011 | 0100 | 0101 | 0111 | 0111 | 0001 | 0001 | 0001 |

Exercises:

1. Explain why the following instructions will cause an error:

    (a) mov eax, D2h

(b) x byte ?

    mov eax, x

(c) mov eax, 3ABDD12E1h

2. For exercise 1, what can be done so D2h can be stored in EAX?

3. Complete the following table, using only binary numbers in EAX.

ASSEMBLY CODE   **EAX**

ASSEMBLY CODE						
mov eax, 2D3Fh						
mov eax, 3h						
mov eax, 1010101b						
mov eax, 434789						
mov eax, 4DFA1101h						
mov eax 2675411o						

4. Complete the following table, using only hexadecimal numbers in EAX.

ASSEMBLY CODE   **EAX**

ASSEMBLY CODE				
mov eax, 2D3Fh				
mov eax, 3h				
mov eax, 1010101b				
mov eax, 434789				
mov eax, 4DFA1101h				
mov eax 2675411o				

It is important to realize, as we demonstrated, that only binary numbers are stored in the variables and registers, irrespective of the number system we are using. However, since binary numbers are difficult to read, most debuggers for the assembly language will display the contents of the registers as well as the variables in the equivalent hexadecimal number system (base 16). The following table gives the equivalent values between the binary digits and the hexadecimal digits.

0000	0001	0010	0011	0100	0101	0110	0111	1000	1001
0	1	2	3	4	5	6	7	8	9

1010	1011	1100	1101	1110	1111
A	B	C	D	E	F

Examples

1. mov edx, 9AB120h

   EDX

BASE 2:	0000	0000	1001	1010	1011	0001	0010	0000
BASE 16:	0	0	9	A	B	1	2	0

2. mov ecx, 5953189d

   ECX

BASE 2:	0000	0000	0101	1010	1101	0110	1010	0101
BASE 16:	0	0	5	A	D	6	A	5

Most of our mathematical experiences has been working with numbers in the base 10. Therefore, if our debugger returns the numbers in our registers as well as variables in hexadecimal, frequently we will need to translate these numbers into the base 10. How do we do this? Well, we could use the methods we have learned so far to find the equivalent hexadecimal numbers in the base 10. However, doing this is not practical. It would be better to use a calculator that will quickly go from one base to another. Microsoft Windows XP and Vista provide such a calculator.

Examples

1. mov eax, 10001100b

EAX

BASE 2:	0000	0000	0000	0000	0000	0000	1000	1100
BASE 16:	0	0	0	0	0	0	8	C
BASE 10:	140							

2. mov ebx, 0DF3h

EBX

BASE 2:	0000	0000	0000	0000	0000	1101	1111	0011
BASE 16:	0	0	0	0	0	D	F	3
BASE 10:	3571							

3. mov ecx, 0111 0111 1101 1110 1110 1110 1011 0111 b

ECX

BASE 2:	0111	0111	1101	1110	1110	1110	1011	0111
BASE 16:	7	7	D	E	E	E	B	7
BASE 10:	2,011,098,807							

Exercises:

1. Complete the following:

   (a) mov eax, 278901

EAX

BASE 2:				
BASE 16:				
BASE 10:				

(b) mov eax, 3ABCD10Fh

EAX

BASE 2:				
BASE 16:				
BASE 10:				

(c) mov edx, 2772101o

EDX

BASE 2:				
BASE 16:				
BASE 10:				

(d) mov eax, 278901

EAX

BASE 2:				
BASE 8:				
BASE 16:				

(e) mov ecx, 3ABCD10Fh

ECX

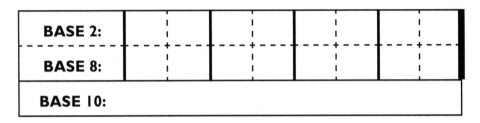

BASE 2:				
BASE 8:				
BASE 10:				

(f) mov edx, 27721010

EDX

BASE 2:				
BASE 8:				
BASE 10:				

2. What is the largest number:

   (a) binary integer of type BYTE?

   (b) octal integer of type BYTE?

   (c) decimal integer associated with type BYTE?

3. What is the largest:

   (a) binary integer of type WORD?

   (b) octal integer of type WORD?

   (c) decimal integer associated with type WORD?

4. What is the largest:

   (a) binary integer of type DWORD?

   (b) octal integer of type DWORD?

   (c) decimal integer associated with type DWORD?

The 16-bit registers

The 16-bit registers are AX, BX, CX, and DX. Each of these registers occupies the right-most part of the corresponding 32-bit registers.

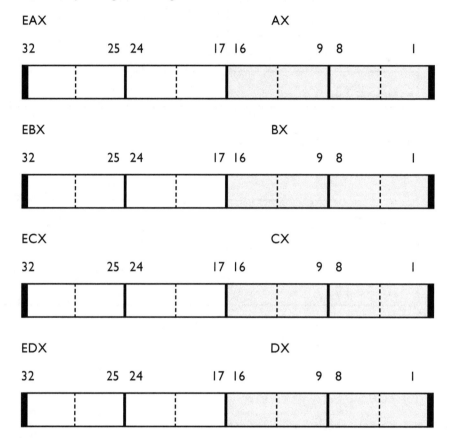

Example:

INSTRUCTIONS	32	25	24	17	16	9	8	1
mov eax, 3C293567h	3	C	2	9	3	5	6	7
mov ax, 9BCh	3	C	2	9	0	9	B	C
mov ax, 56325d	3	C	2	9	**D**	**C**	**0**	**F**

Note: When working with a 16-bit register, the other bits of the 32-bit register are not affected.

The 8-bit registers

The 8-bit registers are AH, AL, BH, BL, CH, CL, DH, and DL. AH occupies the left-most bits of AX, AL occupies the right-most 8 bits of AX, and so on.

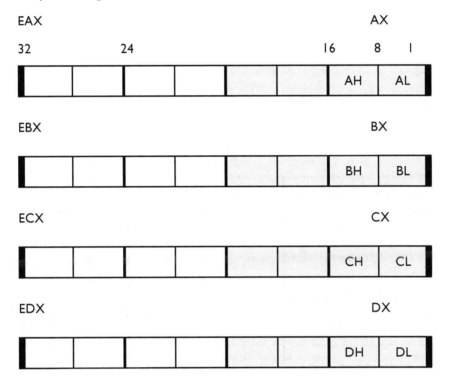

Examples

INSTRUCTIONS	32	25	24	17	16	9	8	1
mov eax, 7293567h	0	7	2	9	3	5	6	7
mov ax, 9BCh	0	7	2	9	0	9	B	C
mov ah, 5	0	7	2	9	0	5	B	C
mov al, 0Eh	0	7	2	9	0	5	0	E
mov al, 251	0	7	2	9	0	5	F	B

Note: When working with an 8-bit register, the other bits of the 16-bit and 32-bit registers are not affected.

Mixing registers

Rule: The assembler will not allow mixing of registers of different data types. The following are examples of errors in programming:

mov eax, bx

mov cx, eax

mov dx, al

Exercises

1. Complete the following tables using hexadecimal numbers only.

	32	25	24	17	16	9	8	1
INSTRUCTIONS								
mov eax, 293567h								
mov ax, 9BCh								
mov ax, 3D32h								
mov ax, 5h								
mov ax, 3h								
mov eax, 1267								
mov ax, 3AF4h								
mov ah, 27h								
mov al, 25								

2.

INSTRUCTIONS	32	25	24	17	16	9	8	1
mov eax, 112937234								
mov ax, 9BCh								
mov al, 5								
mov ah, 0Eh								
mov al, 2								

9.6 TRANSFERRING DATA BETWEEN REGISTERS AND VARIABLES

Rule: The assembler will not allow mixing of registers and variables of different data types. The following are examples of errors in programming.

Examples:

1.

x word 23

mov eax, x

2.

x byte 23

mov ax, x

3.

y byte 2dh

mov eax, y

The following examples demonstrate how integer data is transferred using the *mov* instruction.

Examples:

1.

```
x dword 23

mov eax, x
```

2.

```
x dword 23

y dword ?

mov ebx, x

mov y, ebx
```

3.

```
x dword 3A7Fh

mov ax, x
```

4.

```
x word 3A7Fh

y word ?

mov bx, x

mov y, bx
```

Transferring data from one variable to another variable

The above examples show how to transfer the contents of one variable to another variable. The following algorithm demonstrates x := y.

PSEUDOCODE	AL PSEUDOCODE	ASSEMBLY LANGUAGE CODE
X:= Y	EAX := Y	mov eax, y
	X:= EAX	mov x, eax

The following program will perform the following tasks:

Task 1: Store the number 23 in x.

Task 2: Store the number 59 in y.

Task 3: Store the contents of x in y.

AL PSEUDOCODE	ASSEMBLY LANGUAGE CODE
X := 23	mov x, 23
Y := 59	mov y, 59
EAX := X	mov eax, x
Y := EAX	mov y, eax

Exercises

1. Modify the above program by initializing the values in x and y without using the *mov* instruction.

2. Complete the following table.

AL PSEUDOCODE	AL CODE	X	Y	EAX	EBX
X := 23	mov x, 23				
Y := 59	mov y, 59				
EAX := X	mov eax, x				
EBX := Y	mov ebx, y				
X := EBX	mov x, ebx				
Y := EAX	mov y, eax				

3. In exercise 1, what does the code accomplish?

9.7   ASSEMBLY LANGUAGE STATEMENTS

In assembly language there are three basic statements: *instructions, directives,* and *macros.*

Definition of instructions

An instruction is translated by the assembler into one or more bytes of object code, which will be translated into machine language. The general form of an instruction is:

> label: (optional) mnemonic   operand(s) ; comment (optional)

where *mnemonic* is an instruction and *operands* can be numeric value, variable, or register.

Example:

label: mov eax, 23h ; This is an instruction.

There are two kinds of instructions:

1. nonexecutable codes

2. executable codes

Example of a nonexecutable instruction: the comment

Definition of a comment: A comment is any string of characters preceded by a semicolon (;).

The comment is ignored by the assembler.

Example:

mov eax, 2 ; Transfer the number 2 into the register EAX.

The instruction *mov eax, 2* will be executed by the assembler, but the string following the semicolon will be ignored by the assembler.

The label

All instructions can be preceded by a label ending in a colon (:). The rules for the label are basically the same as variables.

Example:

    xyz: mov eax, -4

Later we will see how labels are used in programing.

Definition of a directive:

A directive instructs the assembler to take a certain action.

Variable data type declarations

A variable has to be designated as one of the following types: *BYTE, WORD,* or *DWORD.*

Definition of a BYTE: A byte consists of 8 bits.

Definition of a WORD: A word consists of 2 bytes (16 bits).

Definition of a DWORD: A double word (DWORD) consists of 4 bytes (32 bits). The form of the variable data type declarations is the following:

    variable name   data type   numeric value assigned or ?

Examples

Num   BYTE 23 ; will define Num as an 8-bit byte and will convert the number 23 to binary and store it in the variable Num.

Num   WORD ?   ; will define Num as a 16-bit word but will not assign a value to Num.

Num   DWORD   0ACD35h   ; will define Num as a 32-bit dword and will convert the number 0ACDE5h to binary and store it in the variable Num.

Note: You may place a label in front of the variable declaration, but the colon (:) is not allowed.

Exercises:

1. What is the largest integer number in the base 10 that can be store in a variable of type BYTE?

2. What is the largest integer number in the base 10 that can be store in a variable of type WORD?

3. What is the largest integer number in the base 10 that can be store in a variable of type DWORD?

4. What is the largest integer number in the base 16 that can be store in a variable of type BYTE?

5. What is the largest integer number in the base 16 that can be store in a variable of type WORD?

6. What is the largest integer number in the base 16 that can be store in a variable of type DWORD?

7. What is the largest integer number in the base 8 that can be store in a variable of type BYTE?

8. What is the largest integer number in the base 8 that can be store in a variable of type WORD?

9. What is the largest integer number in the base 8 that can be store in a variable of type DWORD?

Exercise:

Assume the above program is run. For the table below, fill in the final values stored.

EAX	EBX	A	B	C	D	E	F

9.8   A SAMPLE ASSEMBLY LANGUAGE WRITTEN FOR MASM (MICROSOFT ASSEMBLER)

The following is a complete assembly language program written for the MASM (Microsoft Assembler). For instructions on using this assembler, see References.

```
;This program assigns values to registers
; Last update: 2/10/17

.386

.MODEL FLAT

.STACK 4096

.DATA
a          byte 40
b          byte 30
d          dword 10
e          byte 50
f          word 20

.CODE                     ; start of main program code

_start:
        ;
        ; code inserted here
        ;
    mov ebx, 15h
    mov ecx, 20h
    mov eax, d
    mov ax, f
    mov ah, e
PUBLIC _start

END                       ; end of source code
```

PROJECT

Write an assembly language program that will rearrange numbers so that they are in increasing order, as shown below:

	A	B	C	D	E
BEFORE	40	30	10	50	20
AFTER	10	20	30	40	50

Do not add any additional variables.

CHAPTER TEN

ARITHMETIC EXPRESSIONS

INTRODUCTION

Our next step in becoming assembly language programmers is to learn how to create arithmetic expressions. Those who have studied higher-level programming languages know that assigning arithmetic expressions to variables generally follows the normal assignment statements. For example, in pseudocode we can write instructions such as X =: 2 + 3. However, in assembly language, it is not possible to directly write such an assignment statement. To be able to create arithmetic expressions in assembly language, we first study what are unsigned/signed integer numbers, followed by the arithmetic operations that are available to us. We then learn how to build arithmetic expressions using these types of numbers as needed.

10.1 RING REGISTERS

In chapter 9 (section 9.6), we saw that there are three important rings in the assembly language: byte rings, word rings, and dword rings. The three types of registers—EAX (EBX, ECX, EDX), AX (BX, CX, DX), and AH, AL (BH, BL, CH, CL, DH, DL)—are rings; they conform to the modular rules of arithmetic. The modular formula is:

$r = m \bmod N$ where

$N = 256_{10}$ for the byte rings: AH, AL (BH, BL, CH, CL, DH, DL),

$N = 65{,}536_{10}$ for the word rings: AX (BX, CX, DX),

$N = 4{,}294{,}967{,}296_{10}$ for the dword rings: EAX (EBX, ECX, EDX).

Additive inverses

Since the finite rings do not have negative numbers, as we have with ordinary numbers in the base 10, we need to approach the creation of "negative" numbers in these rings by the following reasoning: In the ordinary base 10 number system, negative numbers are additive inverses of nonnegative numbers, and nonnegative numbers are additive inverses of negative numbers. Therefore, we can create additive numbers in the rings by associating each number of the ring with its corresponding additive inverse. To accomplish this, we begin with the definition of unsigned and signed integers. (See chapter 8 for the definition of additive inverse for a ring and section 8.8 where we first introduce the concept of unsigned and signed binary integers.)

Unsigned and signed binary integers

We start with an arbitrary ring of binary integer numbers:

$R = \{0 \ldots 00, 0 \ldots 01, 0 \ldots 10, 0 \ldots 11, \ldots, 011 \ldots 1, 10 \ldots 00, 10 \ldots 01, 10 \ldots 10, 10 \ldots 011, \ldots, 11 \ldots 1\}$.

For rings of this type, we have the following definitions:

Definition of an unsigned binary integer number:

An unsigned binary integer number has as its extreme left-most bit the bit number zero (0).

Definition of a signed binary integer:

A signed binary integer number has as its extreme left-most bit the bit number one (1).

We see above that the ring R can be divided into two subsets consisting of those binary number that are unsigned:

$$\{0 \ldots 00, 0 \ldots 01, 0 \ldots 10, 0 \ldots 11, \ldots 011 \ldots 1\};$$

and those that signed:

$$\{10 \ldots 00, 10 \ldots 01, 10 \ldots 10, 10 \ldots 011, \ldots, 11 \ldots 1\}.$$

The 8-bit ring as unsigned binary and integer numbers

The following table contains the integer numbers of the base 10 and their 8-bit unsigned binary representation.

NONNEGATIVE INTEGERS BASE 10	UNSIGNED BINARY REPRESENTATION
0	00 00 00 00
1	00 00 00 01
2	00 00 00 10
3	00 00 00 11
4	00 00 01 00
5	00 00 01 01
6	00 00 01 10
7	00 00 01 11

8	00 00 10 00
9	00 00 10 01
:::::	:::::
127	01 11 11 11

Next we need to convert the 8-bit binary numbers to their 8-bit additive inverse numbers. From chapter 8, we use the following formula:

The additive inverse of $a_1 a_2 a_3 a_4 a_5 a_6 a_7 a_8$ equals

$(a_1 a_2 a_3 a_4 a_5 a_6 a_7 a_8)' + 1 = a_1' a_2' a_3' a_4' a_5' a_6' a_7' a_8' + 1$

where

$a_k' = 1$ if $a_k = 0$

and

$a_k' = 0$ if $a_k = 1$.

In the following table, unsigned and signed binary numbers are listed so that each of two columns are additive inverses of each other.

INTEGERS BASE 10	BINARY REPRESENTATION	INTEGERS BASE 10	BINARY REPRESENTATION
0	00 00 00 00	0	00 00 00 00
1	00 00 00 01	255	11 11 11 11
2	00 00 00 10	254	11 11 11 10
3	00 00 00 11	253	11 11 11 01
4	00 00 01 00	252	11 11 11 00
5	00 00 01 01	251	11 11 10 11
6	00 00 01 10	250	11 11 10 10

7	00 00 01 11	249	11 11 10 01
8	00 0010 00	248	11 11 10 00
9	00 00 10 01	247	11 11 01 11
:::::	:::::	::::	::::
127	01 11 11 11	129	10 00 00 01
128	10 00 00 00	128	10 00 00 00

Note: In the above table, the binary numbers in each of the columns are additive inverses of each other.

Examples:

1. Convert the binary number representing 5 to its additive inverse.

   Step 1: The integer number 5: 00000101.

   Step 2: The additive inverse of 00000101 equals 11111010 + 1 = 11111011.

2. Convert the binary number representing 3 to its additive inverse.

   Step 1: The integer number 3: 00000011.

   Step 2: The additive inverse of 00000011 equals 11111100 + 1 = 11111101.

The following table gives the representation of the above table as hexadecimal numbers. Most assemblers will display the binary numbers in registers as their corresponding hexadecimal values.

INTEGERS BASE 10	HEXADECIMAL NUMBERS	INTEGERS BASE 10	HEXADECIMAL NUMBERS
0	00	0	00
1	01	255	FF

2	02	254	FE
3	03	253	FD
4	04	252	FC
5	05	251	FB
6	06	250	FA
7	07	249	F9
8	08	248	F8
9	09	247	F7
::::::	::::::	:::::	::::
127	7F	129	81
128	80	128	80

Note: In the above table, the hexadecimal numbers in each of the columns are additive inverses of each other.

Exercises:

1. Assuming the following numbers are bytes. Find their additive inverse.

   (a) 100101b (b) 2E h (c) 222 d

2. Find the binary representation of the following numbers:

   (a) −81h (b) −1010111b (c) −28h

The 16-bit ring

The following table contains the 16-bit ring divided into columns that are additive inverses of each other.

INTEGERS BASE 10	BINARY REPRESENTATION	INTEGERS BASE 10	BINARY REPRESENTATION
0	00 00 00 00 00 00 00 00	0	00 00 00 00 00 00 00 00
1	00 00 00 00 00 00 00 01	65535	11 11 11 11 11 11 11 11
2	00 00 00 00 00 00 00 10	65534	11 11 11 11 11 11 11 10
3	00 00 00 00 00 00 00 11	65533	11 11 11 11 11 11 11 01
4	00 00 00 00 00 00 01 00	65532	11 11 11 11 11 11 11 00
5	00 00 00 00 00 00 01 01	65531	11 11 11 11 11 11 10 11
6	00 00 00 00 00 00 01 10	65530	11 11 11 11 11 11 10 10
7	00 00 00 00 00 00 01 11	65529	11 11 11 11 11 11 10 01
8	00 00 00 00 00 00 10 00	65528	11 11 11 11 11 11 10 00
9	00 00 00 00 00 00 10 01	65527	11 11 11 11 11 11 01 11
::::	::::	::::	:::
32767	01 11 11 11 11 11 11 11	32769	10 00 00 00 00 00 00 01
32768	10 00 00 00 00 00 00 00	32768	10 00 00 00 00 00 00 00

Note: In the above table, the binary numbers in each of the columns are additive inverses of each other.

The following table gives the representation of the binary numbers as hexadecimal numbers.

INTEGERS BASE 10	HEXADECIMAL NUMBERS	INTEGERS BASE 10	HEXADECIMAL NUMBERS
0	00 00	0	00 00
1	00 01	65535	FF FF

2	00 02	65534	FF FE
3	00 03	65533	FF FD
4	00 04	65532	FF FC
5	00 05	65531	FF FB
6	00 06	65530	FF FA
7	00 07	65529	FF F9
8	00 08	65528	FF F8
9	00 09	65527	FF F7
::::	::::	::::	::::
32767	7F FF	32769	80 01
32768	80 00	32768	80 00

Note: In the above table, the hexadecimal numbers in each of the columns are additive inverses of each other.

Exercises

1. Assume the following numbers are words. Find their additive inverse.

   (a) 100101b   (b) 2E h   (c) 222 d

2. Find the binary representation of the following numbers:

   (a) −81h   (b) −1010111b   (c) -28h

The 32-bit ring

The following table contains the 32-bit ring divided into columns that are additive inverses of each other.

INTEGERS BASE 10	BINARY REPRESENTATION 32 BITS	INTEGERS BASE 10	BINARY REPRESENTATION 32 BITS
0	00—-00 00 00 00	0	00—-00 00 00 00
1	00—-00 00 00 01	4,294,967,295	11—-11 11 11 11
2	00—-00 00 00 10	4,294,967,294	11—-11 11 11 10
3	00—-00 00 00 11	4,294,967,293	11—-11 11 11 01
4	00—-00 00 01 00	4,294,967,292	11—-11 11 11 00
5	00—-00 00 01 01	4,294,967,291	11—-11 11 10 11
6	00—-00 00 01 10	4,294,967,290	11—-11 11 10 10
7	00—-00 00 01 11	4,294,967,289	11—-11 11 10 01
8	00—-00 00 10 00	4,294,967,288	11—- 11 11 00 00
9	00—-00 00 10 01	4,294,967,287	11—- 11 11 01 11
::::	::::	::::	::::
2,147,483,647	01—-11 11 11 11	2,147,483,649	10—-00 00 00 01
2,147,483,648	10—-00 00 00 00	2,147,483,648	10—-00 00 00 00

Note: In the above table, the binary numbers in each of the columns are additive inverses of each other.

The following table gives the representation of the binary numbers as hexadecimal numbers.

INTEGERS BASE 10	HEXADECIMAL NUMBERS	INTEGERS BASE 10	HEXADECIMAL NUMBERS
0	00 00 00 00	0	00 00 00 00
1	00 00 00 01	4,294,967,295	FF FF FF FF
2	00 00 00 02	4,294,967,294	FF FF FF FE
3	00 00 00 03	4,294,967,293	FF FF FF FD
4	00 00 00 04	4,294,967,292	FF FF FF FC
5	00 00 00 05	4,294,967,291	FF FF FF FB
6	00 00 00 06	4,294,967,290	FF FF FF FA
7	00 00 00 07	4,294,967,289	FF FF FF F9
8	00 00 00 08	4,294,967,288	FF FF FF F8
9	00 00 00 09	4,294,967,287	FF FF FF F7
::::	::::	::::	::::::::::
2,147,483,647	7F FF FF FF	2,147,483,649	80 00 00 01
2,147,483,648	80 00 00 00	2,147,483,648	80 00 00 00

Note: In the above table, the hexadecimal numbers in each of the columns are additive inverses of each other.

Exercises:

1. Find the additive inverse of the following numbers in binary as well as the number system:

   (a) 100101b   (b) 2E h   (c) 222 d

2. Find the binary representation of the following numbers:

   (a) −81h   (b) −1010111b   (c) -28h

10.2 WORKING WITH MODULAR ARITHMETIC FOR ADDITION AND SUBTRACTION

Since all registers and data types in assembly language are restricted to three finite rings: bite rings, word rings, and dword rings—it is important to understand how modular arithmetic computes arithmetic expressions. The modular formula is r = m mod N where

Base 10:

$N = 256_{10}$ for the byte rings: AH, AL (BH, BL, CH, CL, DH, DL)

$N = 65,536_{10}$ for the word rings: AX (BX, CX, DX)

$N = 4,294,967,296_{10}$ for the dword rings: EAX (EBX, ECX, EDX)

Base 16:

$N = 100_{16}$ for the byte rings: AH, AL (BH, BL, CH, CL, DH, DL)

$N = 10000_{16}$ for the word rings: AX (BX, CX, DX)

$N = 100000000_{16}$ for the dword rings: EAX (EBX, ECX, EDX)

Exercises:

1. Find N_2 for byte rings, word rings, and dword rings.

2. Find N_8 for byte rings, word rings, and dword rings.

Addition on finite rings

Addition on byte rings:

$$a_{10} \oplus b_{10} = (a_{10} + b_{10}) \bmod 256_{10}$$

Example

PSEUDOCODE	AL PSEUDOCODE	Z	AL
	AL := 205d		205
Z := 205d + 127d	AL := AL + 127d		76
	Z := AL	76	76

Solution:

$$205 \oplus 127 = (205 + 127) \bmod 256 = (332) \bmod 256 = 76$$

$$a_{16} \oplus b_{16} = (a_{16} + b_{16}) \bmod 100_{16}$$

Example:

PSEUDOCODE	AL PSEUDOCODE	Z	AL
Z := 9Dh + 8Fh	AL := 9Dh		**9Dh**
	AL := AL + 8Fh		**2Ch**
	Z := AL	**2Ch**	2Ch

Solution:

$$9D_{16} \oplus 8F_{16} = (9D_{16} + 8F_{16}) \bmod 100_{16} => (157_{10} + 143_{10}) \bmod 256_{10} = 300 \bmod 256 = 44_{10} => 2C_{16}$$

Exercises:

1. Add over a byte ring: $N = 11011101_2 \oplus 01001111_2$

2. Add over a byte ring: $N = 277_8 \oplus 164_8$

Addition on word rings:

$$a_{10} \oplus b_{10} = (a_{10} + b_{10}) \bmod 65{,}536_{10}$$

Example:

PSEUDOCODE	AL PSEUDOCODE	Z	AX
Z := 50,558d + 32,456d	AX := 50558d		**50558**
	AX := AX + 32456d		**17478**
	Z := AX	**17478**	17478

Solution:

$$50558 \oplus 32456 = (50558+32456) \bmod 65{,}536 = 17478$$

$$a_{16} \oplus b_{16} = (a_{16} + b_{16}) \bmod 10000_{16}$$

Example:

PSEUDOCODE	AL PSEUDOCODE	Z	AX
Z := EF7Fh +DDFFh	AX:= EF7Fh		**EF7Fh**
	AX := AX+ DDFFh		**CD7Eh**
	Z := AX	**CD7Eh**	CD7Eh

Solution:

EF7Fh $\oplus$ DDFFh= (EF7Fh + DDFFh) mod 10000_{16} => (61311_{10} + 56831_{10}) mod 65536_{10} => 52606_{10} => CD7Eh

Exercises:

1. Add over a word ring: N = $1100\ 1111\ 1101\ 1101_{2} \oplus 1010\ 1110\ 1001\ 1111_{2}$

2. Add over a word ring: N = $157677_{8} \oplus 177164_{8}$

Addition on dword rings:

$$a_{10} \oplus b_{10} = (a_{10} + b_{10}) \bmod 4{,}294{,}967{,}296_{10}$$

Example:

PSEUDOCODE	AL PSEUDOCODE	Z	EAX
Z := 30132145d + 32456778d	EAX:= 30132145d		**30132145d**
	EAX := EAX + 32456778d		**62588923d**
	Z := EAX	**62588923d**	62588923d

Solution:

$$30132145_{10} \oplus 32456778_{10} = (30132145+32456778) \bmod 4294967296 = 62588923$$

Example

PSEUDOCODE	AL PSEUDOCODE	Z	EAX
Z := FB9EF7Fh +EEDDFFh	EAX:= FB9EF7Fh		F B9 EF 7Fh
	EAX := EAX + EEDDFFh		10 A8 CD 7Eh
	Z := AX	10A8CD7Eh	10 A8 CD 7Eh

Solution:

Since $10A8CD7E_{16} < 100000000_{16}$, it follows that

$$10A8CD7E_{16} \bmod 100000000_{16} = 10A8CD7E_{16}$$

Exercises

1. Add over a dword ring: $N = 1100\ 1111\ 1101\ 1101_2 \oplus 111\ 1110\ 1001\ 1111_2$

2. Add over a dword ring: $N = 215076755_8 \oplus 173757164_8$

Subtraction on finite rings

Subtraction on byte rings:

Definition of ~n:

Given the number n, ~n is defined as the adaptive inverse of n:

$\sim n = 256-n$.

$(n + \sim n) \bmod 256 = [n + (256-n)] \bmod 256$.

Definition of subtraction:

$a_{10} \ominus b_{10} = (a_{10} + \sim b_{10}) \bmod 256_{10}$

Examples:

1. $205_{10} \ominus 15_{10} = (205 + {\sim}15)$ mod $256 = [205 + (256{-}15)\,]$mod $256 = (446)$ mod $256 = 190$

2. $(3_{10} \ominus 150_{10}) = (3 + {\sim}150)$ mod $256 = [3 + (256{-}150)]$ mod $256 = [109]$ mod $256 = 109$

3. $8D_{16} \ominus 6E_{16} = (8D + {\sim}6E)$ mod $100_{16} = [8D + (100_{16}{-}6E)\,]$mod $100_{16} = (11F)$ mod $100_{16} = 1F$

Solution:

$8D_{16} \ominus 6E_{16} => 141_{10} \ominus 110_{10} = (141 + {\sim}110)$ mod $256 = (141 + 146)$mod $256 = 287$ mod 256

$= 31$

Exercises:

Assume a byte ring.

Find:

1. $\sim 201_{10}$

2. $\sim EF$

3. $\sim 277_{8}$

4. $\sim 11\ 11\ 00\ 10_{2}$

5. $(\sim 250_{10}) \ominus 252_{10}$

6. $(\sim A7) \ominus (\sim EE)$

7. $772_{8} \ominus \sim 1427_{8}$

8. $\sim (11\ 11\ 10\ 01_{2} \ominus 10\ 10\ 10\ 11_{2})$

Assume a word ring.

Find:

9. $\sim 6780_{10}$

10. $\sim 35\ ED$

11. $\sim 175673_{8}$

12. $\sim 10\ 10\ 11\ 11\ 11\ 00\ 10_{2}$

13. $(\sim 6550_{10})\ominus 22221_{10}$

14. $(\sim A734) \ominus (\sim EEAD)$

15. $110772_8 \ominus \sim 12642_8$

Assume a dword ring.

Find:

16. $\sim 99456780_{10}$

17. $\sim 567ED24F$

18. $\sim 11124767565_8$

19. $\sim 10\ 10\ 11\ 11\ 11_2$

20. $\sim [43465756_{10})\ominus (\sim 45754_{10})]$

21. $(\sim A734) \ominus (\sim EEAD)$

22. $700772_8 \ominus (\sim 54533_8)$

23. $(11\ 11\ 00\ 11\ 11\ 11\ 10\ 01_2 \ominus 10\ 00\ 01\ 10\ 10\ 10\ 11_2)$

10.3 ASSEMBLY LANGUAGE ARITHMETIC OPERATIONS FOR INTEGERS

The following is a list of the important arithmetic operations for integers.

Addition (+)

Definition: Form of the assembly language add instruction: *add register, source*, where the following rules apply:

Rule 1: The integers may be unsigned or signed.

Rule 2: The source can be a register, variable, or numeric value.

Rule 3: The resulting sum will be stored in the register.

Rule 4: Data types for the register and source must always be the same.

Examples:

1.

PSEUDOCODE	AL PSEUDOCODE	ASSEMBLY CODE
Z := 2 + 3	EAX := 2d	mov eax, 2d
	EAX := EAX + 3d	add eax, 3d
	Z := EAX	mov z, eax

2. Complete the table in hexadecimal numbers.

ASSEMBLY CODE	EAX		AX	AH	AL	X
x dword 2						2h
mov eax, 12345	00 00	30 39h	30 39h	30h	39h	2h
add eax, x	00 00	30 3Bh	30 3Bh	30h	3Bh	2h

3.

ASSEMBLY CODE	EAX		AX	AH	AL	X
x word 1h						1
mov ax, 0ffffh	00 00	ff ff	ff ff	ff	ff	1
add ax, x	00 00	00 00	00 00	00	00	1

4.

ASSEMBLY CODE	EAX		AX	AH	AL	X
x byte 2h						2
mov eax, 0	00 00	00 00	00 00	00	00	2
mov al, 0ffh	00 00	00 ff	00 ff	00	ff	2
add al, x	00 00	00 01	00 01	00	01	2

5.

ASSEMBLY CODE	EAX	AX	AH	AL
mov ah, 200d	200	200	200	
add ah, 150	94	94	94	

6.

ASSEMBLY CODE	EAX		AX	AH	AL	X
x byte 2h						2
mov eax, 0	00 00	00 00	00 00	00	00	2
mov ah, 0ffh	00 00	ff 00	ff 00	ff	00	2
add ah, x	00 00	01 00	01 00	01	00	2

7.

PSEUDOCODE	AL PSEUDOCODE	AL CODE	EAX	AX	X	Y	W
		x word ?					
Y := 223h	Y := 223h	y dword 223h				223	
W := 79223h	W := 79223h	w dword				223	79223
X:= 2h + 3h	AX:= 2h	mov ax, 2h	00 00 00 02	0002		223	79223
	AX := AX + 3h	add ax, 3h	00 00 00 05	0005		223	79223
	X := AX	mov, x, ax	00 00 00 05	0005	5	223	79223
W := W + Y	EAX:= W	mov eax, w	00 07 92 23	9223	5	223	79223
	EAX := EAX+Y	add eax, y	00 07 94 46	9446	5	223	79223
	W := EAX	mov w, eax	00 07 94 46	9446	5	223	79446

Exercises:

1. Complete the following tables.

   Complete the table with hexadecimal numbers.

ASSEMBLY CODE	EAX	AX	AH	AL	X
x dword 2					
mov eax, 12345					
add eax, x					

ASSEMBLY CODE	EAX	AX	AH	AL	X
x word Ah					
mov eax, 0fffffh					
add ax, x					

Complete the table with hexadecimal numbers.

ASSEMBLY CODE	EAX	AX	AH	AL	X
x dword100					
mov eax, 54321					
add eax, x					

ASSEMBLY CODE	EAX	AX	AH	AL
mov eax, 9fffffffh				
add ah, 1h				

2. Complete the table below in hexadecimal.

PSEUDO	AL PSEUDOCODE	AL CODE	EAX	AX	X	Y	W
		x word ? y dword 223h w dword 79223h					
W := W + Y							

X := 2 + 3						

3. Complete the table below in hexadecimal.

PSEUDO	AL PSEUDOCODE	AL CODE	EAX	AX	X	Y	W
		x word ? y dword 223h w dword 79223h					
W := W + Y							
X := 2 + 3							

Subtraction (-)

Definition: Form of the subtraction instruction: *sub register, source,* where the following rules apply:

Rule 1: The integers may be signed or unsigned.

Rule 2: The source can be a register, variable, or numeric value.

Rule 3: The resulting subtraction will be stored in the register.

Rule 4: Data types for the register and source must always be the same.

Examples:

1.

PSEUDO-CODE	AL PSEUDO-CODE	ASSEMBLY CODE
Z:= 2h-3h	EAX := 2h	mov eax, 2h
	EAX := EAX - 3h	sub eax, 3h
	Z:=EAX	mov z, eax

2.

ASSEMBLY CODE	EAX		AX	AH	AL	X
x dword 10h						10
mov eax, 12345678h	12 34	56 78	56 78	56	78	10
sub eax, x	12 34	56 68	56 68	56	68	10

3.

ASSEMBLY CODE	EAX		AX	AH	AL	X
x dword 23544420h						23 54 44 20
mov eax, 12345678h	12 34	56 78	56 78	56	78	23 54 44 20
sub eax, x	EE E0	12 58	12 58	12	68	23 54 44 20

4.

ASSEMBLY CODE	EAX	AX	AH	AL	X
x byte 70h					70
mov eax, 50h	00 00 ¦ 00 50	00 50	00	50	70
sub al, x	00 00 ¦ 00 30	00 E0	00	E0	70

Exercises:

1. Complete the following table in hexadecimal.

PSEUDOCODE	AL PSEUDOCODE	AL CODE	EAX	X	Y	Z
		x dword ? y dword ? z dword ?				
X := CD2h–2h	EAX := 0CD2h					
	EAX := EAX–2h					
	X := EAX					
X := 421h	X := 421h					
Y := 4E75h	Y := 4E75h					
Z:= X – Y	EAX := X					
	EAX := EAX –Y					
	Z := EAX					

2.

ASSEMBLY CODE	EAX	AX	AH	AL	X
x dword 5677h					
mov eax, 0C1234h					
sub eax, x					

3.

ASSEMBLY CODE	EAX	AX	AH	AL	X
x word 0ab9h					
mov eax, 0cca18h					
sub ax, x					

4.

ASSEMBLY CODE	EAX	AX	AH	AL	X
x byte 0dh					
mov eax, 12345678h					
sub al, x					

Multiplication (*)

Definition: There are 2 multiplication instructions we can use: *mul* and *imul*.

- Form of the mul instruction: *mul source*

- Form of the imul instruction: *imul source,* where the following rules apply:

Rule 1: The register used for multiplication is always EAX.

Rule 2a: For the mul instruction, the integers that are multiplied must be unsigned.

Rule 2b: For the imul instruction, the integers can be either unsigned, signed order, or both.

Rule 3: The source can be a register or a variable. The source cannot be a numeric value.

Rule 4: The location of the other number (accumulator) to be multiplied is in one of the following registers:

- AL, if the source is a byte

- AX, if the source is a word

- EAX, if the source is a double word

Rule 5: The resulting product will be located in the accumulator under the following rules:

- If the data type is a byte (8 bits), then the resulting product (16 bits) will be located in AX.

Example:

ASSEMBLY CODE	EAX	AX	AH	AL	X
x byte 10h					10
mov al, 23h	00 00 00 23	00 23	00	23	10
mul x	00 00 02 30	02 30	02	30	10

If the data type is a word (16 bits), then the resulting product (32) bits will have its low-order 16 bits going to the AX register and its high-order 16 bits going to the DX register.

Example:

ASSEMBLY CODE	EAX	AX	DX	X
x word 100h				100
mov ax, 1234h	00 00 12 34	12 34		100
m	00 00 34 00	34 00	00 12	100

If the data type is a dword (32 bits), then the resulting product (64) bits will have its low-order 32 bits going to the EAX register and its high-order 32 bits going to the EDX register.

Example:

ASSEMBLY CODE	EAX	EDX	X
x dword 100h			100
mov eax, 1234567h	01 23 45 67		100
mul x	23 45 67 00	00 00 00 01	100

Exercises:

1. Complete the following tables.

ASSEMBLY CODE	EAX	AX	AH	AL	X
x byte 0EDh					
mov al, 9Fh					
mul x					

ASSEMBLY CODE	EAX	AX	AH	AL	EDX	X
x word 2EF2h						
mov ax, 26DCh						
mul x						

ASSEMBLY CODE	EAX	AX	AH	AL	EDX	X
x dword 46A577DEh						
mov eax, 7EA769Fh						
mul x						

2.

ASSEMBLY CODE	EAX	AX	AH	AL	X
x byte 5Ah					
mov al, 2Fh					
mul x					

ASSEMBLY CODE	EAX	AX	AH	AL	EDX	X
x word 65EEh						
mov al, 2Fh						
mul x						

ASSEMBLY CODE	EAX	AX	AH	AL	EDX	X
x dword 8BB0BB44h						
mov eax, 1DFF872Fh						
mul x						

Division (÷)

For this type of division, we are only performing integer division. The following is the definition of integer division:

Definition of integer division n ÷ m:

Given unsigned integers n and m, we say n is divided by m, where

$n = q*m + r$, where

$0 \leq r < m.$

$n \div m = q$

$n = (n \div m)*m + r.$

Note: The general terminology is as follows:

n: dividend

m: divisor

q: quotient

r: remainder

Examples:

(a) 9 ÷ 4:   9 = 2*4 + 1 where q = 2 and r = 1

9 ÷ 4 = q = 2

(b) 356 ÷ 7: 356 = 50*7 + 6 where q = 50 and r = 6

356 ÷ 7 = q = 50

(c) $78 \div 99$: $78 = 0*99 + 78$ where $q = 0$ and $r = 78$

$78 \div 99 = 0$

Exercises:

1. For the following integer division, find the division form: $n = q*m + r$, base 10:

(a) $143 \div 3$ (b) $3,457 \div 55$ (c) $579 \div 2$ (d) $23 \div 40$

There are 2 division instructions we will use: *div* and *idiv*.

• Form of the div instruction: *div source*

• Form of the idiv instruction: *idiv source*, where the following rules apply:

Rule 1: The register used for integer division is always EAX.

Rule 2: The source is the divisor (m).

Rule 3: The source can be in a register or variable, but it cannot be a numeric value.

Rule 4: The following gives us the locations of n, m, q, and r:

If the source (m) is a byte, then the dividend (n) is stored in the AX register. After execution, the quotient (q) will be stored in the AL register and the remainder (r) in the AH register.

Example;

ASSEMBLY CODE	EAX	AX	AH	AL	X
x byte 10h					10
mov ax, 456h	00 00 04	04 56	04	56	10
div x	00 00 06 45	06 45	06	45	10

If the source (m) is a word, then the dividend (n) is stored in the AX register. Before executing, the EDX must be assigned a numeric value. After execution, the quotient (q) will be stored in AX and the remainder (r) in DX.

Example:

ASSEMBLY CODE	EAX	AX	DX	X
x word 100h				100
mov edx,0			00 00 00 00	100
mov ax, 9378h	00 00 93 78	93 78	00 00 00 00	100
div x	00 00 00 93	00 93	00 00 00 78	100

If the source (m) is a double word, then the dividend (n) is stored in the EAX register. Before executing, the EDX must be assigned a numeric value. After execution, the quotient (q = n ÷ m) will be stored in the EAX register and the remainder(r) in the EDX register.

Example:

ASSEMBLY CODE	EAX	EDX	X
x dword 10h			10
mov edx, 0h		00 00 00 00	10
mov eax, 378h	00 00 03 78	00 00 00 00	10
div x	00 00 00 37	00 00 00 08	10

Note: Whenever we use *div* in this text, we assume the source is a double word.

Rule 5:

- The div instruction should only be used when the dividend and divisor are both unsigned.

- The idiv instruction can be used when the dividend and divisor can be either signed, unsigned, or both.

The following table summarizes rule 3:

DIVIDEND (N)	DIVISOR (M)	Q = N ÷ M	REMAINDER
AX	byte: register or variable	AL	AH
AX	word: register or variable	AX	DX
EAX	dword: register or variable	EAX	EDX

Important: <u>When programming in Visual Studio, one must assign the number 0 to the EDX register before each div or idiv instruction.</u>

Exercises:

Complete the following tables.

1. Complete the following tables in hexadecimal.

ASSEMBLY CODE	EAX	EDX	X
x dword E722Ch			
mov edx, 0			
mov eax, 5670F3AAh			
div x			

ASSEMBLY CODE	EAX	AX	EDX	X
x word 2567h				
mov edx,0				
mov ax, 9D37h				
div x				

ASSEMBLY CODE	EAX	AX	AH	AL	X
x byte 0FDh					
mov ax, 0ABB6h					
div x					

2. Complete the following tables in hexadecimal.

ASSEMBLY CODE	EAX	EDX	X
x dword 95ef 22ch			
mov edx, 0			
mov eax, 0d9def3aah			
div x			

ASSEMBLY CODE	EAX	AX	EDX	X
x word 5f67h				
mov edx,0				
mov ax, 0dacfd378h				
div x				

ASSEMBLY CODE	EAX	AX	AH	AL	X
x byte 0fdh					
mov ax, 0fa56h					
div x					

10.4 SPECIAL NUMERIC ALGORITHMS

In this section, we will study how to write assembly language algorithms for special numeric expressions. To assist us, we will first use pseudocodes and assembly language (AL) pseudocode as our guide. The following are several important algorithms.

• Interchanging values

Algorithm

PSEUDOCODE	AL PSEUDOCODE	AL CODE
TEMP:= X	EAX:= X	mov eax, x
	TEMP:= EAX	mov temp, eax
X:= Y	EAX:= Y	mov eax, y
	X:= EAX	mov x, eax
Y:= TEMP	EAX:= TEMP	mov eax, temp
	Y := EAX	mov y, eax

Example

PSEUDOCODE	AL PSEUDOCODE	AL CODE	X	Y	EAX	T
X := 254h	X := 254h	mov x, 254h	254			
Y := 100h	Y := 100h	mov y, 100h	254	100		
T:= X	EAX := X	mov eax, x	254	100	00 00 02 54	
	T := EAX	mov t, eax	254	100	00 00 02 54	254

X:= Y	EAX:= Y	mov eax, y	254	100	**00 00 01 00**	254
	X:= EAX	mov x, eax	**100**	100	00 00 01 00	254
Y:= T	EAX:= T	mov eax, t	100	100	**00 00 02 54**	254
	Y := EAX	mov y, eax	100	**254**	00 00 02 54	254

The exponential operator: Although we define an exponential operator in assembly, the exponential operator does not exist in the assembly language.

One way to create an exponential operation in assembly language is to perform repetitive multiplication of the same number. The following algorithm will perform such a task:

Algorithm

PSEUDOCODE	AL PSEUDOCODE	AL CODE
P:= 1	P:= 1	mov p, 1
P:= X*P	EAX:= X	mov eax, x
	EAX:= EAX*P	mul p
	P:=EAX	mov p, eax
P:= X*P	EAX:= X	mov eax, x
	EAX:= EAX*P	mul p
	P:=EAX	mov p, eax
....	....	....
P:= X*P	EAX:= X	mov eax, x
	EAX:= EAX*P	mul p
	P:=EAX	mov p, eax

Example

Compute x: $= 10_{16}^{4}$

AL PSEUDOCODE	AL CODE	X	EAX	P
P := 1h	mov p, 1			1
X:=10h	mov x, 10	10		1
EAX:= X	mov eax, x	10	**00 00 00 10**	1
EAX:= EAX*P	mul p	10	00 00 00 10	1
P:= EAX	mov p, eax	10	00 00 00 10	**10**
EAX:= X	mov eax, x	10	00 00 00 10	10
EAX:= EAX*P	mul p	10	**00 00 01 00**	10
P:= EAX	mov p, eax	10	00 00 01 00	**100**
EAX:= X	mov eax, x	10	**00 00 00 10**	100
EAX:= EAX*P	mul p	10	**00 00 10 00**	100
P:= EAX	mov p, eax	10	00 00 10 00	**1000**
EAX:= X	mov eax, x	10	**00 00 00 10**	1000
EAX:= EAX*P	mul p	10	**00 01 00 00**	1000
P:= EAX	mov p, eax	10	00 01 00 00	**10000**

Sum the digits of a positive integer $a_1 a_2 a_3 \ldots a_n$

Example

Sum the digits of 268.

PSEUDOCODE	AL PSEUDOCODE	N	R	EAX	SUM	EDX	T
T := 10d	T := 10d						10
N:= 268d	N := 268d	268					10
SUM := 0d	SUM := 0d	268			0		10
R := N MOD T	EAX:= N	268		268	0		10
	EAX:=EAX ÷ T	268		26	0	8	10
	EDX:= EAX MOD T R:= EDX	268	8	26	0	8	10
N:= N ÷ 10d	N:= EAX	26	8	26	0	8	10
SUM:= SUM + R	EDX:= EDX + SUM	26	8	26	0	8	10
	SUM:= EDX	26	8	26	8	8	10
R:= N MOD T	EAX:=EAX ÷ T	26	8	2	8	6	10
	EDX:= EAX MOD T R:= EDX	26	6	2	8	6	10
N:= N ÷ 10d	N:= EAX	2	6	2	8	6	10
SUM:= SUM + R	EDX:= EDX + SUM	2	6	2	8	14	10
	SUM:= EDX	2	6	2	14	14	10
R:= N MOD T	EAX:=EAX ÷ T	2	6	0	14	2	10
	EDX:= EAX MOD T R:= EDX	2	2	0	14	2	10
N:= N ÷ 10d	N:= EAX	0	2	0	14	2	10
SUM:= SUM + R	EDX:= EDX + SUM	0	2	0	14	16	10
	SUM:= EDX	0	2	0	16	16	10

PSEUDOCODE	AL PSEUDOCODE	AL CODE
TEN := 10d	TEN := 10d	mov ten, 10
N:= 268d	N := 268d	mov n, 268
SUM := 0	SUM := 0	mov sum, 0
R := N MOD TEN	EAX:= N	mov eax, n
	EDX:= 0	mov edx,0
	EAX:= EAX÷TEN	div ten
	R:= EDX	mov r, edx
N:= N ÷ 10	N:= EAX	mov n, eax
SUM:= SUM + R	EDX:= EDX + SUM	add edx, sum
	SUM:= EDX	mov sum, edx
R:= N MOD TEN	EDX:= 0	mov edx,0
	EAX:= EAX÷TEN	div ten
	R:= EDX	mov r, edx
N:= N ÷ 10	N:= EAX	mov n, eax
SUM:= SUM + R	EDX:= EDX + SUM	add edx, sum
	SUM:= EDX	mov sum, edx
R:= N MOD TEN	EDX:= 0	mov edx,0
	EAX:= EAX÷TEN	div ten
	R:= EDX	mov r, edx
N:= N ÷ 10	N:= EAX	mov n, eax
SUM:= SUM + R	EDX:= EDX + SUM	add edx, sum
	SUM:= EDX	mov sum, edx

Algorithm

PSEUDOCODE	AL PSEUDO	AL CODE
SUM := 0	SUM := 0	mov sum, 0
R := N MOD TEN	EAX:= N	mov eax, n
	EDX:= 0	mov edx, 0
	EAX:= EAX ÷ TEN	div ten
	R:= EDX	mov r, edx
N:= N ÷ 10	N:= EAX	mov n, eax
SUM:= SUM + R	EDX:= EDX + SUM	add edx, sum
	SUM:= EDX	mov sum, edx
R:= N MOD TEN	EDX:= 0	mov edx, 0
	EAX:= EAX ÷ TEN	div ten
	R:= EDX	mov r, edx
N:= N ÷ 10	N:= EAX	mov n, eax
SUM:= SUM + R	EDX:= EDX + SUM	add edx, sum
	SUM:= EDX	mov sum, edx
::::::::	::::::::	::::::::::
R:= N MOD TEN	EDX:= 0	mov edx, 0
	EAX:= EAX ÷ TEN	div ten
	R:= EDX	mov r, edx
N:= N ÷ 10	N:= EAX	mov n, eax
SUM:= SUM + R	EDX:= EDX + SUM	add edx, sum
	SUM:= EDX	mov sum, edx

• Factorial $n! = n(n-1)(n-2) \dots (1)$

Example

5! = 5(4)(3)(2)(1) = 120

AL PSEUDOCODE	AL CODE	EAX	EBX
EAX := 5d	mov eax, 5	**00000005**	
EBX := 5d	mov ebx, 5	00000005	**00000005**
EBX := EBX−1d	sub ebx, 1	00000005	**00000004**
EAX := EAX*EBX	mul ebx	**00000020**	00000004
EBX := EBX−1d	sub ebx, 1	**00000020**	**00000003**
EAX := EAX*EBX	mul ebx	**00000060**	00000003
EBX := EBX−1d	sub ebx, 1	00000060	**00000002**
EAX := EAX*EBX	mul ebx	**00000120**	00000002
EBX := EBX−1d	sub ebx, 1	00000120	**00000001**
EAX := EAX*EBX	mul ebx	00000120	**0000001**

Note: See last page for the complete assembly language program.

Algorithm

AL PSEUDOCODE	AL CODE
EAX := N	mov eax , n
EBX : = N	mov ebx , n
EBX := EBX - 1	sub ebx , 1
EAX := EAX*EBX	mul ebx
::::::::::::::::::::	::::::::::::::::::::

$$P(x) = a_n x^n + a_{n-1} x^{n-1} + \ldots + a_1 x + a_0$$

For simplicity, we will evaluate P(x) where n = 5 using the following formula:

$$P(x) = a_5 x^5 + a_4 x^4 + a_3 x^3 + a_2 x^2 + a_1 x + a_0 = ((((a_5 x + a_4) x + a_3) x + a_2) x + a_1) x + a_0$$

$$P(x) = a_n x^n + a_{n-1} x^{n-1} + \ldots + a_3 x^3 + a_2 x^2 + a_1 x + a_0 = (\ldots(((a_n x + a_{4n-1}) x + \ldots + a_3) x + a_2) x + a_1) x + a_0$$

Example

$$p(2) = 7*2^5 + 4*2^4 + 2*2^3 + 10*2^2 + 8*2 + 3 = ((((7*2 + 4)*2 + 2)*2 + 10)*2 + 8)*2 + 3 = 363$$

PSEUDOCODE	AL PSEUDOCODE	AL CODE	P	EAX	X
X:= 2d	X := 2d	mov x, 2			2
P:= 7d	P:= 7d	mov p, 7	7		2
P:= P*X + 4d	EAX:= P	mov eax, p	7	00000007	2
	EAX:= EAX*X	mul x	7	00000014	2
	EAX:= EAX + 4d	add eax, 4	7	00000018	2
	P:= EAX	mov p, eax	18	00000018	2
P:= P*X + 2d	EAX:= P	mov eax, p	18	00000018	2
	EAX:= EAX*X	mul x	18	00000036	2
	EAX:= EAX + 2d	add eax, 2	18	00000038	2
	P:= EAX	mov p, eax	38	00000038	2
P:= P*X + 10d	EAX:= P	mov eax, p	38	00000038	2
	EAX:= EAX*X	mul x	38	00000076	2
	EAX:= EAX + 10d	add eax, 10	38	00000086	2
	P:= EAX	mov p, eax	86	00000086	2

P:= P*X + 8d	EAX:= P	mov eax, p	86	00000086	2
	EAX:= EAX*X	mul x	86	**00000172**	2
	EAX:= EAX + 8d	add eax, 8	86	**00000180**	2
	P:= EAX	mov p, eax	**180**	00000180	2
P:= P*X + 3d	EAX:= P	mov eax, p	180	00000180	2
	EAX:= EAX*X	mul x	180	**00000360**	2
	EAX:= EAX + 3d	add eax, 3	180	**00000363**	2
	P:= EAX	mov p, eax	**363**	00000363	2

Model program

```
;This program computes 5!
.386
.model flat
.stack 4096
.data
factorial dword ?
.CODE
_start:
mov eax , 5
mov ebx, 5
sub ebx, I
mul ebx
sub ebx, I
mul ebx
sub ebx, I
mul ebx
sub ebx, I
mul ebx
mov factorial, eax
public _start
end
```

PROJECT

a. Write a general algorithm that can be used to convert any integer number $N_{10} => N_b$ where b

< 10.

Using this algorithm, write a complete assembly language program, written for the MASM, that will convert the integer 2987_{10} to N_6.

CHAPTER ELEVEN

CONSTRUCTING PROGRAMS IN ASSEMBLY LANGUAGE PART I

INTRODUCTION

Chapters 9 and 10 gave the basics of the assembly language code. From these basics we need to use the syntax to construct complete programs in assembly language. Professional programmers use several different methods for writing programs, such as flow diagrams, pseudocode, and several others. In this chapter we will use pseudocode to guide us in writing assembly language programs. We will employ a four-step process.

Step 1: Analyze the objectives of the program.

Step 2: Convert the objectives of the program into pseudocode algorithm.

Step 3: Convert the algorithm into AL pseudocode.

Step 4: Convert the algorithm AL pseudocode into assembly language code.

To demonstrate these four steps, we will write programs to convert integer numbers from one base to another. In chapter 2, we developed the mathematics to convert bases. From chapter 2, we see that to convert numbers from an arbitrary base to the base 10, we need to evaluate

$$a_n b^n + a_{n-1} b^{n-1} + \ldots + a_3 b^3 + a_2 b^2 + a_1 b + a_0,$$

which is a polynomial of one variable.

However, in assembly language, there is no syntax that will directly allow us to perform exponential operations. The easiest way to evaluate the above expression is to linearize the polynomial.

Definition of linearizing a polynomial:

Given a polynomial of one variable, we write:

$$a_n b^n + a_{n-1} b^{n-1} + \ldots + a_3 b^3 + a_2 b^2 + a_1 b + a_0 = (\ldots(((a_n x + a_{4n-1}) b + \ldots + a_3)b + a_2) b + a_1) b + a_0.$$

In the following number base conversions, we will use the four steps mentioned above.

11.1 AN ASSEMBLY LANGUAGE PROGRAM TO CONVERT A POSITIVE INTEGER NUMBER IN ANY BASE B < 10 TO ITS CORRESPONDING NUMBER IN THE BASE 10.

Step 1: Analyze the objectives of the program.

To convert between an integer number in any base b to its corresponding number in the base 10, we recall from chapter 2 the following formula:

$N_b = a_n a_{n-1} \ldots a_n a_0 \leftrightarrow a_n b^n + a_{n-1} b^{n-1} + \ldots + a_1 b + a_0$ base 10.

Example:

The following manual method will convert the number 2567_8 to its corresponding number in the base 10:

$$N_8 = 2567_8 => ((2*8 + 5)*8 +6)*8 + 7 = ((21)*8 +6)*8 + 7 = 174*8 + 7 = 1399_{10}.$$

To convert the number 2567_8 to the base 10, we first need to write a sample program in pseudocode and assembly language to capture the digits 2, 5, 6, and 7 from the number. The following programs will perform such a task.

Step 2: Convert the objectives of the program into a pseudocode algorithm.

Program: Capture the digits of 2567_8.

PSEUDOCODE	N	A	D
N:= 2567	**2567**		
D:= 1000	2567		**1000**
A:= N ÷ D	2567	**2**	1000
N:= N MOD D	**567**	2	1000
D:= 100	567	2	**100**
A:= N ÷ D	567	**5**	100
N:= N MOD D	**67**	5	100
D:= 10	67	5	**10**
A:= N ÷ D	67	**6**	10
N:= N MOD D	**7**	6	10
D:= 1	7	6	**1**
A:= N ÷ D	7	**7**	1
N:= N MOD D	**0**	7	0

Step 3: Convert the pseudocode algorithm into AL pseudocode.

PSEUDOCODE	AL PSEUDOCODE	N	A	D	EAX	EDX
N:= 2567	N:= 2567	2567				
D:= 1000	D:=1000	2567		1000		
A:= N ÷ D	EAX:= N	2567		1000	2567	
	EAX:= EAX ÷ D	2567		1000	2	
	EDX:= EAX MOD D	2567		1000	2	567
	A:= EAX	2567	2	1000	2	567
N:= N MOD D	N:= EDX	567	2	1000	2	567
D:= 100	D:= 100	567	2	100	2	567
A:= N ÷ D	EAX:=N	567	2	100	567	567
	EAX:=EAX ÷ D	567	2	100	5	567
	EDX:= EAX MOD D	567	2	100	5	67
	A:=EAX	567	5	100	5	67
N:= N MOD D	N:= EDX	67	5	100	5	67
D:= 10	D:= 10	67	5	10	5	67
A:= N ÷ D	EAX:=N	67	5	10	67	67
	EAX:=EAX ÷ D	67	5	10	6	67
	EDX:= EAX MOD D	67	5	10	6	7
	A:=EAX	67	6	10	6	7
N:= N MOD D	N:= EDX	7	6	10	6	7

D:= 1	D:= 1	7	6	1	6	7
A:= N ÷ D	EAX:=N	7	6	1	7	7
	EAX:=EAX ÷ D	7	6	1	7	7
	EDX:= EAX MOD D	7	6	1	7	7
	A:=EAX	7	7	1	7	7
N:= N MOD D	N:= EAX	7	7	1	7	7

Step 4: Convert the AL pseudocode algorithm into assembly language code.

PSEUDOCODE	AL PSEUDOCODE	ASSEMBLY LANGUAGE
N:= 2567	N:= 2567	mov n, 2567
D:= 1000	D:=1000	mov d,1000
A:= N ÷ D	EAX:= N	mov eax, n
	EAX:= EAX ÷ D	mov edx, 0
	EDX:= EAX MOD D	div d
	A:= EAX	mov a, eax
N:= N MOD D	N:= EDX	mov n, edx
D:= 100	D:= 100	mov d, 100
A:= N ÷ D	EAX:=N	mov eax, n
	EAX:=EAX ÷ D	mov edx, 0
	EDX:= EAX MOD D	div d
	A:=EAX	mov a, eax

N:= N MOD D	N:= EDX	mov n, edx
D:= 10	D:= 10	mov d, 10
A:= N ÷ D	EAX:=N	mov eax, n
	EAX:=EAX ÷ D	mov edx, 0
	EDX:= EAX MOD D	div d
	A:=EAX	mov a, eax
N:= N MOD D	N:= EDX	mov n, edx
D:= 1	D:= 1	mov d,1
A:= N ÷ D	EAX:=N	mov eax, n
	EAX:=EAX ÷ D	mov edx, 0
	EDX:= EAX MOD D	div d
	A:=EAX	mov a, eax
N:= N MOD D	N:= EDX	mov n, edx

Note: See model assembly language program. At the end of this chapter.

Step 1: Analyze the objectives of the program.

Program: Write a sample program to compute

$$N_8 = 2567_8 => N = ((2*8 + 5)*8 +6)*8 + 7 = 1399_{10}.$$

Step 2: Convert the objectives of the program into pseudocode algorithm.

PSEUDOCODE	N	A	SUM	D
N:= 2567	**2567**			
SUM:= 0	2567		**0**	

D:= 1000	2567		0	**1000**
A:= N ÷ D	2567	**2**	0	1000
N:= N MOD D	**567**	2	0	1000
SUM:= SUM + A	567	2	**2**	1000
SUM:= SUM*8	567	2	**16**	1000
D:= 100	567	2	16	**100**
A:= N ÷ D	567	**5**	16	100
N:= N MOD D	**67**	5	16	100
SUM:= SUM + A	67	5	**21**	100
SUM:= SUM*8	67	5	**168**	100
D:= 10	67	5	168	**10**
A:= N ÷ D	67	**6**	168	10
N:= N MOD D	**7**	6	168	10
SUM:= SUM + A	7	6	**174**	10
SUM:= SUM*8	7	6	**1392**	10
DIVISOR:= 1	7	6	1392	**1**
A:= N ÷ D	7	**7**	1392	1
SUM:= SUM + A	7	7	**1399**	1

Step 3: Convert the algorithm pseudocode into AL pseudocode.

PSEUDOCODE	AL PSEUDOCOD	N	A	SUM	D	EAX	EDX	E
N:= 2567	N:= 2567	2567						
E:= 8	E:= 8	2567						8
SUM:= 0	SUM:= 0	2567		0				8
D:= 1000	D:= 1000	2567		0	1000			8
A:= N ÷ D	EAX:= N	2567		0	1000	2567		8
	EAX:= EAX÷D	2567		0	1000	2		8
	EDX:= EAX MOD D	2567		0	1000	2	567	8
	A:= EAX	2567	2	0	1000	2	567	8
N:= N MOD D	N:= EDX	567	2	0	1000	2	567	8
SUM:= SUM + A	EAX:= SUM	567	2	0	1000	0	567	8
	EAX:= EAX + A	567	2	0	1000	2	567	8
	SUM:= EAX	567	2	2	1000	2	567	8
SUM:= SUM*E	EAX:= SUM	567	2	2	1000	2	567	8
	EAX:= EAX*E	567	2	2	1000	16	567	8
	SUM:= EAX	567	2	16	1000	16	567	8
D:= 100	D:= 100	567	2	16	100	16	567	8
A:= N ÷ D	EAX:= N	567	2	16	100	567	567	8
	EAX:= EAX ÷ D	567	2	16	100	5	567	8
	EDX:= EAX MOD D	567	2	16	100	5	67	8
	A:= EAX	567	5	16	100	5	67	8
N:= N MOD D	N:= EDX	67	5	16	100	5	67	8

	EAX:= SUM	67	5	16	100	**16**	67	8
SUM:= SUM + A	EAX:= EAX + A	67	5	16	100	**21**	67	8
	SUM:= EAX	67	5	**21**	100	21	67	8
	EAX:= SUM	67	5	21	100	21	67	8
SUM:= SUM*E	EAX:= EAX*E	67	5	21	100	168	67	8
	SUM:= EAX	67	5	168	100	168	67	8
D:= 10	D:= 10	67	5	168	**10**	168	67	8
A:= N ÷ D	EAX:= N	67	5	168	10	**67**	67	8
	EAX:= EAX÷D	67	5	168	10	**6**	67	8
	EDX:= EAX MOD D	67	5	168	10	6	7	8
	A:= EAX	67	**6**	168	10	6	7	8
N:= N MOD D	N:= EDX	7	6	168	10	6	7	8
	EAX:= SUM	7	6	168	10	**168**	7	8
SUM:= SUM + A	EAX:= EAX + A	7	6	168	10	**174**	7	8
	SUM:= EAX	7	6	**174**	10	174	7	8
	EAX:= SUM	7	6	174	10	174	7	8
SUM:= SUM*E	EAX:= EAX*E	7	6	174	10	1392	7	8
	SUM:= EAX	7	6	**1392**	10	1392	7	8
D:= 1	D:= 1	7	6	1392	**1**	1392	7	8
	EAX:= N	7	6	1392	1	7	7	8
A:= N ÷ D	EAX:= EAX ÷ D	7	6	1392	1	7	7	8
	EDX:= EAX MOD D	7	6	1392	1	7	0	8
	A:= EAX	7	7	1392	1	7	0	8
	EAX:= SUM	7	7	1392	1	**1392**	0	8
SUM:= SUM + A	EAX:= EAX + A	7	7	1392	1	1399	0	8
	SUM:= EAX	7	7	**1399**	1	1399	0	8

Step 4: Convert the algorithm AL pseudocode into assembly language code.

PSEUDOCODE	AL PSEUDOCODE	AL CODE
N:= 2567	N:= 2567	mov n, 2567
E:= 8	E:= 8	mov e, 8
SUM:= 0	SUM:= 0	mov sum, 0
D:= 1000	D:= 1000	mov d, 1000
A:= N ÷ D	EAX:= N	mov eax, n
	EAX:= EAX ÷ D	mov edx, 0
	EDX:= EAX MOD D	div d
	A:= EAX	mov a, eax
N:= N MOD D	N:= EDX	mov n, edx
SUM:= SUM + A	EAX:= SUM	mov eax, sum
	EAX:= EAX + A	add eax, a
	SUM:= EAX	mov sum, eax
SUM:= SUM*E	EAX:= SUM	mov eax, sum
	EAX:= EAX*E	mul e
	SUM:= EAX	mov sum, eax
D:= 100	D:= 100	mov d, 100
A:= N ÷ D	EAX:= N	mov eax, n
	EAX:= EAX ÷ D	mov edx, 0
	EDX:= EAX MOD D	div d
	A:= EAX	mov a, eax
N:= N MOD D	N:= EDX	mov n, edx
SUM:= SUM + A	EAX:= SUM	mov eax, sum
	EAX:= EAX + A	add eax, a
	SUM:= EAX	mov sum, eax

SUM:= SUM*E	EAX:= SUM	mov eax, sum
	EAX:= EAX*E	mul e
	SUM:= EAX	mov sum, eax
D:= 10	D:= 10	mov d, 10
A:= N ÷ D	EAX:= N	mov eax, n
	EAX:= EAX ÷ D	mov edx, 0
	EDX:= EAX MOD D	div d
	A:= EAX	mov a, eax
N:= N MOD D	N:= EDX	mov n, edx
SUM:= SUM + A	EAX:= SUM	mov eax, sum
	EAX:= EAX + A	add eax, a
	SUM:= EAX	mov sum, eax
SUM:= SUM*E	EAX:= SUM	mov eax, sum
	EAX:= EAX*E	mul e
	SUM:= EAX	mov sum, eax
D:= 1	D:= 1000	mov d, 100
A:= N ÷ D	EAX:= N	mov eax, n
	EAX:= EAX ÷ D	mov edx,0
	EDX:= EAX MOD D	div d
	A:= EAX	mov a, eax
SUM:= SUM + A	N:= EDX	mov eax, sum
	EAX:= SUM	add eax, a
	EAX:= EAX + A	mov sum, eax

Exercises

1. Use the manual method to linearize the number 230451_6 to convert it to its corresponding number in the base 10.

2. Use the manual method to linearize the number 111101_2 to convert it to its corresponding number in the base 10.

11.2 AN ALGORITHM TO CONVERT ANY INTEGER NUMBER IN THE BASE 10 TO A CORRESPONDING NUMBER IN THE BASE B < 10

Step 1: Analyze the objectives of the program.

Using the Euclidean division theorem, we now review how to use the manual method to convert a number in the base 10 to a number in the base b.

Step 1: We want to write N in the form: $N = a_n b^n + a_{n-1} b^{n-1} + \ldots + a_1 b + a_0$.

Step 2: $N = Qb + R = (a_n b^{n-1} + a_{n-1} b^{n-2} + \ldots + a_1) b + a_0$.

Here, $Q = a_n b^{n-1} + a_{n-1} b^{n-2} + \ldots + a_2 b + a_1 = (a_n b^{n-2} + a_{n-1} b^{n-3} + \ldots + a_2) b + a_1$ and $R = a_0$.

Step 3: Set N = Q.

$Q = Q_1 b + R_1 = (a_n b^{n-2} + a_{n-1} b^{n-3} + \ldots + a_2) b + a_1$

where

$Q_1 = a_n b^{n-2} + a_{n-1} b^{n-3} + \ldots + a_2$

$R_1 = a_1$

Step 4: Continue in this manner, until $Q_n = 0$.

Example

Convert the following decimal numbers to the specified base.

1. $1625 \Rightarrow N_8$

Step 1: $1625 = (1625 \div 8)*8 + 1 = 203*8 + 1$

$a_0 = 1$

Step 2: $203 = (203 \div 8)*8 + 3 = 25*8 + 3$

$a_1 = 3$

Step 3: $25 = (25 \div 8)*8 + 1 = 3*8 + 1$

$a_2 = 1$

Step 4: $3 = (3 \div 8)*8 + 3 = 3$

$a_3 = 3$

Therefore, $1625 => N_8 = 3*8^3 + 1*8^2 + 3*8 + 1 => N_8 = 3131_8$

Program: Convert the integer number 1625 to the base 8.

Step 2: Convert the objectives of the program into pseudocode algorithm.

PSEUDOCODE	N	SUM	TEN	MUL	BASE	R
BASE := 8					8	
N := 1625	1625				8	
SUM := 0	1625	0			8	
MUL := 1	1625	0		1	8	
TEN := 10	1625	0	10	1	8	
R := N MOD BASE	1625	0	10	1	8	1
N:= N ÷ BASE	203	0	10	1	8	1
R := R*MUL	203	0	10	1	8	1
SUM:= SUM + R	203	1	10	1	8	1
MUL:= MUL*TEN	203	1	10	10	8	1
R := N MOD BASE	203	1	10	10	8	3
N:= N ÷ BASE	25	1	10	10	8	3
R := R*MUL	25	1	10	10	8	30
SUM:= SUM + R	25	31	10	10	8	30

MUL:= MUL*TEN	25	31	10	**100**	8	30
R := N MOD BASE	25	31	10	100	8	1
N:= N ÷ BASE	**3**	31	10	100	8	1
R := R*MUL	3	31	10	100	8	100
SUM:= SUM + R	3	**131**	10	100	8	100
MUL:= MUL*TEN	3	131	10	1000	8	100
R := N MOD BASE	3	131	10	1000	8	**3**
N:= N ÷ BASE	0	131	10	1000	8	3
R := R*MUL	0	131	10	1000	8	**3000**
SUM:= SUM + R	0	**3131**	10	1000	8	3000

Step 3: Convert the algorithm pseudocode into AL pseudocode.

PSEUDOCODE	AL PSEUDOCODE	N	S	M	R	EAX	EDX
B := 8	B := 8						
N := 1625	N := 1625	**1625**					
S:= 0	S:= 0	1625	**0**				
M:= 1	M:= 1	1625	0	**1**			
T:= 10	T:= 10	1625	0	1			
R := N MOD B	EAX:= N	1625	0	1		**1625**	
	EAX:= EAX ÷ B	1625	0	1		**203**	
	EDX:= EAX MOD B	1625	0	1		203	**1**
	R:= EDX	1625	0	1	1	203	1

N:= N ÷ B	N:= EAX	203	0	1	1	203	1
	EAX:= R	**203**	0	1	1	**1**	1
R := R*M	EAX:= EAX*M	203	0	1	1	1	1
	R:= EAX	203	0	1	1	1	1
	EAX:= S	203	0	1	1	**0**	1
S:= S + R	EAX:= EAX+ R	203	0	1	1	1	1
	S:= EAX	203	1	1	1	1	1
	EAX:= M	203	1	1	1	1	1
M:= M*T	EAX:= EAX*T	203	1	1	1	**10**	1
	M:= EAX	203	1	10	1	10	1
	EAX:= N	203	1	10	1	**203**	1
	EAX:= EAX ÷ B	203	1	10	1	**25**	1
R := N MOD B	EDX:= EAX MOD B	203	1	10	1	25	3
	R:= EDX	203	1	10	**3**	25	3
N:= N ÷ B	N:= EAX	25	1	10	3	25	3
	EAX:= R	25	1	10	3	**3**	3
R := R*M	EAX:= EAX*M	25	1	10	3	**30**	3
	R:= EAX	25	1	10	**30**	30	3
	EAX:= S	25	1	10	30	**1**	3
S:= S + R	EAX:= EAX + R	25	1	10	30	**31**	3
	S:= EAX	25	31	10	**30**	31	3

M:= M*T	EAX:= M	25	31	10	**30**	**10**	3
	EAX:= EAX*T	25	31	10	30	**100**	3
	M:= EAX	25	31	100	30	100	3
R := N MOD B	EAX:= N	25	31	100	30	**25**	3
	EAX:= EAX ÷ B	25	31	100	30	**3**	3
	EDX:= EAX MOD B	25	31	100	30	3	1
	R:= EDX	25	31	100	**1**	3	1
N:= N ÷ B	N:= EAX	3	31	100	1	3	1
R := R*M	EAX:= R	3	31	100	1	1	1
	EAX:= EAX*M	3	31	100	1	**100**	1
	R:= EAX	3	31	100	**100**	100	1
S:= S + R	EAX:= S	3	31	100	100	**31**	1
	EAX:= EAX + R	3	31	100	100	**131**	1
	S:= EAX	3	**131**	100	100	131	1
M:= M*T	EAX:= M	3	131	100	100	100	1
	EAX:= EAX*T	3	131	100	100	1000	1
	M:= EAX	3	131	**1000**	100	1000	1
R := N MOD B	EAX:= N	3	131	1000	100	3	1
	EAX:= EAX ÷ B	3	131	1000	100	0	1
	EDX:= EAX MOD B	3	131	1000	100	**0**	3
	R:= EDX	3	131	1000	**3**	0	3
N:= N ÷ B	N:= EAX	**0**	131	1000	3	0	3

	EAX:= R	0	131	1000	3	**3**	3
R := R*M	EAX:= EAX*M	0	131	1000	3	**3000**	3
	R:= EAX	0	131	1000	3000	3000	3
	EAX:= S	0	131	1000	3000	**131**	3
S:= S + R	EAX:= EAX + R	0	131	1000	3000	3131	3
	S:= EAX	0	3131	1000	3000	3131	3

$1625 => 3131_8$

Step 4: Convert the algorithm AL pseudocode into assembly language code.

PSEUDOCODE	AL PSEUDOCODE	AL CODE
B := 8	B := 8	mov b, 8
N := 1625	N := 1625	mov n, 1625
S:= 0	S:= 0	mov s, 0
M:= 1	M:= 1	mov m, 1
T:= 10	T:= 10	mov t, 10
	EAX:= N	mov eax, n
R := N MOD B	EAX:= EAX ÷ B EDX:= EAX MOD B	mov edx,0 div b
	R:= EDX	mov r, edx
N:= N ÷ B	N:= EAX	mov n, eax
	EAX:= R	mov eax, r
R := R*M	EAX:= EAX*M	mul m
	R:= EAX	mov r, eax

S:= S + R	EAX:= S	mov eax, s
	EAX:= EAX + R	add eax, r
	S:= EAX	mov s, eax
M:= M*T	EAX:= M	mov eax, m
	EAX:= EAX*T	mul t
	M:= EAX	mov m, eax
R := N MOD B	EAX:= N	mov eax, n
	EAX:= EAX ÷ B EDX:= EAX MOD B	mov edx, 0 div b
	R:= EDX	mov r, edx
N:= N ÷ B	N:= EAX	mov n, eax
R := R*M	EAX:= R	mov eax, r
	EAX:= EAX*M	mul m
	R:= EAX	mov r, eax
S:= S + R	EAX:= S	mov eax, s
	EAX:= EAX + R	add eax, r
	S:= EAX	mov s, eax
M:= M*T	EAX:= M	mov eax, m
	EAX:= EAX*T	mul t
	M:= EAX	mov m, eax
R := N MOD B	EAX:= N	mov eax, n
	EAX:= EAX ÷ B EDX:= EAX MOD B	mov edx,0 div b
	R:= EDX	mov r, edx

N:= N ÷ B	N:= EAX	mov n, eax
R := R*M	EAX:= R	mov eax, r
	EAX:= EAX*M	mul m
	R:= EAX	mov r, eax
S:= S + R	EAX:= S	mov eax, s
	EAX:= EAX + R	add eax, r
	S:= EAX	mov s, eax
M:= M*T	EAX:= M	mov eax, m
	EAX:= EAX*T	mul t
	M:= EAX	mov m, eax
R := N MOD B	EAX:= N	mov eax, n
	EAX:=EAX ÷ B EDX:= EAX MOD B	mov edx,0 div b
	R:= EDX	mov r, edx
N:= N ÷ B	N:= EAX	mov n, eax
R := R*M	EAX:= R	mov eax, r
	EAX:= EAX*M	mul m
	R:= EAX	mov r, eax
S:= S + R	EAX:= S	mov eax, s
	EAX:= EAX + R	add eax, r
	S:= EAX	mov s, eax

Model Assembly Language Program: Capture the digits of 2567_8 (see the program in section 11.1).

```
;This program capture the digits of 25678

.386
.model flat

.stack 4096
.data
n dword ?
d dwoprd ?
a dword ?

.code
_start:
mov n, 2567
mov d, 1000
mov eax, n
div d
mov a, eax
mov n, edx
mov d, 100
mov eax, n
div d
mov a, eax
mov n, edx
mov d, 10
mov eax, n
div d
mov a, eax
mov n, edx

mov d, 1
mov eax, n
div d
mov a, eax
mov n, edx

public _start
end
```

PROJECT

Modify the general algorithm in chapter 10 with appropriate while statement(s) to make the program as general as possible.

CHAPTER TWELVE

BRANCHING AND THE IF-STATEMENTS

INTRODUCTION

We are now ready to study the necessary assembly language instructions to convert the while-conditional and if-then pseudocodes, defined in chapters 5 and 6, to assembly code. To do this conversion, we need two types of jump instructions: conditional jump instructions and unconditional jump instructions.

12.1 CONDITIONAL JUMP INSTRUCTIONS FOR SIGNED ORDER

The basic form in assembly language consists of two instructions:

- The compare instructions: cmp *operand1, operand2*

- The conditional jump instructions: jump *j condition label*

The above instruction are always written in the above order. The operands can be numeric values, registers, or variables.

The compare (cmp) instructions

The following table gives the type of operand1 and operand2 that are allowed. Additional jump instructions in assembly language will be discussed in later chapters.

OPERAND1	OPERAND2
register 8 bits (byte)	numeric byte register 8 bits variable byte
register 16 bits (word)	numeric byte numeric word register 16 bits (word) variable word

register 32 bits (dword)	numeric byte numeric dword register 32 bits (dword) variable dword

variable byte: 8 bits (byte)	numeric byte register 8 bits (byte)
variable word: 16 bits (word)	numeric byte numeric word register word
variable dword: 32 bits	numeric byte numeric dword register 32 bits
AL AX EAX	numeric byte numeric word numeric dword

Note: The instruction cmp x,y are not valid in assembly language.

Examples:

1.

    x dword 236

    cmp eax, x

2.

    cmp ebx, eax

3.

   cmp x, eax

4.

   cmp x, 25767h

Exercises

1. Which of the following are valid? If not, indicate why.

a.	b.	c.	d.	e.
x dword 456h	cmp eax, x	cmp x, eax	cmp x, 235	cmp 235, x
y dword 44444h				
cmp x, y				

The conditional jump instructions for signed order numbers

To perform the pseudocode WHILE statement in assembly language, we now introduce the conditional jump instructions for signed order numbers.

From chapter 8, the following are the signed order of the numbers for the three types of rings:

The binary ring (8 bits)

R_{10}: 128 < 129 < 130 < ... < 254 < 255 < 0 < 1 < 2 < ...< 126 < 127

R_8: 80 < 81 < 82 < ... < FE < FF < 00 < 01 < 02 < ... < 7E < 7F

The word ring (16 bits)

R_{10}: 32768 < 32769 <32770 < ... < 65535 < 0 < 1 < 2 < ... < 32766 < 32767

R_{16}: 80 00 < 80 01 < 80 02 < ... < FF FF < 00 00 < 00 01 < 00 02 < ... < 7F FE < 7F FF

The dword ring (32 bits)

R_{10} : 2147483648 < 2147483649 < ... < 4,294,967,295 < 0 < 1< ... < 2147483647

R_{32} : 80 00 00 00 < 80 00 00 01 < ... < FF FF FF FF < 00 00 00 00 < ... < 7F FF FF FF

The following is a table of the conditional jumps for the signed order of rings in assembly language.

Mnemonic[1]	Description
je	jump to the label if *operand1* = *operand 2*; *jump if equal to*
jne	jump to the label if *operand1* ≠ *operand 2*; *jump if not equal to*
jnge	jump to the label if *operand1* < *operand 2*; *jump if not greater or equal*
jnle	jump to the label if *operand1* > *operand 2*; *jump if not less than or equal*
jge	jump to the label if *operand1* ≥ *operand 2*; *jump if greater than or equal*
jle	jump to the label if *operand1* ≤ *operand 2*; *jump if less than or equal*
jl	jump to the label if *operand1* < *operand 2*; *jump if less than*
jnl	jump to the label if *operand1* ≥ *operand 2*; *jump if not less than*
jg	jump to the label if *operand1* > *operand 2*; *jump if greater than*
jng	jump to the label *if operand1* ≤ *operand 2*; *jump if not greater than*

1. All of the above jump instructions **must** be preceded by the cmp instruction.

Examples:

1.

```
mov al,10; al is operand1

cmp al,2; 2 is operand2

je xyz; since the contents of al is not equal to 2, a jump does not occur.

::::::::::::::::: ; instructions

xyz: ; a label
```

2.

```
mov al, 10; al is operand1

cmp al,2 ; 2 is operand2

jne xyz ; since the contents of al is not equal to 2, a jump occurs.

::::::::::::::::: ; instructions

xyz: ; a label
```

3.

```
mov ax,32770 ; ax is operand1

cmp ax,2; 2 is operand2

jnge xyz ; since the contents of ax is not greater than 2, a jump does occur.

::::::::::::::::: ; instructions

xyz: ; a label
```

4a.

```
mov eax,80000000h; eax is operand1,

cmp al,2; 2 is operand2

jge xyz ; since the contents of al is not greater than or equal to 2, a jump
does not occur

occurs.

::::::::::::::::: ; instructions

xyz: ; a label
```

4b.

```
mov al,0 ; al is operand1

cmp al,129; 129 is operand2

jge xyz ; since the contents of al is greater than or equal to 129, a jump
occurs.

::::::::::::::::: ; instructions

xyz: ; a label
```

5a.

mov al,255 ; al is operand1

cmp al,2; 2 is operand2

jle xyz ; since the contents of al is less than or equal to 2, a jump occurs.

::::::::::::::::: ; instructions

xyz: ; a label

5b.

mov al,2 ; al is operand1

cmp al,255; 255 is operand2

jle xyz ; since the contents of al is greater than 255, a jump does not occurs.

::::::::::::::::: ; instructions

xyz: ; a label

6.

mov al,10 ; al is operand1

cmp al,2; 2 is operand2

jnle al ; since the contents of al is not less than or equal to 2, a jump occurs.

::::::::::::::::: ; instructions

xyz: ; a label

7.

mov al,128 ; al is operand1

cmp al,255; 255 is operand2

jl xyz ; since the contents of al is less than 255, a jump occurs.

::::::::::::::::: ; instructions

xyz: ; a label

8.

mov al,10 ; al is operand1 cmp al,2; 2 is operand2

jnl xyz ; since the contents of al is not less than 2, a jump occurs.

:::::::::::::::::: ; instructions

xyz: ; a label

9.

mov al,10 ; al is operand1

cmp al,2;   2 is operand2

jg xyz ; since the contents of al is greater than 2, a jump occurs.

:::::::::::::::::: ; instructions

xyz: ; a label

10.

mov al,10 ; al is operand1

cmp al,2; 2 is operand2

jng xyz ; since the contents of al is greater than 2, a jump does not occur.

:::::::::::::::::: ; instructions

xyz: ; a label

Exercises: Assume al contains the number 5 and n also contains 5. Which of the following incomplete programs will cause a jump?

1. cmp al, n

je xyz

xyz:

2. cmp al,n

jne xyz

xyz:

3. cmp al, n

   jnge xyz

   xyz:

4. cmp al, n

   jge xyz.

   xyz:

5. cmp al, n

   jle xyz.

   xyz:

6. cmp al, n

   jnle xyz

   xyz:

7. cmp al, n

   jl xyz:

   xyz:

8. cmp al, n

   jnl xyz

   xyz:

9. cmp al, n

   jg xyz

   xyz:

The unconditional jump instruction

The form of the unconditional jump instruction is jmp *label;* a jump will automatically occur.

Example:

jmp xyz ;

::::::::::::::::: ; instructions

xyz: ; a label

The conditional jump instructions for the natural order (unsigned)

From chapter 8, the following are the natural order of the numbers for the three types of rings:

The binary ring (8 bits)

R_{10}: 0 < 1 < 2 < ... < 15 < 16 < 17 < ... < 240 < ... < 254 < ... < 255

R_8: 00 < 01 < 02 < ... < 0F < 10 < 11 < ...< F0 < ... < FE < ... < FF

The word ring (16 bits)

R_{10}: 0 < 1 < 2 < ... < 255 < 256 < ... < 511 < ... < 65280 < ...< 65534 < 65535

R_{16}: 00 00 < 00 01 < 00 02 < ...< 00 FF < 01 00 < ...< 01 FF <... < FF 00 < ... < FF FE < FF FF

The dword ring (32 bits)

R_{10}: 0 < ... < 255 < ... < 65535 < ... < 16777215 < ... < 2147483647

R_{10}: 00 00 00 00 < 00 00 00 FF < ... < 00 00 FF FF < ... < FF FF FF < ... < FF FF FF FF

The following is a table of the conditional jumps for the natural order of rings (unsigned) in assembly language.

Mnemonic	Description
je	jump to the label if *operand1* = *operand 2*; *jump if equal to*
jne	jump to the label if *operand1* ≠ *operand 2*; *jump if not equal to*
jae	jump to the label if *operand1* ≥ *operand 2*; *jump if greater than or equal*
ja	jump to the label if *operand1* > *operand 2*; *jump if greater than*
jbe	jump to the label if *operand1* ≤ *operand 2*; *jump if less than or equal*
jna	jump to the label if *operand1* ≤ *operand 2*; *jump if less than or equal*
jb	jump to the label if *operand1* < *operand 2*; *jump if less than*
jnb	jump to the label if *operand1* ≥ *operand 2*; *jump if greater than or equal*
jnae	jump to the label if *operand1* < *operand 2*; *jump if less than*
jnbe	jump to the label *if operand1* > *operand 2*; *jump if greater than*

Examples:

1.

mov al,10 ; al is operand1

cmp al,2; 2 is operand2

je xyz ; since the contents of al is not equal to 2, a jump does not occur.

:::::::::::::::::: ; instructions

xyz: ; a label

2.

```
mov al,10 ; al is operand1

cmp al,2; 2 is operand2

jne xyz ; since the contents of al is not equal to 2, a jump occurs.

:::::::::::::::::: ; instructions

xyz: ; a label
```

3.

```
mov al,210 ; al is operand1

cmp al,2; 2 is operand2

ja xyz ; since the contents of al is greater than 2, a jump occurs.

:::::::::::::::::: ; instructions

xyz : ; a label
```

4.

```
mov al, 10; al is operand1

cmp al, 2; 2 is operand2

jae xyz; since the contents of al is greater than or equal to 2, a jump
occurs.

::::::::::::::::::::::::::: ; instructions

xyz: ; a label
```

5.

```
mov al, 2; al is operand1

cmp al, 2; 255 is operand2

jbe xyz; since the contents of al is less than or equal to 255, a jump
occurs.

::::::::::::::::::::::::::: ; instructions

xyz: ; a label
```

6.

    mov al, 128; al is operand1

    cmp al, 255; 255 is operand2

    jbe xyz ; since the contents of al is less than 255, a jump occurs.

    ::::::::::::::::::::::::::::: ; instructions

    xyz; ; a label

7.

    mov al, 10; al is operand1

    cmp al, 2; 2 is operand2

    je xyz; since the contents of al is not equal to 2, a jump does not occurs.

    ::::::::::::::::::::::::::::: ; instructions

    xyz; ; a label

8.

    mov al, 10; al is operand1

    cmp al, 2; 2 is operand2

    jne xyz; since the contents of al is not equal to 2, a jump occurs.

    ::::::::::::::::::::::::::::: ; instructions

    xyz ; ; a label

Exercises: Assume al contains the number 5 and n also contains 5. Which of the following incomplete programs will cause a jump?

1.

    cmp al, n

    jbe xyz

    xyz:

2.

    cmp al, n

    jnb xyz

    xyz:

3.

```
cmp al, n
ja xyz
xyz:
```

4.

```
cmp al, n
jnae xyz
xyz:
```

5.

```
cmp al, n
jae xyz
xyz:
```

6.

```
cmp al, n
je xyz
xyz:
```

7.

```
cmp al, n
jb xyz
xyz:
```

8.

```
cmp al, n
jnb xyz
xyz:
```

9.

```
cmp al, n
jnbe xyz
xyz:
```

12.2 CONVERTING THE WHILE-CONDITIONAL STATEMENTS TO ASSEMBLY LANGUAGE

We will use the pseudocode examples from chapter 6 to demonstrate how the jump instructions can be used to convert while statements.

Example:

Write a partial program that will sum the numbers from 1 to 6.

PSEUDOCODE	CYCLE OF INSTRUCTIONS	TOTAL	N
N := 1	N := 1		1
TOTAL := 0	TOTAL := 0	0	1
WHILE N <= 6	WHILE N <= 6	0	1
BEGIN	**BEGIN**	0	1
TOTAL := TOTAL + N	TOTAL := TOTAL + N	1	1
N := N + 1	N := N + 1	1	2
	TOTAL := TOTAL + N	3	2
	N := N + 1	3	3
	TOTAL := TOTAL + N	6	3
	N := N + 1	6	4
	TOTAL := TOTAL + N	10	4
	N := N + 1	10	5
	TOTAL := TOTAL + N	15	5
	N := N + 1	15	6
	TOTAL := TOTAL + N	21	6
	N := N + 1	21	7
END	**END**	21	7

PSEUDOCODE	AL PSEUDOCODE CYCLE OF INSTRUCTION	TOTAL	N	EAX
N := 1	N := 1		1	
TOTAL := 0	TOTAL := 0	0	1	
WHILE N <= 6	WHILE N <= 6	0	1	
BEGIN	**BEGIN**	0	1	
TOTAL := TOTAL + N	EAX := TOTAL	0	1	0
	EAX:= EAX + N	0	1	1
	TOTAL := EAX	1	1	1
N := N + 1	EAX := N	1	1	1
	EAX := EAX + 1	1	2	2
	N:= EAX	1	2	2
	EAX := TOTAL	1	2	1
	EAX:= EAX + N	2	2	3
	TOTAL := EAX	3	2	3
	EAX := N	3	2	2
	EAX := EAX + 1	3	2	3
	N:= EAX	3	3	3
	EAX := TOTAL	3	3	3
	EAX:= EAX + N	3	3	6
	TOTAL := EAX	6	3	6
	EAX := N	6	3	3

	EAX := EAX + 1	6	3	**4**
	N:= EAX	6	4	4
	EAX :=TOTAL	6	4	**6**
	EAX:= EAX + N	6	4	**10**
	TOTAL := EAX	**10**	4	10
	EAX := N	10	4	**4**
	EAX := EAX + 1	10	4	**5**
	N:= EAX	10	5	5
	EAX :=TOTAL	10	5	**10**
	EAX:= EAX + N	10	5	**15**
	TOTAL := EAX	**15**	5	15
	EAX := N	15	5	5
	EAX := EAX + 1	15	5	**6**
	N:= EAX	15	**6**	6
	EAX :=TOTAL	15	6	**15**
	EAX:= EAX + N	15	6	**21**
	TOTAL := EAX	**21**	6	21
	EAX := N	21	6	6
	EAX := EAX + 1	21	6	**7**
	N:= EAX	21	**7**	7
END	**END**	21	7	7

PSEUDOCODE	AL PSEUDOCODE	ASSEMBLY CODE
N:= 1	N := 1	mov n, 1
TOTAL:= 0	TOTAL := 0	mov total, 0
WHILE N <= 6	WHILE N <= 6	while: cmp n, 6
BEGIN	**BEGIN**	jg end1
TOTAL:= TOTAL + N	EAX := TOTAL	mov eax, total
	EAX:= EAX + N	add eax, n
	TOTAL := EAX	mov total, eax
N:= N + 1	EAX := N	mov eax, n
	EAX := EAX + 1	add eax, 1
	N:= EAX	mov n, eax
END	**END**	jmp while end 1:

Exercises

1. Rewrite the above program in a AL pseudocode where only registers (not variables) are used.

2. Modify the above program by replacing jg with jle.

3. Modify the above program by writing an assembly language algorithm that would allow the user to sum arbitrary numbers 1 + 2 + 3 + ... + m.

4. For the number 1 + 2 + 3+ ... + n = n(n + 1)/2, modify the above program to check if the program is adding correctly and inform the user if it is or is not working correctly.

5. Write an assembly language pseudocode algorithm to compute $1^2 + 2^2 + 3^2 + ... + M^2$ for a given positive integer N.

Example

Program: Compute the length of the number 431.

INSTRUCTIONS	CYCLE OF INSTRUCTIONS	N	COUNT
N: = 431	N := 431	**431**	
COUNT := 0	COUNT := 0	431	**0**
WHILE N <> 0	WHILE N <>0	431	0
BEGIN	**BEGIN**	431	0
COUNT := COUNT + 1	**COUNT := COUNT + 1**	431	1
N := N ÷ 10	N := N÷ 10	**43**	1
	COUNT := COUNT + 1	43	**2**
	N := N÷ 10	**4**	2
	COUNT := COUNT + 1	4	**3**
	N := N ÷10	**0**	3
END	**END**	0	3

PSEUDOCODE	AL PSEUDOCODE CYCLE	N	COUNT	EAX	EDX
TEN:= 10	TEN:= 10				
N: = 431	N := 431	**431**			
COUNT := 0	COUNT := 0	431	**0**		
WHILE N <> 0	WHILE N <>0	431	0		
BEGIN	**BEGIN**	431	0		

COUNT := COUNT + 1	EAX: = COUNT	431	0	0	
	EAX:= EAX + 1	431	0	1	
	COUNT:= EAX	431	1	1	
N := N ÷ TEN	EAX:= N	431	1	431	
	EAX:= EAX ÷ TEN	431	1	43	
	EDX:= EAX MOD10	431	1	43	1
	N:= EAX	43	1	43	1
	EAX: = COUNT	43	1	1	1
	EAX:= EAX + 1	43	1	2	1
	COUNT:= EAX	43	2	2	1
	EAX:= N	43	2	43	1
	EAX:= EAX ÷ TEN	43	2	4	1
	EDX:= EAX MOD10	43	2	4	3
	N:= EAX	4	2	4	3
	EAX: = COUNT	4	2	2	3
	EAX:= EAX + 1	4	2	3	3
	COUNT:= EAX	4	3	3	3
	EAX:= N	4	3	4	3
	EAX:= EAX ÷ TEN	4	3	0	4
	N:= EAX	0	3	0	4
	END	0	3	0	4

PSEUDO INSTRUCTIONS	AL PSEUDOCODE	ASSEMBLY CODE
TEN:= 10	TEN:= 10	mov ten, 10
N: = 431	N: = 431	mov n, 431
COUNT := 0	COUNT := 0	mov count, 0
WHILE N <> 0	WHILE N <> 0	while: cmp n, 0
BEGIN	BEGIN	begin: je end1
COUNT:= COUNT + 1	EAX: = COUNT	mov eax, count
	EAX:= EAX + 1	add eax, 1
	COUNT:= EAX	mov count, eax
N ÷ TEN	EAX:= N	mov eax, n
	EAX:= EAX ÷ TEN	mov edx, 0
		div ten
	N:= EAX	mov n, eax
END	END	jmp while end1:

12.3 IF-THEN STATEMENTS

The assembly language does not have an IF-THEN statement as defined in higher programming languages. However, we can obtain many of the same results by using the jump instructions as defined above. The following table gives instructions on how to emulate many of the IF-THEN statements for signed numbers.

PSEUDO IF-THEN INSTRUCTIONS	JUMP INSTRUCTIONS

IF *operand1* > *oprand 2* THEN
BEGIN
(instructions)
END
	cmp *operand1, operand 2*
	begin: jng end
	(instructions)
	end:

IF *operand1* ≥ *oprand 2* THEN
BEGIN
(instructions)
END
	cmp *operand1, operand 2*
	begin: jnge end
	(instructions)
	end:

IF *operand1* = *oprand 2* THEN
BEGIN
(instructions)
END
	cmp *operand1, operand 2*
	begin: jne end
	(instructions)
	end:

IF *operand1* ≠ *oprand 2* THEN
BEGIN
(instructions)
END
	cmp *operand1, operand 2*
	begin: je end
	(instructions)
	end:

IF *operand1* < *oprand 2* THEN
BEGIN
(instructions)
END
	cmp *operand1, operand 2*
	begin: jnl end
	(instructions)
	end:

IF *operand1* ≤ *oprand 2* THEN
BEGIN
(instructions)
END
	cmp *operand1, operand 2*
	begin: jg end
	(instructions)
	end:

The following table gives instructions on how to emulate many of the if-then statements for unsigned numbers.

PSEUDO IF-THEN INSTRUCTIONS	JUMP INSTRUCTIONS

IF *operand1* > *oprand 2* THEN
BEGIN
(instructions)
END
	cmp *operand1, operand 2*
	begin: jbe end
	(instructions)
	end:

IF *operand1* ≥ *oprand 2* THEN
BEGIN
(instructions)
END
	cmp *operand1, operand 2*
	begin: jb end
	(instructions)
	end:

IF *operand1* = *oprand 2* THEN
BEGIN
(instructions)
END
	cmp *operand1, operand 2*
	begin: jne end
	(instructions)
	end:

IF *operand1* ≠ *oprand 2* THEN
BEGIN
(instructions)
END
	cmp *operand1, operand 2*
	begin: je end
	(instructions)
	end:

IF *operand1* < *oprand 2* THEN
BEGIN
(instructions)
END
	cmp *operand1, operand 2*
	begin: jae end
	(instructions)
	end:

IF *operand1* ≤ *oprand 2* THEN
BEGIN
(instructions)
END
	cmp *operand1, operand 2*
	begin: jnbe end
	(instructions)
	end:

Example

1. The following program will perform the following tasks:

Task 1: Check if the number 12103 is divisible by 7.

Task 2: If divisible by 7, then place 0 in x.

PSEUDO-INSTRUCTIONS	Y	X	S
X := 12103		12103	
S := 7		12103	7
Y := (X ÷ S)*S	12103	12103	7
IF X = Y THEN	12103	12103	7
BEGIN	12103	12103	7
X := 0	12103	0	7
END	12103	0	7

PSEUDO-INSTRUCTIONS	AL PSEUDOCODE	Y	X	S	EAX
X := 12103	X:= 12103		12103		
S:= 7	S := 7		12103	7	
Y := (X ÷ S)*S	EAX:= X		12103	7	12103
	EAX:= EAX ÷ S		12103	7	1729
	EDX:= EAX MOD S		12103	7	1729
	EAX:= EAX*S		12103	7	12103
	Y:= EAX	12103	12103	7	12103
IF X = Y THEN	EAX:= X	12103	12103	7	1729
	CMP EAX,Y	12103	12103	7	1729
	JNE END	12103	12103	7	1729
BEGIN	BEGIN	12103	12103	7	1729
X := 0	X := 0	12103	0	7	1729
END	END	12103	0	7	1729

PSEUDO-INSTRUCTIONS	AL PSEUDOCODE	AL INSTRUCTIONS
X := 12103	X:= 12103	mov x, 12103
S:= 7	S := 7	mov s, 7
Y := (X ÷ S)*S	EAX:= X	mov eax, x
	EAX:= EAX÷S EDX:= EAX MOD S EAX:= EAX*S	mov edx, 0
		div s
		mul s
IF X = Y THEN	Y:= EAX	mov y, eax
	EAX:= X	mov eax, x
	CMP EAX, Y	cmp eax, y
	JNE END	jne end
BEGIN	**BEGIN**	;begin
X := 0	X := 0	mov x, 0
END	**END**	end:

Exercises:

1.

From chapter 5, we have the following algorithm.

PSEUDO-INSTRUCTIONS	EXPLANATION
LARGEST :=X1	We start by assuming X1 is the largest

IF X2> LARGEST THEN
BEGIN
LARGEST :=X2
END
	If the contents of X2 is larger than the contents of LARGEST replace LARGEST with the contents of X2

IF X3 > LARGEST THEN
BEGIN
LARGEST :=X3
END
	If the contents of X3 is larger than the contents of LARGEST replace LARGEST with the contents of X3

2. Write the assembly language algorithm to replicate the pseudocode:

IF a < x ≤ b THEN

BEGIN

::::::::::::::::

END

3. Write the assembly language algorithm to replicate the pseudocode:

IF x = a or x = b THEN

BEGIN

::::::::::::::::

END

12.4 IF-THEN-ELSE STATEMENTS

Recall from chapter 5 the form of this conditional statement:

IF *conditional expression* THEN

BEGIN statements 1

END

ELSE

BEGIN

statements 2

END

If the conditional expression is **TRUE**, statements1 following the **THEN** will be carried out and the program will skip statements 2.

If the conditional expression is **FALSE**, statements 1 following the **THEN** will not be carried out and the program will execute statements 2.

Since the assembly language does not have if-then-else statements, the following table shows how the jumps can be used to simulate this type of instruction for signed numbers.

IF-THEN-ELSE PSEUDO-INSTRUCTIONS	SIGN JUMP INSTRUCTIONS

IF *operand1* > *operand 2* THEN
BEGIN
(instructions)
END
ELSE
(instructions)
END
	cmp *operand1, operand 2*
	begin1: jng end1
	(instructions)
	end 1: jg
	(instructions)
	end2:

IF *operand1* ≥ *operand 2* THEN
BEGIN
(instructions)
END
ELSE
(instructions)
END
	cmp *operand1, operand 2*
	begin1: jnge end1
	(instructions)
	end 1:jge end2
	(instructions)
	end2:

IF *operand1* = *operand 2* THEN
BEGIN
(instructions)
END
ELSE
(instructions)
END
	cmp *operand1, operand 2*
	begin1: jne end1
	(instructions)
	end 1:je end2
	(instructions)
	end2:

IF *operand1* ≠ *operand 2* THEN
BEGIN
(instructions)
END
ELSE
(instructions)
END
	cmp *operand1, operand 2*
	begin1: je end1
	(instructions)
	end1: jne end2
	(instructions)
	end2:

IF *operand1* < *operand 2* THEN
BEGIN
(instructions)
END
ELSE
(instructions)
END
	cmp *operand1, operand 2*
	begin1: jnl end1
	(instructions)
	end1: jl end2
	(instructions)
	end2:

IF *operand1* ≤ *operand 2* THEN
BEGIN
(instructions)
END
ELSE
BEGIN
(instructions)
	cmp *operand1*,*operand 2*
	begin1: jg end1
	(instructions)
	end1: jng end2
	(instructions)
	end2:

The following table shows how the jumps can be used to simulate this type of instruction for unsigned numbers.

IF-THEN-ELSE PSEUDO-INSTRUCTIONS	UNSIGN JUMP INSTRUCTIONS

IF *operand1* > *operand 2* THEN
BEGIN
(instructions)
END
ELSE
BEGIN
(instructions)
END
	cmp *operand1*, *operand 2*
	begin1: jna end1
	(instructions)
	end1: jnbe end2
	(instructions)
	end2:

IF *operand1* ≥ *operand 2* THEN
BEGIN
(instructions)
END
BEGIN
ELSE
(instructions)
END
	cmp *operand1*, *operand 2*
	begin1: jb end1
	(instructions)
	end1: jnb end2
	(instructions)
	end2:

IF *operand1* = *operand 2* THEN
BEGIN
(instructions)
END
ELSE
BEGIN
(instructions)
END
	cmp *operand1*, *operand 2*
	begin1: jne end1
	(instructions)
	end1:je end2
	(instructions)
	end2:

IF *operand1* ≠ *operand 2* THEN
BEGIN
(instructions)
END
ELSE
BEGIN
(instructions)
END
	cmp *operand1*, *operand 2*
	begin1: je end1
	(instructions)
	end1:jne end2
	(instructions)
	end2:

IF *operand1* < *operand 2* THEN
BEGIN
(instructions)
END
ELSE
(instructions)
END
	cmp *operand1*, *operand 2*
	begin1: jnb end1
	(instructions)
	end1:jb end2
	(instructions)
	end2:

IF *operand1* ≤ *operand 2* THEN
BEGIN
(instructions)
END
ELSE
BEGIN
(instructions)
END
	cmp *operand1*, *operand 2*
	begin1: jg end1
	(instructions)
	end1: jna end2
	(instructions)
	end2:

Example

PSEUDO-INSTRUCTIONS	ASSEMBLY CODE
N := 7	mov n, 7
M := 5	mov m, 5

IF N = 2 THEN
 	
BEGIN
 	
N := N + 5
 	
END
	begin1: cmp n, 2

	jne end1
	mov eax, n
	add eax, 5
	mov n, eax
	end1:

ELSE
 	
BEGIN
 	
M = N + 5
 	
END
	begin2: je end2

	mov eax, n
	add eax, 5
	mov m, eax
	end2:

Exercise

1. Assume n is a nonnegative integer. We define n factorial as:
   $n! = n(n - 1)(n - 2) \ldots (2)(1)$ for $n > 0$ and $0! = 1$. Write an assembly language pseudocode program that will compute the value of 10!

2. Modify the above problem as an algorithm for an arbitrary n integer.

   Application: Assume we have N distinct objects, and r of these objects are randomly selected.

3. The number of ways that this can be done, where order is important, is $_NP_r = N!/(N - r)!$.

   Write an assembly language pseudocode algorithm that will perform the following tasks:

   Task1: Assign the integer N and r.

   Task2: compute: $_NP_r = N!/(N - r)!$.

4. The number of ways that this can be done, where order is not important, is

   $$\frac{N!}{r!(N - r)!}$$

   Write an assembly language pseudocode algorithm that will perform the following tasks:

   Task 1: Assign the integer N and r.

   Task 2: compute: $\dfrac{N!}{r!(N - r)!}$

5. Write an assembly language algorithm that will compute the absolute value of $|x - y|$.

12.5 TOP-DOWN STRUCTURED MODULAR PROGRAMMING

To program using top-down structured modular programming, we first begin with a list of tasks that we want to process in the specified order:

Task 1: ———

Task 2: ———

Task 3: ———

::::::::::::::::::::

Task n: ———

Next we write pseudocode for each task in a given module as follows.

```
Task 1: Module 1

::::::::::::::::::::::
```

↓

```
Task 2: Module 2

::::::::::::::::::::
```

↓

```
Task 3: Module 3

::::::::::::::::::::
```

↓

::

::::::::::::::::::::

```
Task n: Module n

::::::::::::::::::::::
```

Finally, we rewrite the pseudocode in assembly language.

Basic rules

1. After writing the tasks, first we write the code for module 1 and check for errors. Once all errors, if any, are corrected, we write module 2 and check for errors. We continue in this manner.

2. We only use jumps to perform branching within the same module. If we need to jump to outside the module, we can branch down to another module, or if the program is menu driven, we can jump to the module that contains the menu.

PROJECT

Write an AL algorithm that will find the correspondence for the given number $N_\alpha => M_\beta$ where

α, β are selected base numbers; $\alpha, \beta = 2, 3, ..., 9, 16; \alpha \neq \beta$.

CHAPTER THIRTEEN

CONSTRUCTING PROGRAMS IN ASSEMBLY LANGUAGE PART II

INTRODUCTION

Now that we can create logical and while statements in assembly language, we return to the programs and algorithms in chapter 11 to rewrite them in the most general form. Therefore, the following algorithms and programs will be modeled after those in chapter 11.

13.1 AN ASSEMBLY LANGUAGE PROGRAM TO CONVERT A POSITIVE INTEGER NUMBER IN ANY BASE B < 10 TO ITS CORRESPONDING NUMBER IN THE BASE 10

Examples

1. The following method will convert the number 2567_8 to its corresponding number in the base 10:

$$N_8 = 2567_8 => ((2*8 + 5)*8 + 6)*8 + 7 = ((21)*8 + 6)*8 + 7 = 174*8 + 7 = 1399.$$

To convert the number 2567_8 to the base 10, we first need to write a sample program in pseudocode and assembly language to capture the digits 2, 5, 6, and 7 from the number. The following programs will perform such a task.

Program: Capture the digits of 2567_8.

PSEUDO-INSTRUCTIONS	N	A	D
N:= 2567	**2567**		
D:= 1000	2567		**1000**
A:= N÷D	2567	2	1000
N:= N MOD D	**567**	2	1000
D:= D÷10	567	2	**100**
A:= N÷D	567	5	100
N:= N MOD D	**67**	5	100

D:= D÷10	67	5	10
A:= N÷D	67	6	10
N:= N MOD D	7	6	10
D:= D÷10	7	6	1
A:= N÷D	7	7	1
N:= N MOD D	0	7	0

CYCLE OF CODES	AL PSEUDOCODE	N	A	EAX	EDX	D	T
N:= 2567	N:= 2567	2567					
T:= 10	T:= 10	2567					10
D:= 1000	D:= 1000	2567		0		1000	10
WHILE N <> 0	WHILE N <> 0	2567				1000	10
BEGIN	BEGIN	2567				1000	10
A:= N ÷ D	EAX := N	2567		2567		1000	10
	EAX := EAX ÷ D EDX:= EAX MOD D	2567		2	567	1000	10
	A := EAX	2567	2	2	567	1000	10
N:= N MOD D	N:= EDX	567	2	2	567	1000	10
D:= D ÷ T	EAX := D	567	2	1000	567	1000	10
	EAX:= EAX ÷ T EDX := EAX MOD T	567	2	100	0	1000	10
	D := EAX	567	2	100	0	100	10

A:= N ÷ D	EAX := N	567	2	**567**	0	100	10
	EAX := EAX ÷ D EDX:= EAX MOD D	567	2	**5**	**67**	100	10
	A := EAX	567	5	5	67	100	10
N:= N MOD D	N:= EDX	**67**	5	5	67	100	10
D:= D÷ 10	EAX := D	67	5	**100**	67	100	10
	EAX := EAX ÷ T EDX := EAX MOD T	67	5	**10**	**0**	100	10
	D := EAX	67	5	10	0	10	10
A:= N ÷ D	EAX := N	67	5	67	0	10	10
	EAX := EAX ÷ D EDX := EAX MOD D	67	5	**6**	**7**	10	10
	A:= EAX	67	6	6	7	10	10
N:= N MOD D	N:= EDX	**7**	6	6	7	10	10
D:= D ÷ 10	EAX := D	7	6	10	7	10	10
	EAX := EAX ÷ T EDX := EAX MOD T	7	6	**1**	**0**	10	10
	D:= EAX	7	6	1	0	1	10
A:= N ÷ D	EAX := N	7	6	**7**	0	1	10
	EAX := EAX ÷ D EDX := EAX MOD D	7	6	7	0	1	10
	A := EAX	7	**7**	7	0	1	10
N:= N MOD D	N:= EDX	**0**	7	7	0	1	10
END	**END**	0	7	7	0	1	10

PSEUDOCODE	AL PSEUDOCODE	AL CODE
N:= 2567	N:= 2567	mov n, 2567
T:= 10	T:= 10	mov t, 10
D:= 1000	D:= 1000	mov d, 1000
WHILE N <> 0	WHILE N <> 0	while: cmp n, 0
		je end1
BEGIN	**BEGIN**	;begin
A:= N ÷ D	EAX := N	mov eax, n
	EAX := EAX ÷D EDX:= EAX MOD D	mov edx, 0
		div d
	A := EAX	mov a, eax
N:= N MOD D	N:= EDX	mov n, edx
D:= D ÷ T	EAX := D	mov eax, t
	EAX:= EAX÷T EDX := EAX MOD T	mov edx, 0
		div t
	D := EAX	mov d, eax
		jmp while
END	**END**	end1:

Exercise

1. Let $N_{10} = a_0a_1a_2 \ldots a_m$. Write an assembly language algorithm that will sum the digits of N.

2. **Program:** Write a sample program to compute

   $N_8 = 2567_8 \Rightarrow N_{10} = ((2*8 + 5)*8 + 6)*8 + 7 = 1399$.

PSEUDO-INSTRUCTIONS	N	A	SUM	D	T
N:= 2567	**2567**				
SUM:= 0	2567		**0**		
T:= 10	2567		0		10
D:= 1000	2567		0	1000	10
A:= N%D	2567	**2**	0	1000	10
SUM:= SUM + A	2567	2	**2**	1000	10
SUM:= SUM*8	2567	2	**16**	1000	10
N:= N MOD D	**567**	2	16	1000	10
D:= D%T	567	2	16	100	10
A:= N%D	567	**5**	16	100	10
SUM:= SUM + A	567	5	21	100	10
SUM:= SUM*8	567	5	168	100	10
N:= N MOD D	**67**	5	168	100	10
D:= D%T	67	5	168	**10**	10
A:= N%D	67	**6**	168	10	10
SUM:= SUM + A	67	6	**174**	10	10
SUM:= SUM*8	67	6	**1392**	10	10
N:= N MOD D	7	6	1392	10	10
D:= D%T	7	6	1392	**1**	10
A:= N%D	7	7	1392	1	10
SUM:= SUM + A	7	7	**1399**	1	10

CYCLE OF CODES	AL PSEUDO CODES	N	A	S	EAX	EDX	D	E	T
N:= 2567	N:= 2567	2567						8	
E:= 8	E:= 8	2567						8	

CYCLE OF CODES	AL PSEUDO CODES	N	A	S	EAX	EDX	D	E	T
S := 0	S := 0	2567		0				8	
T:=10	T:= 10	2567		0				8	10
D := 1000	D := 1000	2567		0			1000	8	10
WHILE D <> 1	WHILE D <> 1	2567		0			1000	8	10
BEGIN	BEGIN	2567		0			1000	8	10
A:= N ÷ D	EAX := N	2567		0	2567		1000	8	10
	EAX := EAX ÷ D	2567		0	2	567	1000	8	10
	A := EAX	2567	2	0	2	567	1000	8	10
S:= S + A	EAX := S	2567	2	0	0	567	1000	8	10
	EAX := EAX + A	2567	2	0	2	567	1000	8	10
	S := EAX	2567	2	2	2	567	1000	8	10
S:= S*E	EAX := S	2567	2	2	2	567	1000	8	10
	EAX := EAX *E	2567	2	2	16	567	1000	8	10
	S := EAX	2567	2	16	16	567	1000	8	10
N := N MOD D	EAX := N	2567	2	16	2567	567	1000	8	10
	EAX := EAX ÷ D	2567	2	16	2	567	1000	8	10
	N := EDX	567	2	16	2	567	1000	8	10

D:= D ÷ 10	EAX :=D	567	2	16	**1000**	567	1000	8	10
	EAX:= EAX ÷ T	567	2	16	100	**0**	1000	8	10
	D:= EAX	567	2	16	100	0	100	8	10
A:= N ÷ D	EAX := N	567	2	16	**567**	0	100	8	10
	EAX := EAX ÷ D	567	2	16	**5**	**67**	100	8	10
	A := EAX	**2567**	**5**	16	5	67	100	8	10
S:= S + A	EAX := S	2567	5	16	**16**	67	100	8	10
	EAX:= EAX + A	**567**	5	16	**21**	67	100	8	10
	S:= EAX	567	5	21	21	67	100	8	10
S:= S*E	EAX := S	567	5	21	21	67	100	8	10
	EAX := EAX *E	567	5	21	**168**	**0**	100	8	10
	S := EAX	567	5	**168**	168	0	100	8	10
N:= N MOD D	EAX := N	567	5	168	**567**	0	100	8	10
	EAX := EAX ÷ D	567	5	168	**5**	**67**	100	8	10
	N := EDX	67	5	168	5	67	100	8	10
D:= D ÷ 10	EAX :=D	67	5	168	**100**	67	100	8	10
	EAX:= EAX ÷ T	67	5	168	10	0	100	8	10
	D:= EAX	67	5	168	10	0	10	8	10
A:= N ÷ D	EAX := N	67	5	168	**67**	0	10	8	10
	EAX := EAX ÷ D	67	5	168	6	**7**	10	8	10
	A := EAX	67	6	168	6	7	10	8	10

S:= S + A	EAX:= S	67	6	168	168	7	10	8	10
	EAX:= EAX + A	67	6	168	174	7	10	8	10
	S:= EAX	67	6	174	174	7	10	8	10
S:= S*E	EAX := S	67	6	174	174	7	10	8	10
	EAX := EAX *E	67	6	174	1392	0	10	8	10
	S := EAX	67	6	1392	1392	0	10	8	10
N:= N MOD D	EAX := N	67	6	1392	67	0	10	8	10
	EAX := EAX ÷ D	7	6	1392	6	7	10	8	10
	N := EDX	7	6	1392	6	7	10	8	10
D:= D ÷ 10	EAX :=D	7	6	1392	10	7	10	8	10
	EAX:= EAX ÷ T	7	6	1392	1	0	10	8	10
	D:= EAX	7	6	1392	1	0	1	8	10
END	END	7	6	1392	1	0	1	8	10
S:= S + A	EAX := S	7	7	1392	1392	0	1	8	10
	EAX:= EAX + A	7	7	1392	1399	0	1	8	10
	S:= EAX	7	7	1399	1399	0	1	8	10

PSEUDOCODE	AL PSEUDOCODES	AL CODE
N := 2567	N:= 2567	mov n, 2567
E:=8	E:= 8	mov e, 8
S := 0	S := 0	mov s, 0
T:= 10	T:= 10	mov t, 10

D := 1000	D := 1000	mov d, 1000
WHILE D <> 1	WHILE D <> 1	while: cmp d,1 je end1
BEGIN	**BEGIN**	;begin
A:= N ÷ D	EAX := N	mov eax, n
	EAX := EAX ÷ D	mov edx, 0
		div d
	A := EAX	mov a, eax
S:= S + A	EAX := S	mov eax, s
	EAX := EAX + A	add eax, a
	S := EAX	mov s, eax
S:= S*E	EAX := S	mov eax, s
	EAX := EAX *E	mul e
	S := EAX	mov s, eax
N:= N MOD D	EAX := N	mov eax, n
	EAX := N ÷ D	mov edx,0 div d
	N := EDX	mov n, edx
D:= D ÷ 10	EAX :=D	mov eax, d
	EAX:= EAX ÷ T	mov edx, 0
		div t
	D:= EAX	mov d, eax
END	**END**	jmp while
S:= S + A	EAX := S	end: mov eax, s
	EAX:= EAX + A	add eax, a
	S:= EAX	mov s, eax

13.2 AN ALGORITHM TO CONVERT ANY INTEGER NUMBER IN THE BASE 10 TO A CORRESPONDING NUMBER IN THE BASE B < 10

Using the Euclidean division theorem, we now review how to use the manual method to convert a number in the base 10 to a number in the base b.

Step 1: We want to write N in the form:

$$N = a_n b^n + a_{n-1} b^{n-1} + \ldots + a_1 b + a_0$$

Step 2:

$$N = Qb + R = (a_n b^{n-1} + a_{n-1} b^{n-2} \ldots + a_1)b + a_0$$

Here, $Q = a_n b^{n-1} + a_{n-1} b^{n-2} \ldots + a_2 b + a_1 = (a_n b^{n-2} + a_{n-1} b^{n-3} \ldots + a_2)b + a_1$
And $R = a_0$

Step 3: Set N = Q.

$$Q = Q_1 b + R_1 = (a_n b^{n-2} + a_{n-1} b^{n-3} \ldots + a_2)b + a_1$$

Where $Q_1 = a_n b^{n-2} + a_{n-1} b^{n-3} \ldots + a_2$

$R_1 = a_1$

Step 4: Continue in this manner until $Q_n = 0$.

Example:

Convert the following decimal numbers to the specified base.

1. $1625 \Rightarrow N_8$

   Step 1: $1625 = (1625 \div 8)*8 + 1 = 203*8 + 1$

   $a_0 = 1$

   Step 2: $203 = (203 \div 8)*8 + 3 = 25*8 + 3$

   $a_1 = 3$

   Step 3: $25 = (25 \div 8)*8 + 1 = 3*8 + 1$

   $a_2 = 1$

   Step 4: $3 = (3 \div 8)*8 + 3 = 3$

   $a_3 = 3$

Therefore, $1625 => N_8 = 3*8^3 + 1*8^2 + 3*8 + 1 \leftrightarrow N_8 = 3131_8$.

Program: Pseudocode to convert the integer number 1625 to the base 8.

PSEUDOCODE	N	SUM	TEN	MUL	BASE	R
BASE := 8					8	
N := 1625	1625				8	
SUM := 0	1625	0			8	
MUL := 1	1625	0		1	8	
TEN := 10	1625	0	10	1	8	
R := N MOD BASE	1625	0	10	1	8	1
N:= N ÷ BASE	203	0	10	1	8	1
R := R*MUL	203	0	10	1	8	1
SUM:= SUM + R	203	1	10	1	8	1
MUL:= MUL*TEN	203	1	10	10	8	1
R := N MOD BASE	203	1	10	10	8	3
N:= N ÷ BASE	25	1	10	10	8	3
R := R*MUL	25	1	10	10	8	30
SUM:= SUM + R	25	31	10	10	8	30
MUL:= MUL*TEN	25	31	10	100	8	30
R := N MOD BASE	25	31	10	100	8	1
N:= N ÷ BASE	3	31	10	100	8	1
R := R*MUL	3	31	10	100	8	100

SUM:= SUM + R	3	**131**	10	100	8	100
MUL:= MUL*TEN	3	131	10	**1000**	8	100
R := N MOD BASE	3	131	10	1000	8	3
N:= N ÷ BASE	**0**	131	10	1000	8	3
R := R*MUL	0	131	10	1000	8	3000
SUM:= SUM + R	0	**3131**	10	1000	8	3000

CYCLE OF CODES	AL PSEUDOCODE	N	S	M	R	EAX	EDX	B
B := 8	B := 8							8
N := 1625	N := 1625	**1625**						8
S:= 0	S:= 0	1625	**0**					8
M:= 1	M:= 1	1625	0	1				8
T:= 10	T:= 10	1625	0	1				8
WHILE N <> 0	WHILE N <> 0	1625	0	1				8
BEGIN	**BEGIN**	1625	0	1				8
R:= N MOD	EAX:= N	1625	0	1		**1625**		8
	EAX:= EAX ÷ B	1625	0	1		**203**		8
	EDX:= EAX MOD	1625	0	1		203	1	8
	R:= EDX	1625	0	1	1	203	1	8
N:= N ÷ B	N:= EAX	**203**	0	1	1	203	1	8
R := R*M	EAX:= R	203	0	1	1	**1**	1	8
	EAX:= EAX*M	203	0	1	1	1	1	8
	R:= EAX	203	0	1	1	1	1	8

S:= S + R	EAX:= S	203	0	I	I	0	I	8
	EAX:= EAX + R	203	0	I	I	I	I	8
	S:= EAX	203	I	I	I	I	I	8
M:= M*T	EAX:= M	203	I	I	I	I	I	8
	EAX:= EAX*T	203	I	I	I	10	I	8
	M:= EAX	203	I	10	I	10	I	8
R:= N MOD	EAX:= N	203	I	I	I	203	I	8
	EAX:= EAX ÷ B	203	I	I	I	25	3	8
	R:= EDX	203	I	I	3	25	3	8
N:= N ÷ B	N:= EAX	25	I	10	3	25	3	8
R := R*M	EAX:= R	25	I	10	3	3	3	8
	EAX:= EAX*M	25	I	10	3	30	3	8
	R:= EAX	25	I	10	30	30	3	8
S:= S + R	EAX:= S	25	I	10	30	I	3	8
	EAX:= EAX + R	25	I	10	30	31	3	8
	S:= EAX	25	31	10	30	31	3	8
M:= M*T	EAX:= M	25	31	10	I	10	3	8
	EAX:= EAX*T	25	31	10	I	100	3	8
	M:= EAX	25	31	100	I	100	3	8
R:= N MOD	EAX:= N	25	31	100	I	25	3	8
	EAX:= EAX ÷ B	25	31	100	I	3	3	8
	EDX:= EAX MOD B	25	31	100	I	3	I	8
	R:= EDX	25	31	100	I	3	I	8
N:= N ÷ B	N:= EAX	3	31	100	I	3	I	8

R := R*M	EAX:= R	3	31	100	1	1	1	8
	EAX:= EAX*M	3	31	100	1	100	1	8
	R:= EAX	3	31	10	100	100	1	8
S:= S + R	EAX:= S	3	31	100	100	31	1	8
	EAX:= EAX + R	3	31	100	100	131	1	8
	S:= EAX	3	131	100	100	131	1	8
M:= M*T	EAX:= M	3	131	100	100	100	1	8
	EAX:= EAX*T	3	131	100	1	1000	1	8
	M:= EAX	3	131	1000	1	1000	1	8
R:= N MOD	EAX:= N	3	131	1000	1	3	1	8
	EAX:= EAX ÷ B	3	131	1000	1	0	1	8
	EDX:= EAX MOD B	3	131	1000	1	0	3	8
	R:= EDX	3	131	1000	3	0	3	8
N:= N ÷ B	N:= EAX	0	131	1000	3	0	3	8
R := R*M	EAX:= R	0	131	1000	3	3	3	8
	EAX:= EAX*M	0	131	1000	3	3000	3	8
	R:= EAX	0	131	1000	3000	3000	3	8
S:= S + R	EAX:= S	0	131	1000	3000	131	3	8
	EAX:= EAX + R	0	131	1000	3000	3131	3	8
	S:= EAX	0	3131	1000	3000	3131	3	8
M:= M*T	EAX:= M	0	3131	1000	3000	1000	3	8
	EAX:= EAX*T	0	3131	1000	3000	10000	3	8
	M:= EAX	0	3131	10000	3000	10000	3	8
END	END	0	3131	10000	3000	10000	3	8

$1625 \Rightarrow 3131_8$

PSEUDOCODE	AL PSEUDOCODE	AL CODE
B := 8	B := 8	mov b, 8
N := 1625	N := 1625	mov n, 1625
S:= 0	S:= 0	mov s, 0
M:= 1	M:= 1	mov m, 1
T:= 10	T:= 10	mov t, 10
WHILE N <> 0	WHILE N <> 0	while: cmp n, 0
BEGIN	**BEGIN**	begin: je end1
R := N MOD B	EAX:= N	mov eax, n
	EAX:= EAX÷B	mov edx, 0
	EDX:= EAX MOD B	div b
	R:= EDX	mov r, edx
N:= N ÷ B	N:= EAX	mov n, eax
R := R*M	EAX:= R	mov eax, r
	EAX:= EAX*M	mul m
	R:= EAX	mov r, eax
S:= S + R	EAX:= S	mov eax, s
	EAX:= EAX + R	add eax, r
	S:= EAX	mov s, eax
M:= M*T	EAX:= M	mov eax, m
	EAX:= EAX*T	mul t
	M:= EAX	mov m, eax
		jmp while
END	END	end:

$1625 \Rightarrow 3131_8$

Note: See following model program.

```
;This program converts 1625 ⇒ 3131₈
.386

.MODEL FLAT

.STACK 4096

.DATA
n dword ?
s dword ?
m dword ?
r dword ?
b dword ?
t dword ?

.CODE

_start:

;start assembly language code

mov b, 8

mov n, 1625

mov s, 0

mov m, 1

mov t, 10

While1: cmp n, 0

begin: je end1

mov eax, n

mov edx,0

div b

mov r, edx

mov n, eax

mov eax, r
```

```
mul m

mov r, eax

mov eax, s

add eax, r

mov s, eax

mov eax, m

mul t

mov m , eax

jmp while1
end1:

;end of assembly language code

PUBLIC_start

END
```

PROJECTS

1. *Definition of prime numbers:* A positive integer number N > 1 is said to be a prime number if N mod(k) = 0 only for k = 1 and k = N.

   Definition of a pair-wise odd sequence: An infinite pair of numbers (2N + 1, 2N + 3); N = 1, 2, 3, ...

   Definition of pair-wise prime numbers: Those number pairs in the above sequence where both numbers are prime.

   Examples: (3, 5), (5, 7), (11, 13), ...

   (a) Write an AL algorithm that checks an arbitrary pair-wise number to determine if it is a pair-wise prime number.

   (b) From the algorithm, write an AL program to determine if (3335787, 3335789) is a pair-wise prime numbers.

2. The Fibonacci numbers

   The Fibonacci numbers are a sequence of integer numbers generated as follows:

   Step 1: Start with 0, 1.

   Step 2: The next number is generated by adding the previous two numbers: 0, 1, 1.

   Step 3: To generate the next number, continue by adding the previous two numbers: 0, 1, 1, 2, 3, 5, 8, 13, 21, …

   Write an assembly language program that will generate a sequence N Fibonacci numbers.

CHAPTER FOURTEEN

LOGICAL EXPRESSIONS, MASKS, AND SHIFTING

14.1 INRODUCTION: LOGICAL EXPRESSIONS

Logical expressions and values are similar to conditional expressions as defined in chapters 5 and 6. However, due to the nature of the applications, we will use different terminology in this chapter.

Definition of logical values:

Logical values are of two types: true and false.

Definition of logical identifiers:

Logical identifiers are registers and variables that are assigned only values true and false.

Definition of logical operators:

There are three binary logical operators and one unary logical operator:

The binary logical operators are .AND., .OR., and .XOR. The unary logical operator is .NOT.

Definition of logical expressions:

A logical expression is made up of logical values, logical identifiers connected by logical operators.

The following table gives the logical values that result from the four logical operators.

OPERATORS	RESULTING VALUE
.OR.	*true* .OR. *true* = *true* *true* .OR. *false* = *true* *false* .OR. *true* = *true* *false* .OR. *false* = *false*
.AND.	*true* .AND. *true* = *true* *true* .AND. *false* = *false* *false* .AND. *true* = *false* *false* .AND. *false* = *false*
.XOR.	*true* .XOR. *true* = *false* *true* .XOR. *false* = *true* *false* .XOR. *true* = *true* *false* .XOR. *false* = *false*
.NOT.	.NOT. *true* = *false* .NOT. *false* = *true*

Examples

1. Logical value:

    5 = 2 + 3

    takes on the value *true*.

2. Logical identifiers: X where

    X := (5 = 1–4)

    X takes on the value *false*.

3. *true* .AND. (X = *false*) takes on the value *false*.

    Y ;= 5

    VALUE := *true*

    (.NOT. (VALUE = *true*)) .OR. (Y < 3)

    The above expression takes on the value *false* .OR. *false* = *false*.

4. Z := 0

    Y = *true*

    .NOT. ((Z < 2) .XOR. (Y = *false*))

    takes on the value *false*.

Relational operators

The following six relational operators connect the logical values and identifiers.

Definition of six relational operators:

The six relational operators are:

	Operator	**Interpretation**
1.	=	Equality
2.	<>	Inequality
3.	<	Less than
4.	>	Greater than
5.	<=	Less than orequal to
6.	>=	Greater than or equal to

Examples	Values
5 = 2 + 3	*true*
9 <> 3*3	*false*
4 <= 4	*true*
-17 < -7	*true*
(7 = 2 + 3) .OR. (4 < 1)	*false*

LOGICAL EXPRESSIONS	VALUES
(5 = 2–4) .OR. (2 <> 3)	*false* .OR. *true* = *true*
(5 = 2–4) .AND. (2 <> 3)	*false* .AND. *true* = *false*
(5 = 2–4) .XOR. (2 <> 3)	*false* .XOR. *true* = *true*
.NOT. (5 = 2–4)	.NOT. (5 = 2–4) = *true*

Logical Statements

Definition of logical statements:

A logical statement is a an instruction where the variables are declared to be logical identifiers, and these variables can be assigned logical values resulting from logical expressions.

Example:

PSEUDOCODE	X	Y	L	Z
X := 4	4			
Y := 6	4	6		
L:= (X + Y = 10)	4	6	**true**	
Z := L .XOR. (X–Y <> 0)	4	6	true	**False**
Z := Z .AND. L	4	6	true	**False**

Exercise:

Complete the following.

PSEUDOCODE	X	Y	L	Z
X := 2				
Y := 5				
L:= (X + 2*Y > 2)				
Z := .NOT. (L .OR. (.NOT. (X–Y <> 0)))				
Z := (.NOT. (L .AND. (Z .OR. L)) .XOR. Z				

Example:

The following program demonstrates how these logical expressions can be used in a program.

Task1: Assign three integer numbers.

Task 2: If the sum of these numbers is greater than 10 but less than 20, divide the sum by 2; otherwise, compute the average of these numbers.

For the following program, assume the numbers 3, 4, and 9 are assigned.

PSEUDOCODE	X	Y	Z	S	L
X:= 3	3				
Y:= 4	3	4			
Z:= 9	3	4	9		
S := X + Y + Z	3	4	9	16	
L: = (S > 10) .AND. (S < 20)	3	4	9	16	true
IF L = true THEN	3	4	9	16	true
BEGIN	3	4	9	16	true

S:= S%2	3	4	9	**8**	*true*
END	3	4	9	8	*true*
ELSE	3	4	9	8	*true*
BEGIN	3	4	9	8	*true*
S:= S%3	3	4	9	8	*true*
END	3	4	9	8	*true*

Exercises

1. In the following program, indicate if the following statements are correct or incorrect.

   X: = 2

   Z: = *true*

   V: = .NOT. (*true* .OR. *false*)

   V: = (.NOT. (V .OR. V)) .AND. V

2. Evaluate the following expressions:

   (a) (.NOT. (*true* .XOR *true*)) .AND. (.NOT. (*false* .OR. *true*))

   (b) (.NOT. (*true* .XOR *false*)) .OR. (.NOT. (*true* .OR. *false*))

   (c) .NOT. ((NOT.(*true* .XOR. *false*)) .AND. ((*true* .OR. *false*)))

3. Evaluate the following expressions:

   (a) (.NOT. (*true* .AND. *true*) = *false*) .OR. *false*

   (b) (.NOT. (*false* .AND. *true*) = *true*) .XOR. *false*

   (c) (.NOT. (*false* .AND. *false*) = *true*) .OR. *true*

   (d) (.NOT. (*true* .OR. *true*) = *false*) .AND. *false*

   (e) (.NOT. (*false* .OR. *true*) = *true*) .AND. *false*

   (f) (.NOT. (*false* .OR *false*) = *true*) .AND. *true*

4. Is the following statement true or false?

   (.NOT. (*false* .XOR. *true*) = *true*) .AND. *false*

14.2 LOGICAL EXPRESSIONS IN ASSEMBLY LANGUAGE

In assembly language the value *true* is associated with the integer number 1, and the value *false* is associated with the integer number 0. The four logical operations in assembly language are given by the following table.

PSEUDO LANGUAGE LOGICAL OPERATORS	ASSEMBLY LANGUAGE LOGICAL OPERATORS
.AND.	And
.OR.	Or
.XOR.	Xor
.NOT.	Not

The following table gives the logical values in assembly language that result from the above four logical operators.

ASSEMBLY LANGUAGE LOGICAL OPERATORS	RESULTING VALUE
and	1 and 1 = 1
	1 and 0 = 0
	0 and 1 = 0
	0 and 0 = 0
or	1 or 1 = 1
	1 or 0 = 1
	0 or 1 = 1
	0 or 0 = 0
xor	1 xor 1 = 0
	1 xor 0 = 1
	0 xor 1 = 1
	0 xor 0 = 0
not	not 1 = 0
	not 0 = 1

The Format Of The Assembly Language Logical Operators

The following are the formats of the four assembly language logical operators:

and *destination, source*

or *destination, source*

xor *destination, source*

not *destination*

Definition of destination:

A destination is always a register where the logical value is assigned.

Definition of source:

The source is a logical identifier, logical value (0 or 1), or register containing a logical value. If the source is an identifier variable or register, then the source must be of the same data type as the destination data type.

Important: The *not* logical instruction will change, in the register, the 0 bits to the 1 bits and the 1 bits to the 0 bits.

Examples

The *and* operator

ASSEMBLY LANGUAGE	AL
mov al, 1	**00 00 00 01**
and al, 1	00 00 00 01
and al, 0	00 00 00 00
mov al, 0	00 00 00 00
and al, 0	00 00 00 00

The *or* operator

ASSEMBLY LANGUAGE	AL
mov al, I	**00 00 00 0I**
or al, I	00 00 00 0I
or al, 0	00 00 00 0I
mov al, 0	**00 00 00 00**
or al, 0	00 00 00 00

The *xor* operator

ASSEMBLY LANGUAGE	AL
mov al, I	**00 00 00 0I**
xor al, I	00 00 00 00
xor al, 0	00 00 00 00
xor al, I	00 00 00 0I

The *not* operator

ASSEMBLY LANGUAGE	AL
mov al, I	**00 00 00 0I**
not al	II II II I0
not al	00 00 00 0I
mov al, 0	**00 00 00 00**
not al	II II II II
not al	00 00 00 00

14.3 ASSIGNING LOGICAL EXPRESSIONS A LOGICAL VALUE IN ASSEMBLY LANGUAGE

The following examples will demonstrate how to create logical expressions and assign their logical values.

Examples:

1. Calculate the union of two logical variables where X is *true* and Y is *false*.

PSEUDO-CODE	AL PSEUDOCODE	ASSEMBLY LANGUAGE	X	Y	Z	AL
X:= *true*	X:= *true*	mov x, 1	1			
Y:= *false*	Y:= *false*	mov y, 0	1	0		
Z:= X .OR. Y	AL:=X	mov al, x	1	0		1
	.OR. AL, Y	or al, y	1	0		1
	Z:= AL	mov z, al	1	0	1	1

2. The following is an assembly language algorithm that evaluates

   (A .AND. B) .OR. (A .AND. C).

Solution:

```
mov al, a
and al, b
mov bl, a
and bl, c
or al, bl
```

Exercises:

1. Complete the following table.

PSEUDO-CODE	AL PSEUDOCODE	ASSEMBLY LANGUAGE	X	Y	Z	AL
X:= true						
Y:= false						
Z:= X .AND.Y						

2. Write an assembly language algorithm that evaluates

   A .AND. (B .OR. C).

When programming in assembly language, we cannot use logical statements directly. To perform logical statements, we need to use the compare and jump statements described in chapter 12. This is done by assigning values 1 or 0 so that the compare and the appropriate jump statements can properly evaluate and carry out the logical statements desired. The following example shows how this is done.

Example:

We wish to write an assembly language program that will perform the following tasks:

   Task 1: Assign two numbers to x and y.

   Task 2: If both numbers are greater than 10, compute the sum of the two numbers.

   Task 3: If at least one of the numbers is less than or equal to 10, compute the product of the two numbers.

PSEUDOCODE	X	Y	Z	LOG
X:= 5	5			
Y:= 60	5	60		
LOG:= (X > 10) .AND. (Y > 10)	5	60		*false*
IF LOG = *true* THEN	5	60		*false*
BEGIN	5	60		*false*
Z:= X + Y	5	60		*false*
END	5	60		*false*
ELSE	5	60		*false*
BEGIN	5	60		*false*
Z:= X*Y	5	60	300	*false*
END	5	60	300	*false*

PSEUDOCODE	AL	X	Y	Z	LOG	EAX	EBX
X:= 5	mov x, 5	5					
Y:= 60	mov y, 60	5	60				
LOG := (X > 10) .AND. (Y > 10)	mov eax, 0	5	60			0	
	mov ebx, 0	5	60			0	0
	cmp x, 10	5	60			0	0
	jng L1	5	60			0	0
	mov eax, 1	5	60			0	0
	L1: cmp y, 10	5	60			0	0
	jng L2	5	60			0	0
	mov ebx, 1	5	60			0	1
	L2: and eax, ebx	5	60			0	1
	mov log, eax	5	60		0	0	1

IF LOG = *true* THEN	cmp log, 1	5	60		0	0	1
BEGIN	begin1 : jne end1	5	60		0	0	1
Z:= X +Y	mov eax, x	5	60		0	0	1
	add eax, y	5	60		0	0	1
	mov z, eax	5	60		0	0	1
END	end1 :	5	60		0	0	1
ELSE	je end2	5	60		0	0	1
BEGIN	begin2:	5	60		0	0	1
Z:= X*Y	mov eax, x	5	60		5	0	1
	mul y	5	60		5	**300**	1
	mov z, eax	5	60	**300**	5	300	1
END	end2:	5	60	300	0	300	1

Exercises

1. For the above program, assume x = 20 and y = 30. With these values, change the above program.

2. For the above program, assume x = 2 and y = 3. With these values, change the above program.

3. Write an assembly language algorithm that will perform the following tasks:

   Task1: Assign two positive integer numbers x and y.

   Task 2: If x > 10 and y > 10, then compute x + y.

   Task 3: If x > 10 and y $\leq$ 10, then compute x*y.

   Task 4: If x $\leq$ 10 and y > 10, then compute 2*(x + y).

   Task 5: If x $\leq$ 10 and y $\leq$ 10, then compute 3*(x + y).

14.4 MASKS

Definition of a mask:

A mask is a binary integer number (BYTE, WORD, DWORD) used with a selected logical operator (and, or, xor) that will be matched bit-by-bit with the corresponding binary number contained in a selected register.

The Mask Instruction

Definition of the mask instruction:

    logical operator   destination, source,

where the destination and source are defined above. If the source is an identifier, the destination and source must be of the same data type.

For this instruction, matching the following resulting values will hold the following.

ASSEMBLY LANGUAGE LOGICAL OPERATORS	RESULTING VALUE
and	1 and 1 = 1 1 and 0 = 0 0 and 1 = 0 0 and 0 = 0
or	1 or 1 = 1 1 or 0 = 1 0 or 0 = 0
xor	1 xor 1 = 0 1 xor 0 = 1 0 xor 1 = 1 0 xor 0 = 0

Examples:

Assume AX and BX contain the following binary numbers:

       AX: 0110 1110 1100 0011

       BX: 1001 1100 0101 1011

Here, BX will be the mask.

The following examples will show how the mask works, resulting in changing of bits in AX:

and ax, bx;

       AX: 0110 1110 1100 0011

       BX: 1001 1100 0101 1011

              ↓

       AX: 0000 1100 0100 0011

       :::::::::::::::::::::::::::::

or ax, bx;

       AX: 0110 1110 1100 0011

       BX: 1001 1100 0101 1011

               ↓

       AX: 1111 1110 1101 1011

       :::::::::::::::::::::::::::::

xor ax, bx;

       AX: 0110 1110 1100 0011

       BX: 1001 1100 0101 1011

               ↓

       AX: 1111 0010 1001 1000

Exercises:

Assume CX contains an arbitrary number. For the following assembly instructions, explain what changes to CX, if any, result from the following masks:

1. and cx, cx

2. or cx, cx

3. xor cx, cx

4. and cx, (not cx)

5. or cx, (not cx)

6. xor cx, (not cx)

14.5 SHIFTING INSTRUCTIONS

There are two types of shifting instructions: the shift instructions and the rotation instructions.

The Shift Instructions

The shift instructions move the bits in a register to the left or to the right by a designated number. The following are the shift instructions:

shl *register,* n; will shift the bits in the register to the left by n places. The extreme left bits will fall out of the register. Added bits will be the bit 0. The added bit(s) will be in bold.

shr *register,* n; will shift the bits in the register to the right by n places. The extreme right bits will fall out of the register, but the left added bits will be the bit 0. The added bit(s) will be in bold.

Examples

For the following examples, assume the register AX contains 1011 0100 1110 1011.

       shl ax, 1 ; 1011 0100 1110 1011

                      ⇐

        0110 1001 1101 011**0**

     ::::::::::::::

shl ax, 4 1011 0100 1110 1011

$$\Leftarrow$$

0100 1110 1011 **0000**

::::::::::::

shr ax, 1 ; 1011 0100 1110 1011

$$\Rightarrow$$

0101 1010 0111 0101

:::::::::::

shr ax, 4 1011 0100 1110 1011

$$\Rightarrow$$

0000 1011 0100 1110

Multiplication and Division Applications

One important application of the left shift results in multiplying the original number by a power of 2.

Examples:

1. Assume AX contains 0000 0000 0000 0011, which is equal to the number 3d.

   shl ax, 1 will result in AX changed to 000 0000 0000 00110, which is equal to the number 6d.

2. Assume AX contains 0000 0000 0000 0011, which is equal to the number 3d.

   shl ax, 2 will result in AX changed to 0000 0000 0000 1100, which is equal to the number 12d.

One important application of the right shift results in dividing the original number by a power of 2.

3. Assume AX contains 0000 0000 0000 0110, which is equal to the number 6d.

   shr ax, 1 will result in AX changed to 0000 0000 0000 0011, which is equal to the number 3d.

The Rotation Instructions

There are two types of rotation instructions:

rol *destination,* n; *rotate* the bits to the left n places. The bits that are shifted off the left-hand side replace the bits that are added on the right-hand side.

ror *destination,* n; rotate the bits to the right n places. The bits that are shifted off the right-hand side replace the bits that are added on the left-hand side.

Examples

1. Assume AX contains 1100 0000 0000 0101.

   rol ax, 2 will result in AX changed to 0000 0000 0001 0111.

2. Assume AX contains 1100 0000 0000 0101.

   ror ax, 3 will result in AX changed to 1011 1000 0000 0000.

```
;This is the above program.
.386

.model flat

.stack 4096

.data
n dword ?
s dword ?
m dword ?
r dword ?
b dword ?
t dword ?

.code

_start:

;start assembly language code

mov x, 5

mov y, 60

mov eax, 0
```

```
mov ebx, 0

cmp x, 10

jng L1

mov eax, 1

L1: cmp y, 10

jng L2

mov ebx, 1

L2: and eax, ebx

mov log, eax

cmp log, 1

begin1: jne end1

mov eax, x

add eax, y

mov z, eax

end1:

je end2

begin2:

mov eax, x

mul y

mov z, eax
end2:

;end of assembly language code

public _start

End
```

278 • ASSEMBLY LANGUAGE PROGRAMMING MADE CLEAR

PROJECTS

1. There are important equations in logical expression:

   Morgan's law I: .NOT. (A .OR. B) = (.NOT. A) .AND. (.NOT. B)

   Morgan's law II: .NOT. (A .AND. B) = (.NOT. A) .OR. (.NOT. B)

   For each law, write an AL program that 'proves' the two laws are true for all possible values of A and B.

2. A .AND. (B .OR. C) = (A .AND. B) .OR. (A .AND. C)

   is referred to as the distributive law. Write an AL program that proves the law is true for all possible values of A, B, and C.

3. Two different positive integer numbers are said to be relatively prime if both numbers have no common divisors other than the number 1.

Examples

The numbers 51 and 32 are relatively prime, since they have no common divisors.

The numbers 22 and 40 are not relatively prime, since 2 divides both numbers.

Write an assembly language algorithm that will determine if 1,048,576 and 387,420,489 are relatively prime.

CHAPTER FIFTEEN

INTEGER ARRAYS

INTRODUCTION

So far, we have seen that we can save integer numeric values in variables such as x, y, z, and so on. Restricting ourselves to only variables of this type does not allow us to effectively store large amount of data. To accomplish this, we need to define arrays (tables). We first introduce one-dimensional arrays in pseudocode.

15.1 REPRESENTING ONE-DIMENSIONAL ARRAYS IN PSEUDOCODE

Definition of a one-dimensional array:

A one-dimensional array is a collection of cells that all have the same name but are distinguished from one another by the use of subscripts. A subscript is a positive integer number in parentheses that follows the array's name.

Examples

1. a(1), a(2), a(3), ..., a(99), a(100)

2. num(1), num(2), ..., num(999), num(1000)

In the first example, the array named a can store 100 pieces of data, and the in the second example, the array named num can store 1,000 pieces of data.

Rules for arrays

1. The array name is a valid identifier.

2. Each subscript must be a positive integer.

3. Integer numeric values can be stored in these array cells.

Examples

a(10) := 3

num(100) := –7

sum := a(10) + num(100)

Programming examples

The following program in pseudocode will perform the following tasks:

Task 1: Store the numbers 2, 4, 6, ..., 1000 in array cells.

Task 2: Add the numbers in the cells.

Task 3: Compute the average.

Task 4: Store all the numbers that are greater than the average.

Task 1:

```
k:= 1
j:= 0
WHILE j ≤ 1000
BEGIN
j:= 2*K
num(k) := j
k:= k + 1
END
```

Task 2:

```
total:= 0
k := 0
WHILE k ≤ 500
k := k + 1
total := total + num(k)
END
```

Task 3:

```
average : = total/500
```

Task 4:

```
k := 0
WHILE k ≤ 500
k := k + 1
IF num(k) > average THEN
Store(k) := num(k)
END
```

Exercises:

1. Write a pseudocode algorithm that will perform the following tasks:

   Task 1: Store the numbers $2, 2^2, 2^3, \ldots, 2^n$ in array cells.

   Task 2: Add the numbers in the cells.

   Task 3: Compute the integer average (the average without the remainder).

2. Finding the largest value: Write a pseudocode algorithm that will perform the following tasks:

   Task 1: Store n nonnegative integers in an array.

   Task 2: Find the largest value.

3. Converting positive decimal integers into binary: Write a pseudocode algorithm that will perform the following task:

   Task 1: Convert a nonnegative integer number into binary and store the binary digits in an array.

4. Writing numbers backward: Write a pseudocode algorithm that performs the following tasks:

   Task 1: Store a positive integer number.

   Task 2: Store the digits in an array backward.

5. A proper divisor of a positive integer N is an integer that is not equal to 1 or N and divides N without a remainder. For example, the proper divisors of 21 are 3, and 7.

   Write a pseudocode algorithm that performs the following tasks:

   Task 1: Store a positive integer number N.

   Task 2: Find and store in an array all the proper divisors of N.

6. The Fibonacci number sequence: The Fibonacci numbers are the following:

   0, 1, 1, 2, 3, 5, 8, 13, ...,

   where $0 + 1 = 1, 1 + 1 = 2, 1 + 2 = 3, 2 + 3 = 5$, and so on.

The general rule is to add the previous two numbers in the sequence to get the next number. Write a pseudocode algorithm that will perform the following tasks:

Task 1: Store a positive integer N.

Task 2: Compute and store in an array all Fibonacci numbers less than or equal to N.

15. 2 CREATING ONE-DIMENSIONAL INTEGER ARRAYS IN ASSEMBLY LANGUAGE

There are several ways to create a one-dimensional integer array. We begin by starting an array at the location of a given variable. We define an array using the directive instruction in the data portion of the program. We will use the directive

variable name data type ?

to establish the location in memory of the cell a(1).

Since the assembler will determine the beginning location of the first cell of the array, we can capture the location with the lea instruction. The following is the definition of the lea instruction in the instruction portion of the program:

The lea 32-bit register, variable name of the array instruction

Definition of the lea instruction:

The lea instruction will store into any 32-bit register, the first byte location of a variable.

Example

x byte ?

lea ebx, x

In this example the lea instruction will store in ebx, the first byte location of the variable x. Before we discuss arrays in assembly language, we need to better understand how data is stored in main memory. All integer data are represented as bytes, words, or dwords. All of these are made up of bytes: the double word (DWORD) is made up of 4 bytes (32 bits); the word (WORD) is made up of 2 bytes, and the byte (BYTE) is made up of 1 byte. We can think of the main memory as a large memory table made up of columns and rows; each cell of the table is a byte, each identified with a numeric location.

1		2		3		4	
5		6		7		8	
9		10		11		12	
13		14		15		16	
·········	·········	·········	·········	·········	·········	·········	·········

For example, assume the identifiers x and y are defined as double words and assigned the values 3h and 5875h, respectively:

x dword 3h

y dword 5875h

Assume the assembler selects in memory cell locations 1 to 4 for x and 13 to 16 for y. Our memory table would look something like the following.

1		2		3		4	
0	0	0	0	0	0	0	3
····	····	····	····	····	····	····	····
13		14		15		16	
0	0	0	0	5	8	7	5
····	····	····	····	····	····	····	····

Creating a one-dimensional array of a given data type

When we create an array, we can store the array elements as three types of data: byte, word, and dword.

The following steps will define and set up the array.

Step 1: Define the variable name and its data type byte.

Step 2: Using the lea instruction, store the first byte location in a 32-bit register.

Examples

1.

x byte ?

lea ebx, x

2.

y word ?

lea eax, y

3.

z dword ?

lea edx, z

Storing data in the array using a variable's location

The following definition is the assignment statement that will allow us to perform data assignments to and from memory cells:

mov [register], source instruction.

where the **register** must be a 32-bit register, and the **source** can be a register of the same data type as the variable.

Definition: mov [register], source

The *mov [register], source* instruction will store the number in the source register directly in the memory location indicated by the contents of the register, where the following rules apply:

Rule 1: The lea instruction will establish the first byte location.

Rule 2: The register must be EAX, EBX, ECX, or EDX.

Rule 3: The *source* can be a register of the same data type as the variable.

Rule 4: The *[register]* indicates the cell location where the bytes are to be located.

The *[register]* is called the indirect register.

For all examples in this chapter, we assume all numbers are represented as hexadecimals.

Examples

The following examples show how arrays of different data types are created and data is stored.

1.

AL CODE	AL	X
x byte 68h		**68**
lea ebx, x		68
mov al, 9Ah	**9A**	68
mov [ebx], al	9A	**9A**

2.

AL CODE	AX	X
x word ?		
lea ebx, x		
mov ax, 237Ah	**23 7A**	
mov [ebx], ax	23 7A	**23 7A**

3.

AL CODE	EAX	X
x dword 17223FDh		**01 72 23 FD**
lea ebx, x		01 72 23 FD
mov eax, 0A637Ah	**00 0A 63 7A**	01 72 23 FD
mov [ebx], eax	00 0A 63 7A	**00 0A 63 7A**

4. The following program will store numbers 13h, 29h, 25h into the array X of type BYTE.

PSEUDOCODE	AL CODE	AL	X		
			byte 1	byte 2	byte 3
Array X	x byte ? lea ebx,x				
X(1) := 13h	mov al, 13h	**13**			
	mov [ebx], al	13	**13**		
	add ebx, 1	13	13		
X(2):= 29h	mov al, 29h	**29**	13		
	mov [ebx], al	29	13	**29**	
	add ebx, 1	29	13	29	
X(3):= 25h	mov al, 25h	**25**	13	29	
	mov [ebx], al	25	13	29	**25**

Important: Since we are storing in individual bytes, we increment by 1.

5. The following program will store numbers 13h, 29h, and 25h in the array of type WORD.

PSEUDOCODE	AL CODE	AX	X		
			word 1	word 2	word 3
Array X	x word ? lea ebx,x				
X(1) := 13h	mov ax, 13h	**00 13**			
	mov [ebx], ax	00 13	**00 13**		
	add ebx, 2	00 13	00 13		

X(2):= 29h	mov ax, 29h	**00 29**	00 13		
	mov [ebx], ax	00 29	00 13	**00 29**	
	add ebx, 2	00 29	00 13	00 29	
X(3):= 25h	mov ax, 25h	**00 25**	00 13	00 29	
	mov [ebx], ax	00 25	00 13	00 29	**00 25**

Important: Since we are storing in individual bytes for each word, <u>we increment by 2.</u>

6. The following program will store numbers 13h, 29h, and 25h in the array of type DWORD.

PSEUDOCODE	AL CODE	EAX	X		
			dword 1	dword 2	dword 3
Array X	x dword ? lea ebx, x				
X(1) := 13h	mov eax, 13h	**00 00 00 13**			
	mov [ebx], eax	00 00 00 13	**00 00 00 13**		
	add ebx, 4	00 00 00 13	00 00 00 13		
X(2):= 29h	mov eax, 29h	**00 00 00 29**	00 00 00 13		
	mov [ebx], eax	00 00 00 29	00 00 00 13	**00 00 00 29**	
	add ebx, 4	00 00 00 29	00 00 00 13	00 00 00 29	
X(3):= 25h	mov eax, 25h	**00 00 00 25**	00 00 00 13	00 00 00 29	
	mov [ebx], eax	00 00 00 25	00 00 00 13	00 00 00 29	**00 00 00 25**

Important: Since we are storing in individual bytes for each dword, <u>we increment by 4.</u>

Exercise

1. Write an assembly language program that will store the first 50 positive odd numbers.

Storing data in the array without a variable's location

Arrays can also be created without using a variable location by simply using the

mov [register], source instruction

where the source is a register, contain the location where the first byte of the array is to be stored. For this instruction the following rules apply:

Rule 1: The register must be EAX, EBX, ECX, or EDX.

Rule 2: The *source* can be a register of any data type.

Rule 3: The *[register]* indicates the cell location where the bytes are to be located.

The *[register]* is called the indirect register.

Examples

1.

AL CODE	EBX	AL	[EBX]
mov ebx, 403030h	**00 40 30 30**		
mov al, 9Ah	00 40 30 30	**00 9A**	
mov [ebx], al	00 40 30 30	00 9A	00 00 00 **9A**

2.

AL CODE	EBX	AX	[EBX]
mov ebx, 403030h	**00 40 30 30**		
mov ax, 569Ah	00 40 30 30	**56 9A**	
mov [ebx], ax	00 40 30 30	56 9A	00 00 **56 9A**

3.

AL CODE	EBX	EAX	[EBX]
mov ebx, 403030h	00 40 30 30		
mov eax, 2AC6756Ah	00 40 30 30	2A C6 75 6A	
mov [ebx], eax	00 40 30 30	2A C6 75 6A	2A C6 75 6A

4.

AL CODE	EAX	EBX	BYTES 1	2	3	4	5	6	7	8
mov eax, 1h	1									
mov ebx, 7D712Eh	1	007D712E								
mov [eax], ebx	1	007D712E	0 0	7 D	7 1	2 E				
mov eax, 5h	5	007D712E	0 0	7 D	7 1	2 E				
mov ebx.	5	00568923	0 0	7 D	7 1	2 E				
mov [eax], ebx	5	00568923	0 0	7 D	7 1	2 E	0 0	5 6	8 9	2 3
mov ebx, 3h	5	00000003	0 0	7 D	7 1	2 E	0 0	5 6	8 9	2 3
mov [eax], ebx	5	00000003	0 0	7 D	7 1	2 E	0 0	0 0	0 0	0 3

Exercise:

1. Write an assembly language program that will perform the following tasks:

   Task 1: Store the first 50 positive odd numbers.

   Task 2: Retrieve the first 50 positive odd numbers stored in task 1.

Retrieving data from an array

The elements of an array can be retrieved using the following instruction:

mov source, [register]

The *mov source, [register]* instruction will retrieve the number in the array at its beginning location and store it in the source, where the following rules apply:

Rule 1: The register must be EAX, EBX, ECX, or EDX.

Rule 2: The *source* must be a register of the same data type as the original array.

Rule 3: The *[register]* indicates the cell location where the bytes are to be located.

The *[register]* is called the indirect register.

Examples:

1.

AL CODE	EBX	AL	[EBX]	CL
mov ebx, 403030h	**00403030**			
mov al, 9Ah	00403030	**9A**		
mov [ebx], al	00403030	9A	**9A**	
mov cl, [ebx]	00403030	9a	9A	**9A**

2.

AL CODE	EBX	AX	[EBX]	CX
mov ebx, 403030h	**00403030**			
mov ax, 569Ah	00403030	**569A**		
mov [ebx], ax	00403030	569A	**569A**	
mov cx, [ebx]	00403030	569A	569A	**569A**

3.

AL CODE	EBX	EAX	[EBX]	ECX
mov ebx, 403030h	**00403030**			
mov eax, 2AC6756Ah	00403030	**2AC6756A**		
mov [ebx], eax	00403030	2AC6756A	**2AC6756A**	
mov ecx, [ebx]	00403030	2AC6756A	2AC6756A	**2AC6756A**

The following example is an extension of the above example and shows how the data from the array can be retrieved.

4.

AL CODE	AL	X		
x byte ? lea ebx,x		byte 1	byte 2	byte 3
mov al, 13h	**13**			
mov [ebx], al	13	**13**		
add ebx, 1	13	13		
mov al, 29h	**29**	13		
mov [ebx], al	29	13	**29**	
add ebx, 1	29	13	29	
mov al, 25h	**25**	13	29	
mov [ebx],a l	25	13	29	**25**
sub ebx, 2; Retrieving data	25	13	**29**	25
mov al, [ebx]	**13**	13	29	25
add ebx, 1	13	13	29	25
mov al, [ebx]	**29**	13	29	25
add ebx, 1	29	13	29	25
mov al, [ebx]	**25**	13	29	25

Exercise:

1. Extend the following program so that the array data stored can be retrieved to the register ax.

AL CODE	EAX	X		
x dword ? lea ebx, x		dword 1	dword 2	dword 3
mov eax, 13h	**00 00 00 13**			
mov [ebx], eax	00 00 00 13	**00 00 00 13**		
add ebx, 4	00 00 00 13	00 00 00 13		
mov eax, 29h	**00 00 00 29**	00 00 00 13		
mov [ebx], eax	00 00 00 29	00 00 00 13	**00 00 00 29**	
add ebx, 4	00 00 00 29	00 00 00 13	00 00 00 29	
mov eax, 25h	**00 00 00 25**	00 00 00 13	00 00 00 29	
mov [ebx], eax	00 00 00 25	00 00 00 13	00 00 00 29	**00 00 00 25**

Array lists

An alternative way to create one-dimensional arrays is to list the array elements in the following directive:

variable name data type $n_1, n_2, ..., n_m$, where the list is of the same data type.

There are three directives of this type:

variable name byte type $n_1, n_2, ... , n_m$

variable name word type $n_1, n_2, ... , n_m$

variable name dword type $n_1, n_2, ... , n_m$

Examples

The following examples show how to retrieve listed arrays.

1.

AL CODE	AL	X		
		byte 1	byte 2	byte 3
x byte 3h, 7dh, 99h		**03**	**7d**	**99**
lea ebx, x		03	7d	99
mov al, [ebx]	**03**	03	7d	99
add ebx, 1	03	03	7d	99
mov al, [ebx]	**07**	03	7d	99
add ebx, 1	07	03	7d	99
mov al, [ebx]	**99**	03	7d	99

2.

AL CODE	AX	X		
		word 1	word 2	word 3
x word 37f2h, 723dh, defah		**37 f2**	**72 3d**	**de fa**
lea ebx, x		37 f2	72 3d	de fa
mov ax, [ebx]	**37 f2**	37 f2	72 3d	de fa
add ebx, 2	37 f2	37 f2	72 3d	de fa
mov ax, [ebx]	**72 3d**	37 f2	72 3d	de fa
add ebx, 2	72 3d	37 f2	72 3d	de fa
mov ax, [ebx]	**de fa**	37 f2	72 3d	de fa

3.

AL CODE	EAX	X		
		dword	dword	dword 3
x dword 4437f2h, 21723dh, d276efah		4437f2	21723d	d276efa
lea ebx, x		4437f2	21723d	d276efa
mov eax, [ebx]	00 44 37 f2	4437f2	21723d	d276efa
add ebx, 4	00 44 37 f2	4437f2	21723d	d276efa
mov eax, [ebx]	00 2 1 72 3d	4437f2	21723d	d276efa
add ebx, 4	00 21 72 3d	4437f2	21723d	d276efa
mov eax, [ebx]	0d 27 6e fa	4437f2	21723d	d276efa

15.3 RESERVING STORAGE FOR AN ARRAY USING THE DUP DIRECTIVE

There are times when it is important to set aside a block of memory that array values will be stored in. The reason is that without reserving a block of memory, data or code can be destroyed when cells are filled by an array. In fact, it is recommended that, where possible, the DUP directive be used when creating arrays. To accomplish this, we define an array A(dimension) using the following directive instruction in the data portion of the program:

variable name type dimension DUP (?)

Examples:

1. x byte 100   dup (?)

   will create an array with a dimension of 100 byte cells.

2. x word 100   dup (?)

   will create an array with a dimension of 100 WORD cells, consisting of 200 bytes.

3. x dword 100 dup (?)

will create an array with a dimension of 100 DWORD cells, consisting of 400 bytes.

Note: The lea *instruction* will still be used to determine the first byte position of the array.

Exercise:

1. Write an assembly language program that will perform the following task: store in a dimensioned array the first 100 positive numbers.

15.4 WORKING WITH DATA

The following instruction will allow data to be directly stored in an array cell:

mov *DATA TYPE* PTR.

In order to avoid ambiguity about the data type, this instruction informs the assembler that the numeric value to be stored is to be identified as a given data type.

This instruction is defined as

mov data type PTR *[register], numeric value.*

For this move instruction, the following are the three different forms of the instruction:

• mov *byte* PTR *[register], numeric value;*

will define the size *of the numeric value* to be stored as a byte.

• mov *word* PTR *[register], numeric value;*

will define the *size of the numeric value* to be stored as a word.

• mov d*word* PTR *[register], numeric value;*

will define the *size of the numeric value* to be stored a dword.

Note: mov *[register]*, source does not modify the contents of the register in question.

Examples:

1.

AL CODE	EBX	[EBX]
mov ebx, 403030h	**00 40 30 30**	
mov byte ptr [ebx], 9ah	00 40 30 30	**00 00 00 9a**

2.

AL CODE	EBX	[EBX]
mov ebx, 403030h	**00 40 30 30**	
mov word ptr [ebx], 679ah	00 40 30 30	**679a**

3.

AL CODE	EBX	[EBX]
mov ebx, 403030h	**403030**	
mov dword ptr [ebx], 231abc9ah	403030	**23 1a bc 9a**

Arithmetic operators using [*register*]

For the following two integer arithmetic operators—addition and subtraction—the indirect register *[register]* can be a source for the following arithmetic instructions:

- add register *[register]*
- add *[register]*, register
- sub register, *[register]*
- sub *[register]*, register

Examples:

I.

AL CODE	EAX	X
x byte 6h		**06**
lea ebx, x		06
mov eax, 2h	**00 00 00 02**	06
add eax, [ebx]	**00 00 00 08**	06

2.

AL CODE	EAX	X
x byte 2h		**02**
lea ebx, x		02
mov eax, 8h	**00 00 00 08**	02
sub eax, [ebx]	**00 00 00 06**	02

Exercises:

1. Complete the following table.

BYTES

AL INSTRUCTIONS	Eax	ebx	10	11	12	13	14	15	16	17	18
mov eax, 2ACD16 h											
mov ebx, 10h											
add ebx, 1h											
mov [ebx], eax											
add [ebx], ebx											
add eax, ebx											

2. Assume we have two arrays, x and y, containing the elements:

x: 2, 7, 9, 10

y: 123, 56, 11, 9.

Write an assembly language program that will multiply the corresponding array elements and store the resulting product in an array z.

The cmp using [*register*]

The cmp instruction can be used to compare array elements. The instruction is of the following forms:

cmp [register], register

cmp register, [register]

Example:

AL CODE	EAX	X
x byte 6h		**06**
lea ebx, x		06
mov eax, 7h	**00 00 00 07**	06
cmp eax, [ebx]	00 00 00 07	06
ja bigger	00 00 00 07	06
jp not_bigger	00 00 00 07	06
bigger: mov eax, 0h	**00 00 00 00**	06
jmp finished	00 00 00 00	06
not_bigger: mov eax, 1h	00 00 00 00	06
finished:	00 00 00 00	06

15.5 REPRESENTING TWO-DIMENSIONAL ARRAYS IN PSEUDOCODE

Definition of a two-dimensional arrays name(r,c):

A two-dimensional array is a collection of cells that all have the same name but are distinguished from one another by the use of two subscripts. A subscript is a positive integer number in parentheses that follows the array's name. The two-dimensional array can be indicated by *name*(r,c) where r is the number of rows and c the number of columns.

The following are the way the values of the two-dimensional array are written:

a(1,1), a(1,2), a(1,3), ..., a(1,c),

a(2,1), a(2,2), a(2,3), ..., a(2,c),

:::

a(r,1), a(r,2), a(r,3), ..., aa (r,c)

Such an array is said to have r rows and c columns.

The following table shows the structure of the two-dimensional array.

row/c ol	1	2	3	4	5	6	7		--k--	c
1	a(1,1)	a(1,2)	a(1,3)	a(1,4)	a(1,5)	a(1,6)	a(1,7)	a(1,8)	a(1,k)	a(1,c)
2	a(2,1)	a(2,2)	a(2,3)	a(2,4)	a(2,5)	a(2,6)	a(2,7)	a(2,8)	a(2,k)	a(2,c)
3	a(3,1)	a(3,2)	a(3,3)	a(3,4)	a(3,5)	a(3,6)	a(3,7)	a(3,8)	a(3,k)	a(3,c)
4	a(4,1)	a(4,2)	a(4,3)	a(4,4)	a(4,5)	a(4,6)	a(4,7)	a(4,8)	a(4,k)	a(4,c)
5	a(5,1)	a(5,2)	a(5,3)	a(5,4)	a(5,5)	a(5,6)	a(5,7)	a(5,8)	a(5,k)	a(5,c)
::::::::	::::	::::	::::	::::	::::	::::	::::	::::	::::	::::
j	a(j,1)	a(j,2)	a(j,3)	a(j,4)	a(j,5)	a(j,6)	a(j,7)	a(j,8)	a(j,k)	a(j,c)
::::::::	::::	::::	::::	::::	::::	::::	::::	::::	::::	::::
r	a(r,1)	a(r,2)	a(r,3)	a(r,4)	a(r,5)	a(r,6)	a(r,7)	a(r,8)	a(j,k)	a(r,c)

where a(j,k) are the numerical values of the array.

However, we have one small problem: The assembly language really only provides storing of data for one-dimensional arrays. Therefore, to program two-dimensional arrays, we need to change the two-dimensional array into a one-dimensional array. To do this, first we note that the two-dimensional array is made up of rows that are stacked one on top of each other. To convert the two-dimensional array into a one-dimensional array, take each row and connectively arrange them one by one to make the new one-dimensional array. To demonstrate how this is done, we use as an example a two-dimensional array consisting of 3 rows and 10 columns:

r/c	1	2	3	4	5	6	7	8	9	10
1	a(1,1)	a(1,2)	a(1,3)	a(1,4)	a(1,5)	a(1,6)	a(1,7)	a(1,8)	a(1,9)	a(1,10)
2	a(2,1)	a(2,2)	a(2,3)	a(2,4)	a(2,5)	a(2,6)	a(2,7)	a(2,8)	a(2,k)	a(2, 10)
3	a(3,1)	a(3,2)	a(3,3)	a(3,4)	a(3,5)	a(3,6)	a(3,7)	a(3,8)	a(3,k)	a(3,10)

Row 1	**Row 2**	**Row 3**
a(1,1) a(1,2) a(1,3) ... ... a(1,10)	a(2,1) a(2,2) a(2,3) ... ... a(2,10)	a(3,1) a(3,2) a(3,3) ... ... a(3,10)

Now we need to change a(i,j) into an array element of one subscript for the above one-dimensional array. We define a(t) as the following:

$$a(10r - 10 + c) = a(r,c) \text{ for}$$

$$1 \leq r \leq 3$$

$$1 \leq c \leq 10$$

Using the above formula, we have:

r = 1: a(1) = a(1,1); a(2) = a(1,2); a(3) = a(1,3); a(4) = a(1,4); a(5) = a(1,5); a(6) = a(1,6)

a(7) = a(1,7); a(8) = a(1,8); a(9) = a(1,9); a(10) = a(1,10)

r = 2: a(11) = a(2,1); a(12) = a(2,2); a(13) = a(2,3); a(14) = a(2,4); a(15) = a(2,5);

a(16) = a(2,6) a(17) = a(2,7); a(18) = a(2,8); a(19) = a(2,9); a(20) = a(2,10);

r = 3: a(21) = a(3,1); a(22) = a(3,2); a(23) = a(3,3); a(24) = a(3,4); a(25) = a(3,5);

a(26) = a(3,6) a(27) = a(3,7); a(28) = a(3,8); a(29) = a(3,9); a(30) = a(3,10);

Which gives our one-dimensional array:

Row 1	Row 2	Row 3
a(1) a(2) a(3) ... a(10)	a(11) a(12) a(13) ... a(20)	a(21) a(22) a(23) ... a(30)

Example

The following program in pseudocode will perform the following task:

Task: Assign array values $a(r, c) = r + 2c$, for $1 \leq r \leq 100$; $1 \leq c \leq 10$

Program

```
r := 1

r ≤ 100

BEGIN

c := 1

WHILE c ≤ 10

BEGIN

a(r, c) := r + 2*c

c := c + 1

END

r := r + 1

END
```

Exercise:

1. Write an assembly language program that will generate the above array.

Model program

```
;The following program is a partial program that will store numbers 2,4,6,..., 10,000 into
an array a.
.386
.MODEL FLAT
.STACK 4096
.DATA

a dword 5000 dup (?) ; Array a(dim 5000)

.CODE
_start:
lea ebx, a
mov k, 1
while1: cmp k, 5000
begin: jg  end
; begin
mov eax, k
mul  2
mov [ebx], eax
mov eax, k
add eax, 1
mov k, eax
add ebx, 4
jmp while1
end:
;end of assembly language code

PUBLIC_start

end
```

PROJECTS

1. Write a assembly language algorithm to convert a number N in the base a to its corresponding number M in the base 10 by performing the following tasks:

   Task 1: Store each digit of N in a separate cell of an array.

   Task 2: From these digits, convert N to M.

   Task 3: Store each digit of M in a separate cell of another array.

   Task 4: Store the number M in a dword variable.

   Hint: Use the method in chapter 2 that shows how to convert $N_{10} => N_b$.

2.

   (a) Write an assembly language algorithm that will find and store the first N prime numbers in an array.

   (b) Write an assembly language program that will find and store the first 100 prime numbers in an array.

   Assume an array was already created with N elements located at a declared data type. Write an assembly language algorithm that will do the following:

3. Find and retrieve a single value of the array.

4. Find the largest value of the array.

CHAPTER SIXTEEN

PROCEDURES

16.1 INTODUCTION: PSEUDOCODE PROCEDURES

As in higher programming languages, we will need to use procedures (subroutines) repeatedly in many of our assembly language programs. These procedures in a sense can be thought of as algorithms, in that they can stand alone and be used repeatedly in different programs. For pseudocode, the following will be the definition of the main body of the procedure:

DEFINITION OF PSEUDCODE PROCEDURES

PROCEDURE *name of procedure*

BEGIN

(instructions)

END

We will assume the following rules apply to procedures:

>   Rule 1: All procedures will be local to the main program.

>   Rule 2: All procedures will be located at the end of the main program.

>   Rule 3: All variables are global.

>   Rule 4: The procedure will be ignored by the assembler, unless it is called by the call instruction.

Definition of the call instruction

CALL *name of procedure*

We will assume the following rules apply to the call instruction:

>   Rule 1: All call instructions can be inserted anywhere inside the main program.

>   Rule 2: When the call instruction is activated, transfer is made to the first instruction of the procedure.

>   Rule 3: The END at the end of the procedure will transfer back to the instruction immediately following the call instruction.

Examples:

1. *The exponential operator $p = a^N$.* Although we define an exponential operator in pseudocode, the exponential operator does not exist in the assembly language. Therefore, we need to create a procedure that will perform the exponential operator that we have in our pseudocode. For the following procedure, we will compute $p = a^n$, where

$$a > 0$$

$$n \geq 0$$

PROCEDURE exponential

BEGIN

P := 1

K:= 1

WHILE K≤ N

BEGIN

P:= A*P

K:= K + 1

END

IF N:= 0 THEN

BEGIN

P:= A

END

1. The following program will use the above procedure and will perform the following task:

Task: Compute and store 5^7, 2^{10}.

PSEUDOCODE
A:= 5
N:= 7
CALL EXPONENTIAL
EXP1:= P
A:= 2
N:= 10

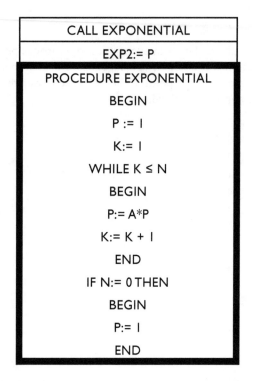

CALL EXPONENTIAL
EXP2:= P
PROCEDURE EXPONENTIAL
BEGIN
P := I
K:= I
WHILE K ≤ N
BEGIN
P:= A*P
K:= K + I
END
IF N:= 0 THEN
BEGIN
P:= I
END

2. The following procedure will perform the following tasks:

   Task 1: Compare the relative size of two different integer numbers x and y.

   Task 2: Return the larger of the two numbers.

PROCEDURE compare

BEGIN

IF x > y THEN

BEGIN

larger := x

ELSE

BEGIN

larger := y

END

Write a program using the above procedure that will perform the following task:

   Task 1: Compare two pairs of different integer numbers and store the
   larger in different variables.

PSEUDOCODE	X	Y	LARGER	LARGER1	LARGER2
X := 5	5				
Y := 10	5	10			
CALL COMPARE	5	10			
LARGER1:= LARGER	5	10	10	10	
X : = 12	12	10	10	10	
Y : = 7	12	7	10	10	
CALL COMPARE	12	7	10	10	
LARGER2 := LARGER	12	7	12	10	12

```
PROCEDURE COMPARE
    BEGIN
    IF X > Y THEN
        BEGIN
        LARGER := X
        END
    ELSE
        BEGIN
        LARGER := Y
        END
```

3. The following procedure will perform the following task:

    Task: For any positive integer N, compute the value sum = 1 + 2 + 3 + ... + N.

```
PROCEDURE sum
BEGIN
total := 0
k : = 1
WHILE k ≤ N
BEGIN
total := total + k
k := k + 1
END
END
```

Write a program using the above the procedure that will perform the following tasks:

Task 1: Store the sum of the numbers 1, 2, 3, ..., 100.

Task 2: Store the sum of the numbers 1, 2, 3, ..., 150.

Task 3: Store the sum of the numbers 1, 2, 3, ..., 250.

PSEUDOCODE	N	TOTAL	TOTAL1	TOTAL2	TOTAL3
N:= 100	100				
CALL SUM	100				
TOTAL1 := TOTAL	100	5050	5050		
N:= 150	150	5050	5050		
CALL SUM	150	11325	5050		
TOTAL2:= TOTAL	150	11325	5050	11325	
N := 250	250	11325	5050	11325	
CALL SUM	250	11325	5050	11325	
TOTAL3:= TOTAL	250	125500	5050	11325	125500
PROCEDURE SUM BEGIN TOTAL := 0 K := 1 WHILE K ≤ N BEGIN TOTAL := TOTAL + K K := K + 1 END END					

4. The following procedure will perform the following tasks:

Task 1: Compare four array integer values.

Task 2: Find and return the smallest integer value.

PROCEDURE array

BEGIN

smallest := a(1)

IF a(2) < smallest THEN

BEGIN

smallest := a(2)

END

IF a(3) < smallest THEN

BEGIN

smallest := a(3)

END

IF a(4) < smallest THEN

BEGIN

smallest := a(4)

END

END

Write a program using the above procedure that will perform the following tasks:

Task 1: Find and store the smallest of the numbers 5, 7, 2, and 10.

Task 2: Find and store the smallest of the numbers 57, 1001, 2222, and 43.

PSEUDOCODE	A(1)	A(2)	A(3)	A(4)	SMALLEST	S1	S2
A(1) := 5	5						
A(2) := 7	5	7					
A(3) := 2	5	7	2				
A(4) := 10	5	7	2	10			
CALL ARRAY	5	7	2	10			
S1:= SMALLEST	5	7	2	10	2		
A(1) := 57	57	7	2	10	2		
A(2) := 1001	57	1001	2	10	2		
A(3) := 2222	57	1001	2222	10	2		
A(4) := 43	57	1001	2222	43	2		
CALL ARRAY	57	1001	2222	43	2		
S2:= SMALLEST	57	1001	2222	43	43		

```
PROCEDURE ARRAY
     BEGIN
SMALLEST := A(1)

IF A(2) < SMALLEST THEN
   BEGIN
   SMALLEST := A(2)
   END

IF A(3) < SMALLEST THEN
BEGIN
SMALLEST := A(3)
   END

IF A(4) < SMALLEST THEN
BEGIN
SMALLEST := A(4)
   END
        END
```

Exercises

1. Write an algorithm and procedure in pseudocode that will perform the following tasks:

   Task 1: Store the following positive integer numbers in an array:

   $$n, n + 1, n + 2, n + 3, ..., n + m, m > 0.$$

   Task 2: Add the numbers stored in the array.

2. Rewrite exercise 1 in assembly language.

16.2 WRITING PROCEDURES IN ASSEMBLY LANGUAGE

The assembly language syntax is very similar to pseudocode:

Body of the procedure

identifier   PROC NEAR 32;   *identifier:* the procedure's name

   (instructions)

ret   ; will jump to the code following the call instruction.

identifier ENDP; Terminates the body of the procedure.

The call instruction is simply:

        call *identifier*

Examples:

1. From example 1 above, complete the table below.

PSEUDOCODE	AL PSEUDOCODE	ASSEMBLY LANGUAGE CODE
A:= 5	A:= 5	mov a, 5
N:= 7	N:= 7	mov n, 7
CALLEXPONENTIAL	CALL EXPONENTIAL	call exponential
EXP1:= P	EAX:= P	mov eax, p
	EXP1:= EAX	mov exp1, eax

A:= 2	A:= 2	mov a, 2
N:= 10	N:= 10	mov n, 10
CALL EXPONENTIAL	CALL EXPONENTIAL	call exponential
EXP2:= P	EAX:= P	mov eax, p
	EXP2:= EAX	mov exp2, eax
PROCEDURE EXPONENTIAL	**PROCEDURE EXPONENTIAL**	exponential PROC NEAR 32
BEGIN	BEGIN	begin:
P := 1	P:= 1	mov p, 1
K:= 1	K:= 1	mov k, 1
WHILE K ≤ N	WHILE K≤ N	while1: cmp k, n
		jg end1
BEGIN	BEGIN	begin1:
P:= A*P	EAX:= P	mov eax, p
	MUL A	mul a
	P:= EAX	mov p, eax
K:= K + 1	EAX:= K	mov eax, k
	EAX:= EAX + 1	add eax, 1
	K:= EAX	mov k, eax
END	END	jmp while1
		end1:
IF N:= 0 THEN	IF N:= 0 THEN	cmp ebx, 0
		jg end2
BEGIN	BEGIN	begin2:
P:= 1	P:= 1	mov p, 1
END	END	end2:
		ret expontential ENDP

2. From example 3 above, complete the table below.

PSEUDOCODE	AL PSEUDOCODE	ASSEMBLY LANGUAGE CODE
N := 100	N:= 100	mov n, 100
CALL SUM	CALL SUM	call sum
TOTAL1:= TOTAL	TOTAL1 := TOTAL	mov eax, total mov total1, eax
N:= 150	N:= 150	mov n, 150
CALL SUM	CALL SUM	call sum
TOTAL2:= TOTAL	TOTAL2:= TOTAL	mov eax, total mov total2, eax
N := 250	N:= 250	mov n, 250
CALL SUM	CALL SUM	call sum
TOTAL3:= TOTAL	TOTAL3:= EBX	mov eax, total mov total2, eax

PROCEDURE SUM
BEGIN
 	
TOTAL := 0
K : = 1
WHILE K ≤ N
BEGIN
 	
TOTAL := TOTAL + K
K := K + 1
 	
END
END
	PROCEDURE SUM
	
	BEGIN
	
	TOTAL := 0
	
	K:= 1
	WHILE TOTAL ≤ N
	
	BEGIN
	EAX:= TOTAL
	EAX:= EAX + 1
	TOTAL:= EAX
	
	END
	END
		sum PROC NEAR 32
		
		mov total, 0
		
		mov k, 1
		cmp total, n
		begin:
		
		mov eax, total
		add eax, 1
		
		mov total, eax
		jle begin
		ret
		sum ENDP

Exercise:

1. Write an assembly language algorithm that computes

$$1 + a + a_2 + \ldots + a^N$$

where $a > 0$ and $N > 0$.

PROJECT

Write an algorithm that will compute and add all prime numbers from N to M by using a procedure. Have the main algorithm set the values of N and M, and let the procedure compute the prime numbers and their sum.

From the algorithm, write a program that sums all prime numbers from 10 to 200.

II. WORKING WITH DECIMAL NUMBERS

CHAPTER SEVENTEEN

DECIMAL NUMBERS

INTRODUCTION

So far we have only worked with integers in assembly language. For many assembly language compilers, decimal numbers are also available. In order be become a proficient assembly language programmer, one needs to have a good understanding of how decimal numbers are represented in the assembler. To accomplish this, we start with the basic ideas of decimal numbers in the base 10. In later chapters, we will expand these numbers to the various forms that are needed.

17.1 DEFINITION OF DECIMAL NUMBERS AND FRACTIONS

Definition of decimal numbers in the base 10:

Decimal numbers are numbers of the following forms:

$$m.a_1a_2a_3 \ldots a_n$$

or

$$m.a_1a_2a_3 \ldots a_na_1a_2a_3 \ldots a_n \ldots a_1a_2a_3 \ldots a_n \ldots$$

where m is an integer and a_1, a_2, a_3 ... are nonnegative integers.

There are three types of decimal numbers: positive, negative, and zero.

Examples:

0.123,   −0.06143,   4.54,   33.248248...,   −72.77777777777

Definition of fractions:

Fractions are defined as ± N/M, where N and M represent arbitrary integers, with the restriction that M ≠ 0.

2/3,   −4/7,   1/3,   124/456,   −7/7,   0/4,   400/200

There are two types of fractions: proper and improper.

Definition: A proper positive fraction N/M is a fraction where 0 < N < M.

Examples:

2/3,   −4/7,   1/3,   124/456

Definition: An improper positive fraction N/M is a fraction where N ≥ M > 0.

5/2,   −7/6,   10/ 5

Note: In this chapter, we are primarily interested in positive proper fractions.

Exercises:

1. Which of the following fractions can be reduced to integer numbers?

   (a) 1446/558   (b) 12356/2333   (c) 458/3206   (d) 1138/569

2. Rewrite the following numbers as fractions:

   (a) (1/2)/(5/7)   (b) (212/124)/(5)   (c) (1/3)/(2/3)

3. Which of the following fractions are proper?

   (a) 3/2   (b) 234/567   (c) ½

Note: For the following presentation, we will only consider decimal numbers that are generated from positive fractions.

17.2 REPRESENTING POSITIVE DECIMAL NUMBERS CORRESPONDING TO PROPER FRACTIONS IN EXPANDED FORM

Any fraction can be represented by a decimal number. Since we are mainly interested in fractions that are proper, this means that all corresponding decimal numbers we study will be less than 1.

There are two types of decimal numbers: finite and infinite.

Definition of finite decimal numbers:

Finite decimal numbers are written in the form:

$0.a_1a_2a_3 \ldots a_n$

where

$0.a_1a_2a_3 \ldots a_n = a_1/10 + a_2/10^2 + a_3/10^3 + \ldots + a_n/10^n$

and

a_k (k = 1, 2, ..., n) are nonnegative integers.

Note: Finite decimal numbers can also be negative numbers.

Examples

$0.579 = 5/10 + 7/100 + 9/1000$

$0.3579 = 0.3579 = 3/10 + 5/100 + 7/1000 + 9/10000$

$0.49607 = 4/10 + 9/100 + 6/1000 + 0/10000 + 7/100000$

$0.005411 = 0/10 + 0/100 + 5/1000 + 4/10000 + 1/100000 + 1/1000000 =$

$5/1000 + 4/10000 + 1/100000 + 1/1000000$

Definition of infinite decimal numbers:

Infinite decimal numbers are written in the form:

$0.a_1a_2a_3 \ldots a_n a_1a_2a_3 \ldots a_n \ldots a_1a_2a_3 \ldots a_n \ldots$

where

$0.a_1a_2a_3 \ldots a_n a_1a_2a_3 \ldots a_n \ldots a_1a_2a_3 \ldots a_n \ldots =$

$a_1/10 + a_2/10^2 + a_3/10^3 \ldots + a_n/10^n + a_1/10^{n+1} + a_2/10^{n+2} + a_3/10^{n+3} + \ldots + a_n/10^{2n} + \ldots$

and

a_k (k = 1, 2, ...,) are nonnegative integers.

To avoid the complications of working with infinite expansions, we will use the following notation:

$0.a_1a_2a_3 \ldots a_n a_1a_2a_3 \ldots a_n \ldots a_1a_2a_3 \ldots a_n \ldots = 0.\overline{a_1a_2 \ldots a_n}$

Also, we will assume that all the laws of arithmetic work when applied to infinite decimal numbers.

Examples:

$0.798798\ldots = 0.\overline{798}$

$0.015981598\ldots = 0.0\overline{1598}$

$0.66\ldots = 0.\overline{6},$

$0.13241324\ldots = 0.0\overline{1324}$

$0.25897897897\ldots = 0.25\overline{897}$

Examples:

$$1/2 = 0.5, 2/3 = 0.666... = 0.\overline{6} \qquad 1/4 = 0.25, \qquad 1/3 = 0.333...0.\overline{3}$$

$$213/999 = 0.213213213... = 0.\overline{213}, 16/3 = 5.333... = 5.\overline{3}$$

Exercises

1. Expand the following in the form: $0.\overline{a_1 a_2 ... a_n} = 0.a_1 a_2 a_3 ... a_n a_1 a_2 a_3 ... a_n ...$

   (a) $0.2\overline{357}$ (b) $0.\overline{0097}$

2. Expand the following in the form
   $0.a_1 a_2 a_3 ... a_n\ a_1 a_2 a_3 ... a_n ... a_1 a_2 a_3 ... a_n ... =$

   (a) 0.0768907689... (b) 0.00235559055590...

3. Write the following fractions as decimal numbers using the upper bar notation where necessary:

   (a) 5/12   (b) −7/8   (c) 5/6   (d) 1/7   (e) −3/7

17.3 CONVERTING DECIMAL NUMBERS TO FRACTIONS

Finite decimal numbers can easily be converted to fractions by writing them first in the form:

$$0.a_1 a_2 a_3 ... a_n = a_1/10 + a_2/10^2 + a_3/10^3 + ... + a_n/10^n =$$

$$(a_1 *10^{n-1} + a_2 *10^{n-2} + ... + a_k *10^{n-k} + ... + a)/10^n$$

and then summing the terms with a common denominator.

Examples

$0.5 = 5/10$

$0.579 = 5/10 + 7/100 + 9/1000 = (5*100 + 7*10 + 9)/1000 = 579/1,000$

$0.3579 = 3/10 + 5/100 + 7/1000 + 9/10000 = (3*1000 + 5*100 + 7*10 + 9)/10000$

   $= 3,579/10,000$

$0.49607 = (4/10 + 9/100 + 6/1000 + 0/10000 + 7/100,000) = 49607/100,000$

$0.005411 = 0/10 + 0/100 + 5/1000 + 4/10000 + 1/100000 + 1/1000000 =$

$(5*1000 + 4*100 + 1/10 + 1)/1000000 = 5411/1,000,000$

Exercises

1. Write the decimal numbers as fractions:

   (a) 0.0235   (b) 0.1111215   (c) 0.999999

Infinite decimal numbers of type $0.\overline{a_1 a_2 \dots a_n}$ can also be converted into a fraction. The following algorithm will demonstrate how this is done:

Step 1: $x = 0.\overline{a_1 a_2 \dots a_n}$

Step 2: $10^n * x = a_1 a_2 a_3 \dots a_n . \overline{a_1 a_2 a_3 \dots a_n}$

By subtracting x from $10^n * x$ we can incorporate the above algorithm into a single basic formula:

$$0.\overline{a_1 a_2 \dots a_n} = \frac{a_1 a_2 \dots a_n}{10^n - 1}$$

Example:

Convert $0.\overline{21657}$ to a fraction:

$$0.\overline{21657} = \frac{21657}{10^5 - 1} = \frac{21657}{100000 - 1} = \frac{21657}{99999}$$

Exercises

1. Write the following decimal numbers as fractions:

   (a) $0.\overline{23}$

   (b) $0.\overline{73}$

   (c) $0.\overline{8}$

   (d) $0.\overline{101}$

   (e) $0.\overline{3}$

   (g) 23.468

   (h) 2.0078

   (i) $0.24\overline{679852}$

2. Write the following decimal numbers as a single fraction p/q where p and q are integers:

   (a) $0.\overline{7323} + 0.\overline{83}$

(b) $0.\overline{7323} - 0.\overline{83}$

(c) $0.\overline{7323} * 0.\overline{83}$

(d) $0.\overline{7323} / 0.\overline{83}$

3. Write the following decimal numbers as a decimal number $0.\overline{a_1 a_2 a_3 \ldots a_n}$

(a) $0.\overline{7323} + 0.\overline{0083}$

(b) $0.\overline{7323} - 0.\overline{0083}$

17.4 CONVERTING FRACTIONS TO DECIMAL NUMBERS

Assume that N/M is a positive proper fraction. We define the decimal representation of N/M as:

$$M/N = a_1/10 + a_2/10^2 + a_3/10^3 + \ldots.$$

where a_k are nonnegative integers.

The following example will demonstrate the conversion from a fraction to a decimal number.

Example

Convert 3/7 to its decimal representation.

$$3/7 = a_1/10 + a_2/10^2 + a_3/10^3 + a_4/10^4 + a_5/10^5 + a_6/10^6 + a_7/10^7 + \ldots$$

Step 1:

$$10(3/7) = 30/7 = (28 + 2)/7 = 4 + 2/7 =$$

$$a_1/10 + a_2/10 + a_3/10^2 + a_4/10^3 + a_5/10^4 + a_6/10^5 + a_7/10^6 + \ldots$$

$$a_1 = 4$$

$$2/7 = a_1/10 + a_2/10 + a_3/10^2 + a_4/10^3 + a_5/10^4 + a_6/10^5 + a_7/10^6 + \ldots$$

Step 2:

$$10(2/7) = 20/7 = (14 + 6)/7 = 2 + 6/7 =$$

$$a_2 + a_3/10^2 + a_4/10^3 + a_5/10^4 + a_6/10^5 + a_7/10^6 + \ldots$$

$$a_2 = 2$$

$$6/7 = a_3/10 + a_4/10^2 + a_5/10^3 + a_6/10^4 + a_7/10^5 + \ldots$$

Step 3:

$$10(6/7) = 60/7 = (56 + 4)/7 = 8 + 4/7 = a_3 + a_4/10 + a_5/10^2 + a_6/10^3 + a_7/10^4 + \ldots$$

$$a_3 = 8$$

$$4/7 = a_4/10 + a_5/10^2 + a_6/10^3 + \ldots$$

Step 4:

$$10(4/7) = 40/7 = (35 + 5)/7 = 5 + 5/7 = a_4 + a_5/10 + a_6/10^2 + \ldots$$

$$a_4 = 5$$

$$5/7 = a_5/10 + a_6/10^2 + \ldots$$

Step 5:

$$10(5/7) = 50/7 = (49 + 1)/7 = 7 + 1/7 = a_5 + a_6/10 + a_7/10^2 + \ldots$$

$$a_5 = 7$$

$$1/7 = a_6/10 + a_7/10^2 + \ldots$$

Step 6:

$$10(1/7) = 10/7 + (7 + 3)/7 = 1 + 3/7 = a_6 + a_7/10 + \ldots$$

$$a_6 = 1$$

$$3/7 = a_7/10 + \ldots$$

Since we cycled back to 3/7, we can write:

$$3/7 = 0.428571428571428571428571428571143\ldots = 0.\overline{428571}$$

Exercise

Convert the following fractions to decimals:

1. 4/9

2. 3/8

3. 67/5

17.5 REPRESENTATION OF DECIMAL NUMBERS

Every finite decimal number has two representations.

Examples

(a) $0.\overline{9}$

Step 1: $x = 0.\overline{9} = 0.99...$

Step 2: $10x = 9.99...$

Step 3: Subtract the equation in step 1 from the equation in step 2:
$9x = 9$

Step 4: $x = 0.\overline{9} = 1$

(b) $0.00\overline{9}$

Step 1: $0.00\overline{9} = \overline{9}/100 = 1/100 = 0.01$

(c) $24.\overline{9}$

$24.\overline{9} = 24 + 0.\overline{9} = 24 + 1 = 25$

(d) $0.2354\overline{9}$

$0.2354\overline{9} = 0.2354 + 0.0000\overline{9} = 0.2354 + 0.0001 = 0.2355$

Exercises

1. Convert the following into integer form:

   (a) $281.\overline{9}$ (b) $41256.\overline{9}$

2. Write the following in fraction form:

   (a) $0.23\overline{8}$ (b) $0.00\overline{791}$ (c) $0.1\overline{110000}$

3. Explain why we cannot convert, using the above algorithm, the following number into a fraction:

   $0.272772777277772777772...$

From your analysis, does such a number exist?

DIFFERENT NUMBER BASES FOR FRACTIONS

INTRODUCTION

In chapters 1 and 2, we restricted our studies to integer numbers of different bases. We now move on to the study of decimal numbers of different bases. It is important to understand that to become a successful assembly programmer, one has to have a complete understanding of how both integer and decimal numbers work within the assembler system.

17.6 DEFINITION OF DECIMAL AND FRACTIONS

In the first part of this chapter, we defined finite and infinite decimal numbers in expanded form in the base 10 as:

$$a_{10} = 0.a_1a_2a_3...a_n = a_1/10 + a_2/10^2 + ... + a_n/10^n$$

$$\overline{a}_{10} = (0.a_1a_2a_3...a_n \ a_1a_2a_3...a_n \ ...)_{10} = (0.\overline{a_1a_2 \ ... \ a_n})_{10} =$$

$$a_1/10 + a_2/10^2 + ... + a_n/10^n + a_1/10^{n+1} + a_2/10^{n+2} + ... + a_n/10^{2n} +...$$

Examples

$0.25 = 2/10 + 5/10^2$

$0.0625 = 6/10^2 + 2/10^3 + 5/10^4$

$\quad\quad 0.3333... = 3/10 + 3/10^2 + 3/10^3 + ...$

$0.\overline{285714} = 2/10 + 8/10^2 + 5/10^3 + 7/10^4 + 1/10^5 + 4/10^6 + 2/10^7 + 8/10^8 + 5/10^9 + 7/10^{10} + 1/10^{11} + 4/10^{12} + ... +$

In a similar manner, we can define finite and infinite decimal numbers less than 1 for any base b in expanded form:

Definition: A finite nonnegative decimal number less than 1 can be written in the base b as:

$$a_b = (0.a_1a_2a_3...a_n)_b = a_1/10_b + a_2/10_b^2 + ... + a_n/10_b^n$$

where

$0 \leq a_k < b \ (k = 1, 2, ...,n),$

$a_b = a_1/10_b + a_2/10_b^2 + ... + a_n/10_b^n = 0.a_1 + 0.0a_2 + ... + 0.00...0a_n$

Definition: An infinite decimal number less than 1 can be written in the base b as:

$$\overline{a}_b = (0.a_1a_2a_3...a_n\ a_1a_2a_3...a_n...)_b = (0.\overline{a_1a_2...a_n})_b = a_1/10_b + a_2/10_b^2 + ... +$$

$$a_n/10_b^n + a_1/10_b^{n+1} + a_2/10_b^{n+2} + ... + a_n/10_b^{2n} + ...$$

where

$$0 \le a_k < b\ (k=1, 2, ...)$$

$$\overline{a}_b = a_1/10_b + a_2/10_b^2 + ... + a_n/10_b^n + ... = 0.a_1 + 0.0a_2 + ... + 0.00...0a_n + ...$$

Note: We are only using these decimal expansions to indicate the various positions of the decimal point, not for computational values.

Examples

$$0.11101_2 = 1/10_2 + 1/10_2^2 + 1/10_2^3 + 0/10_2^4 + 1/10_2^5$$

$$0.02756_8 = 0/10_8 + 2/10_8^2 + 7/10_8^3 + 5/10_8^4 + 6/10_8^5$$

$$0.\overline{98C7DF}_{16} = 9/10_{16} + 8/10_{16}^2 + C/10_{16}^3 + 7/10_{16}^4 + D/10_{16}^5 + F/10_{16}^6 + ...$$

Exercises

1. Write the following numbers in expanded form:

    (a) 0.231120_4 (b) 0.11111101_2 (c) 0.232323_8 (d) $0.ABC2_{16}$

An alternative way of representing infinite expansion of numbers of the base b is:

$$0.\overline{(a_1a_2...a_n)}_b = \frac{(a_1a_2...a_n)_b}{10_b^n - 1}$$

where $10_b^n - 1 = b_1b_2 ... b_n$; $b_k = b - 1$; $k = 1, 2, ..., n$

Examples

    (a) $0.\overline{97865}_{10} = 97865_{10}/99999_{10}$; where $b = 10$; $10^5 - 1 = 99999_{10}$

    (b) $0.\overline{632}_8 = 632_8/777_8$; where $b = 8$; $10_8^3 - 1 = 777_8$

    (c) $0.\overline{12EA29}_{16} = 12EA29_{16}/FFFFFF_{16}$; where $b = 16$; $10_{16}^6 - 1 = FFFFFF_{16}$

    (d) $0.\overline{101}_2 = 101_2/111_2$; where $b = 2$; $10_2^3 - 1 = 111_2$

17.7 CONVERTING DECIMAL NUMBERS BETWEEN THE BASE 10 AND AN ARBITRARY BASE

As we stated in chapter 2, it is important to be able to convert integer numbers from a given number base to corresponding integer numbers in any other base. Similarly, we wish to do the same for fractions. First we will define the corresponding decimal number ($n_b < 1$) that corresponds to a unique decimal number in the base 10.

Converting a finite decimal number in any base b to its corresponding decimal number in the base 10

From chapter 2, when converting from a number in base b to a number in base 10, we have $10_b \rightarrow b_{10}$ and therefore $10_b^n \rightarrow b_{10}^n$.

It follows that the following formula gives a one-to-one correspondence from a finite decimal number in the base b to a unique finite decimal number in the base 10:

$$n_b = (0.a_1 a_2 \ldots a_n)_b = a_1/10_b + a_2/10_b^2 + \ldots + a_n/10_b^n \Rightarrow a_1/b_{10} + a_2/b_{10}^2 + \ldots + a_n/b_{10}^n = n_{10}$$

Note: All computation is done in decimals.

Examples:

(a)

$$0.321_4 \Rightarrow 3/4 + 2/4^2 + 1/4^3 = 3/4 + 2/16 + 1/64 = 0.75 + 0.125 + 0.015625 = 0.890625_{10}$$

(b)

$$0.11011_2 \Rightarrow 1/2 + 1/2^2 + 1/2^4 + 1/2^5 = 0.5 + 0.25 + 0.0625 = 0.03125 = 0.84375_{10}$$

(c)

$$0.9AF_{16} \Rightarrow 9/16 + 10/16^2 + 15/16^3 = 0.5625 + 0.0390625 + 0.003662109375$$

$$= 0.605224609375_{10}$$

Exercises:

1. Convert the following numbers to the base 10:

    (a) 0.231120_4 (b) 0.11111101_2 (c) 0.232323_8 (d) $ABC2_{16}$

Converting an infinite decimal number in any base b to its corresponding decimal number in the base 10

The following formula will convert any infinite decimal number in the base b to its corresponding decimal number in the base 10:

$$\overline{a}_b = 0.\overline{a_1 a_2 a_3 \ldots a_n} = (0.a_1 a_2 a_3 \ldots a_n\, a_1 a_2 a_3 \ldots a_n \ldots)_b = a_1/10_b + a_2/10_b^2 + \ldots + a_n/10_b^n +$$
$$a_1/10_b^{n+1} + a_2/10_b^{n+2} + \ldots + a_n/10_b^{2n} + \ldots$$

$$\overline{a}_b = 0.\overline{a_1 a_2 \ldots a_n} => a_1/b + a_2/b^2 + \ldots + a_n/b^n + a_1/b^{n+1} + a_2/b^{n+2} + \ldots + a_n b^{2n} + \ldots$$

Here we use the formula:

$$\overline{a}_b = 0.\overline{a_1 a_2 \ldots a_n} = \frac{(a_1 a_2 a_3 \ldots a_n)_b}{10_b^n - 1} => N_{10}/(b_{10}^n - 1)$$

Examples

   (a) Find $0.\overline{3}_4 => N_{10}$

       Step 1: b = 4

       Step 2: n = 1

       Step 3: $0.\overline{3}_4 = 3_4/(10_4 - 1) => 3_{10}/(4-1)_{10} = 1_{10}$

   (b) Find $0.\overline{101}_2 \Rightarrow N_{10}$

       Step 1: b = 2

       Step 2: n = 3

       Step 3: $0.\overline{101} = 101_2/(10^3_2 - 1) \Rightarrow 5_{10}/(2^3_{10} - 1) = (5/7)_{10}$

Exercises:

   1. Convert the following numbers to the base 10:

      (a) $0.\overline{6}_8$ (b) $0.\overline{01001}_2$ (c) $0.\overline{A5C}_{16}$ (d) $0.\overline{00365}_8$

Converting a finite decimal number in the base 10 to its corresponding decimal number in any base b

$$n_{10} = (a_1/10 + a_2/10^2 + \ldots + a_n/10^n) \rightarrow (0.a_1 a_2 \ldots a_n \ldots)_b$$

In converting from base b to base 10, we have the equation

$$a_1/b_{10} + a_2/b_{10}^2 + \ldots + a_n/b_{10}^n = n_{10}.$$

The following examples will demonstrate how to solve the values a_k:

Examples:

Convert the following decimal numbers to the indicated base.

(a) Convert 0.2_{10} to the base 4.

Step 1: $0.2_{10} = a_1/4 + a_2/4^2 + a_3/4^3 + \ldots$

Step 2: $4*(0.2) = 0.8 = a_1 + a_2/4 + a_3/4^2 + \ldots$

Step 3: Since a_1 is an integer, $a_1 = 0$.

Step 4: $0.8 = a_2/4 + a_3/4^2 + \ldots$

Step 5: $4*(0.8) = 3.2 = a_2 + a_3/4 + \ldots$

Step 6: $a_2 = 3$

Step 7: $0.2 = a_3/4 + a_4/4^2 + \ldots$

Since we are back to step 1, the decimal number in the base 4 can be written as:

$$0.2_{10} \Rightarrow n_4 = 0.0303\ldots \quad 0.\overline{(a_1 a_2)_4} = 0.\overline{03}_4$$

(b) Convert 0.9_{10} to the base 16.

Step 1: $0.9 = a_1/16 + a_2/16^2 + a_3/16^3 + \ldots$

Step 2: $16*(0.9) = 14.4 = a_1 + a_2/16 + a_3/16^3 + \ldots$

Step 3: Since a_1 is an integer, $14 \rightarrow a_1 = E$

Step 4: $0.4 = a_2/16 + a_3/16^2 + \ldots$

Step 5: $16*(0.4) = 6.4 = a_2 + a_3/16 + \ldots$

Step 6: $a_2 = 6$

Step 7: $0.4 = a_3/16 + a_4/16^2 + \ldots$

Step 8: Since we are back to step 4, the decimal number can be written as:

$$0.9_{10} \leftrightarrow N_{16} = 0.E666\ldots = 0.E\overline{6}$$

(c) Convert 0.8_{10} to the base 2.

Step 1: $0.8 = a_1/2 + a_2/2^2 + a_3/2^3 + \ldots$

Step 2: $2*(0.8) = 1.6 = a_1 + a_2/2 + a_3/2^2 + \ldots$

Step 3: $a_1 = 1$

Step 4: $0.6 = a_2/2 + a_3/2^2 + \ldots$

Step 5: $2*(0.6) = 1.2 = a_2 + a_3/2 + \ldots$

Step 6: $a_2 = 1$

Step 7: $0.2 = a_3/2 + a_4/2^2 + \ldots$

Step 8: $2*(0.2) = 0.4 = a_3 + a_4/2 + \ldots$

Step 9: $a_3 = 0$

Step 10: $0.4 = a_4/2 + a_5/2^2 + \ldots$

Step 11: $2*(0.4) = 0.8 = a_4 + a_5/2 + \ldots$

Step 12: $a_4 = 0$

Step 13: $0.8 = a_5/2 + a_6/2^2 + \ldots$

At this point, we are back to step 1:

Step 14: Therefore,

$$0.8 \Rightarrow 0.\overline{a_1 a_2 a_3 a_4} = 0.1100_2$$

Checking out computation

By applying the above formula:

$$\overline{a}_b \Rightarrow \frac{(a_1 a_2 \ldots a_n)_{10}}{10^n - 1}$$

we can check to see if we correctly converted the finite decimal number.

Example

Let us check to see that we correctly converted 0.8_{10} to binary $0.\overline{1100}_2$.

Step 1: $a_2 = 0.\overline{1100}$

Step 2: $b = 2$

Step 3: $n = 4$

Step 4: Substituting in the above formula gives

$$0.\overline{1100}_2 = 1100_2/(10_2^4 - 1) = 1100_2/1111_2 \rightarrow 12_{10}/15_{10} = 0.8.$$

Exercises:

1. Convert 0.6_{10} to the following:

    (a) base 2   (b) base 4   (c) base 8   (d) base 16

2. Show $0.0\overline{21}_4 \leftrightarrow 0.15_{10}$

Converting an infinite decimal number in the base 10 to its corresponding decimal number in any base b

We will use the same method of converting a finite decimal number in the base 10 to any number in the base b by replacing the finite decimal number by an infinite decimal number.

Example

1. Convert and check your results.

Convert: $0.\overline{2}_{10}$ to base 2

$$0.\overline{2}_{10} = 2/9 = a_1/2 + a_2/2^2 + a_3/2^3 + \ldots$$

$$2(2/9) = 4/9 = a_1 + a_2/2 + a_3/2^2 + a_4/2^3 + \ldots$$

$$a_1 = 0$$

$$4/9 = a_2/2 + a_3/2^2 + a_4/2^3 + \ldots$$

$$2(4/9) = 8/9 = a_2 + a_3/2 + a_4/2^2 + a_5/^32^3 + \ldots$$

$$a_2 = 0$$

$$(8/9) = a_3/2 + a_4/2^2 + a_5/2^3 + \ldots$$

$$2(8/9) = 16/9 = (9 + 7)/9 = a_3 + a_4/2 + a_5/2^2 + \ldots$$

$$a_3 = 1$$

$$7/9 = a_4/2 + a_5/2^2 + a_5/2^3 + \ldots$$

$$2(7/9) = 14/9 = (9 + 5)/9 = a_4 + a_5/2 + a_6/2^2 + \ldots$$

$$a_4 = 1$$

$$5/9 = a_5/2 + a_6/2^2 + \ldots$$

$$2(5/9) = 10/9 = (9 + 1)/9 = a_5 + a_6/2^2 + \ldots$$

$$a_5 = 1$$

$$2(1/9) = 2/9 = + a_6/2^2 + a_7/2^3 + \ldots$$

$$a_6 = 0$$

$$0.\overline{2}_{10} \Rightarrow 0.\overline{001110}_2$$

Check: $\overline{001110}_2 = \dfrac{\overline{1110}_2}{\overline{111111}_2} \Rightarrow 14_{10}/63_{10} = 0.\overline{2}_{10}$

Exercise:

1. Convert $0.\overline{1}_{10}$ to base 5

17.8 CONVERTING DECIMAL NUMBERS IN A GIVEN BASE TO FRACTIONS IN THE SAME BASE

Finite decimal numbers in the base b can easily be converted to fractions by writing them first in the form:

$$(0.a_1a_2a_3 \ldots a_n)_b = a_{1b}/10_b + a_{2b}/10_b^2 + a_{3b}/10_b^3 + \ldots + a_{nb}/10_b^n$$

$$= [(a_{1b}*10_b^{n-1} + a_{2b}*10_b^{n-2} + \ldots + a_{kb}*10_b^{n-k2} + \ldots + a_{1b})]/10^n]_b.$$

Examples:

$$0.5_8 = (5/10)_8$$

$$0.1011_2 = 1/10_2 + 0/100_2 + 1/1000_2 + 1/10000_2$$

$$= (1*1000_2 + 1*10_2 + 1)/10000_2$$

$$= (1011/10000)_2$$

$$0.3DF2_{16} = 3/10_{16} + D/100_{16} + F/1000_{16} + 2/10000_{16} = (3*1000_{16} + D*100_{16}$$

$$+ F*10_{16} + 2)/10000 = (3DF2/10000)_{16}$$

Exercise:

1. Write the following decimal numbers as fractions:

   (a) 0.0235_8 (b) 0.110111_2 (c) 0.999999_{16}

Infinite decimal numbers of type $0.\overline{a_1a_2 \ldots a_n}_b$ can also be converted into a fraction by using the basic formula developed in this chapter:

$$0.\overline{(a_1a_2 \ldots a_n)_b} = \dfrac{(a_1a_2 \ldots a_n)_b}{10_b^n - 1}$$

where $10^n - 1 = d_1d_2 \ldots d_n$

and $d_k = b - 1$ $(k = 1, 2, \ldots, n)$, the largest digit in the base b.

Examples

$$0.\overline{723}_8 = 723_8/(1000_8 - 1) = 723_8 /777_8$$

$$0.\overline{10}_2 = 10_2/(100_2 - 1) = 10_2 /11_2$$

$$0.\overline{3FA9}_{16} = 3FA9_{16}/(10000_{16} - 1) = 3FA9_{16}/FFFF_{16}$$

Exercise

1. Write the following decimal numbers as fractions in the same base:

(a) $0.\overline{0101}_2$ (b) $0.\overline{000723}_8$ c. $0235.\overline{7237}_8$ d. $02C5.\overline{7239}_{16}$

17.9 CONVERTING NUMBERS BETWEEN DIFFERENT BASES

There exists a one-to-one correspondence between different bases. This can be shown by converting a number in one base to the base 10 and then convert this number to the other base.

Examples

(a) $0.2_4 \Rightarrow N_6$

$0.2_4 \Rightarrow N_{10} = 2/4 = 0.5$

$0.5_{10} = a_1/6 + a_2/6^2 + a_3/6^3 + \ldots$

$6*0.5 = a_1 + a_2/6 + a_3/6^2 + \ldots = 3.0$

$a_1 = 3, a_2 = 0, a_3 = 0, \ldots$

$0.5 \Rightarrow 0.3_6$

$0.2_4 \Rightarrow 0.3_6$

(b) $0.6_8 \rightarrow N_2$

$0.6 \rightarrow N_{10} = 6/8 = .75$

$0.75 = a_1/2 + a_2/2^2 + a_3/2^3 + \ldots$

$2*(0.75) = a_1 + a_2/2 + a_3/2^2 + \ldots = 1.5$

$a_1 = 1$

$0.5 = a_2/2 + a_3/2^2 + \ldots$

$2*0.5 = a_2 + a_3/2 + \ldots = 1$

$a_2 = 1, a_3 = 0, a_4 = 0, \ldots$

$0.5 \rightarrow 0.11_2$

$0.68 \rightarrow 0.11_2$

(c) $0.A_{16} \rightarrow N_2$

$0.A \rightarrow N_{10} = 10/16 = 0.625_{10}$

$0.625 = a_1/2 + a_2/2^2 + a_3/2^3 + \ldots$

$2*(0.625) = a_1 + a_2/2 + a_3/2^2 + \ldots = 1.25$

$a_1 = 1$

$2*(0.25) = a_2 + a_3/2 + \ldots = 0.5$

$a_2 = 0$

$2*(0.5) = a_3 + a_4/2 + \ldots = 1$

$a_3 = 1$

$0.625_{10} \rightarrow 0.101_2$

$0.A_{16} \rightarrow 0.101_2$

Quick conversions between the base 2 and base 16

With no computation, we can convert a number in the base 2 to its corresponding number in the base 16.

To convert from the base 2 to the base 16 or conversely, we need to construct the following table.

BASE 2 DIGITS Binary	BASE 16 DIGITS Hexadecimal
0000	0
0001	1
0010	2
0011	3

0100	4
0101	5
0110	6
0111	7
1000	8
1001	9
1010	A
1011	B
1100	C
1101	D
1110	E
1111	F

Converting a finite decimal number less than 1

The following two rules show how to convert a finite binary number to a hexadecimal number:

1. From left to right, group the digits of the binary number in groups of four; adding zeros at the end if necessary.

2. Match each group of these four digits with the corresponding hexadecimal digits from the above table.

Example:

Convert 0.1101111011_2 to its corresponding hexadecimal digit.

We first write: $0.1101111011_2 = 0.\underline{1101} \ \underline{1110} \ \underline{1100}_2$.

Next we match from the above table the corresponding hexadecimal digit:

$$0.1101111011_2 = 0.\underline{1101} \ \underline{1110} \ \underline{1100} => 0.DEC_{16}$$

$$0. \quad D \quad \quad E \quad \quad C_{16}$$

To convert a finite hexadecimal number to a binary number, just match each hexadecimal digit with the corresponding binary digits in the above table.

Example

Convert 0.F3DB$_{16}$ to its corresponding binary number.

0.F3DB$_{16}$ =	0.	F	3	D	B →	0.1111 0011 1101 1011$_2$
	0.	1111	0011	1101	1011	

Exercises:

1. Using this quick conversion, convert the following binary numbers to hexadecimal:

   (a) 0.011010101$_2$ (b) 0.0001111101$_2$

2. Using this quick conversion, convert the following hexadecimal numbers to binary:

   (a) 0.5623$_{16}$ (b) 0.ACF230A$_2$

3. In the example above, we converted 0.110111011$_2$ → 0.DEC$_{16}$

   Use another conversion method. Is the result the same?

4. Set up a quick conversion system between the base 2 and the base 8.

5. Convert   (a) 0.110111011$_2$ to the base 8.

   (b) Convert 0.23461$_8$ to the base 2.

6. Use quick conversion to convert 0.76123$_8$ to the base 16.

Converting an infinite decimal number less than 1

When converting an infinite binary number to hexadecimal, we to use the following rules:

1. From left to right, group the digits of the binary number in groups of four; adding zeros at the end if necessary. If we cannot group the digits in groups of four, expand the binary number to a minimal number of digits that will allow the grouping.

2. Match each group of these four digits with the corresponding hexadecimal digits from the above table.

Example

Convert $0.\overline{1001}_2$ to hexadecimal.

$0.\overline{1001}_2 = 0.\underline{1001}$ $\underline{1001}$ $\underline{1001}$ ... $\Rightarrow 0.\overline{9}_{16}$

$\qquad\qquad\quad 0.9 \qquad 9 \qquad 9$ ...

Example

Convert $0.\overline{11011011}_2$ to hexadecimal.

$0.\overline{11011011} = 0.1101$ 1011 1101 1011 1101 1011 ... $\Rightarrow 0.\overline{DB}_{16}$

$\qquad\qquad\qquad\quad 0.D \qquad B \qquad D \qquad B \qquad D \qquad B$ ...

Example

Convert $0.\overline{10}_2$ to hexadecimal.

Since we don't have a multiple of four digits, we expand:

$0.1010_2 = 0.101010101010101010... => 0.\overline{A}_{16}$

$\qquad\qquad\qquad 0.A \qquad A \qquad A \qquad A$ ....

Example

Convert $0.\overline{101}_2$ to hexadecimal.

Since we don't have a multiple of four digits, we expand:

$0.\overline{101} = 0.101101101101...$ 0.1011 0110 1101 ... $\Rightarrow 0.\overline{B6D}_{16}$

$\qquad\qquad\qquad\qquad\qquad\qquad\quad 0.B \qquad 6 \qquad D$

Example

Convert $0.\overline{9A3DD}_{16}$ to binary.

$0.\overline{9A3DD}_{16}$

$\Leftrightarrow 0.\underline{1001}$ $\underline{1010}$ $\underline{0011}$ $\underline{1101}$ $\underline{1101}$ $= \overline{0.1001\ 1010\ 0011\ 1101\ 1101}_2$

Exercises:

1. Convert $0.\overline{1011}_2$ to a hexadecimal number.

2. Convert the following binary numbers to hexadecimal:

   (a) $0.\overline{1}_2$

   (b) $0.\overline{10111}_2$

   (c) $0.\overline{101101101}_2$

3. Convert $0.\overline{11011}_2$ to a hexadecimal number.

4. Show that the largest positive 32-bit number $0.1111...1_2$ corresponds to the decimal number

   $1 - 1/2^{32}$.

5. Explain why we cannot convert, using our above algorithm, the following number into a fraction:

   $0.2727727772777727777772...$

PROJECT

Find each expression and a_k and c_k for $k = 1, 2, 3, 4, 5$.

$$\frac{0.\overline{ABCDE}_{16}}{0.\overline{654321}_{16}} = \frac{N_{16}}{M_{16}} \Rightarrow \frac{N_{10}}{M_{10}} = \left(\frac{a_1}{10} + \frac{a_2}{10^2} + \frac{a_3}{10^3} + ...\right)_{10} \rightarrow$$

$$\left(\frac{c_1}{10} + \frac{c_2}{10^2} + \frac{c_3}{10^3} + ...\right)_{16}$$

CHAPTER EIGHTEEN

WORKING WITH DECIMAL NUMBERS IN ASSEMBLY

18.1 INTRODUCTION: REPRESENTATION OF DECIMAL NUMBERS

So far in assembly language, we have only worked with integer numbers. We will now study how we can represent and work with fractions represented as numbers with a decimal point. These numbers will be called decimal numbers. When such numbers are used in assembly language programming, they are frequently represented as ordinary decimal numbers or scientific notation.

Definition of ordinary decimal numbers

An ordinary decimal number is of the form $\pm a_0.a_1a_2 \ldots a_n$, where a_k are nonnegative integers.

Examples:

      23.4,   -55.0101,   0.00154,   9.0

Definition of scientific representation of decimal numbers

The representation of a decimal number in a scientific format is of the form $\pm n*10^k$ where n is an integer, * represents the multiplication operation, and k is always a non-positive integer. The value k is called the exponent, and the factional part is called the mantissa.

Definition of floating-point representation of decimal numbers

In assembly language, decimal numbers represented in the form

$$\pm a_0.a_1a_2 \ldots a_n \times E \pm n$$

and are called floating-point numbers, where a_0 is a positive digit.

Examples:

ORDINARY DECIMAL NUMBER REPRESENTATION	SCIENTIFIC REPRESENTATION	FLOATING-POINT REPRESENTATION
23.4	$234*10^{-1}$	2.34 E1
−55.0101	$-550101*10^{-4}$	−5.50101E 1
0.00154	$154*10^{-5}$	1.54 E −3
−79.0	$-79*10^{0}$	−7.9 E 1
9.0	$9*10^{0}$	9 E 0

Exercise:

1. Write the following in scientific and floating-point representation:

0.00234   45.356   −32

18.2 ARITHMETIC OPERATIONS USING SCIENTIFIC REPRESENTATION

Multiplication

To multiply two numbers in scientific notation, we simply multiply the integer numbers and add the exponents:

$(N*10^n)(M*10^m) = (N*M)*10^{n+m}$

Examples:

$(0.234)(0.05667) = (234*10^{-3})(5667*10^{-5}) = (234)(5667)*10^{-8} = 1326078*10^{-8} =$

1326078 E -8

The following partial assembly language code will compute $(0.234)(0.05667)$:

    mov eax, 234

    mov ebx, -3

    mul 5667

    add ebx, -5

Exercises:

1. Write the following using scientific representation.

    - 575.345*0.00234   678*0.03*2.135   0.0034*0.221

2. Write assembly language codes that will compute the above.

Addition and subtraction

To add or subtract two numbers using scientific representation, the exponents must be equal:

$$N*10^n \pm M*10^m = (N \pm M)*10^n$$

Example:

$0.234 + 0.05667 = 234*10^{-3} + 5667*10^{-5} = 23400*10^{-5} + 5667*10^{-5} =$

$(23400 + 5667)*10^{-5} = 29067*10^{-5}$

The following assembly language code will compute $0.234 + 0.05667$:

    mov eax, 23400

    mov ebx, −5

    add eax, 5667

Exercises:

Write the following using scientific representation:

1. −575.345 + 0.00234   678 + 0.03 + 2.135   0.0034 − 0.221

2. Write assembly language codes that will compute the above.

Long division

To divide two decimal numbers using scientific representation, we have the following form:

$$(N * 10^n)/(M * 10^m) = (N/M) * 10^{n-m}.$$

Example:

1. $0.00258/23.456 = (258*10^{-5}) / (23456*10^{-3}) = (258/23456)10^{-5+3} = (258/23456)10^{-2}$

18.3 80X86 FLOATING-POINT ARCHITECTURE

The MASM compiler has the ability to handle ordinary and floating-**point** decimal numbers. The following are definitions of the representation given by MASM for decimal numbers.

Definition of float:

An ordinary decimal representation. The number is represented as a 32-bit number.

Definition of double decimal:

An ordinary decimal representation. The number is represented as a 64-bit number.

Definition of long double:

A floating-point representation. The number is represented as an 80-bit number.

The following are data type registers that are available: **TBYTE, REAL4, REAL8, REAL10.** The *table* below gives the specifications for each of these data types.

DIRECTIVE	# OF BYTES	NUMBER TYPE
REAL4	4	float decimal
REAL8	8	double decimal
REAL10	10	long double, floating point
QWORD	8	integer
TBYTE	10	long double, floating point

Along with these data types, we still can use the integer data types: **BYTE, WORD, DWORD.**

Important: Except the QWORD data type, all the above data types are only represented in the base 10. The QWORD follows the data type representation for integer numbers.

Examples:

.DATA

w	TBYTE	0.236;	will assign the number 2.36 to the identifier w as 2.36E-1.
x	real4	2.34;	will assign the number 2.34 to the identifier x as 2.34.
y	real8	0.00678;	will assign 0.00678 to the identifier y as 0.00678.
z	real10	23554.5678	will assign 23554.5678 to the identifier z as 2.35545678E4.
q	qword	10	will assign 10 to the identifier q as an integer.

Rules for assigning floating-point numbers

The following are rules for assigning floating-point numbers:

- All identifiers are initially assigned floating-point numbers, where they are defined in the data part of the program.

- All other assignments are done by passing the contents of the variables to the various floating-point registers.

Floating-point registers

The registers EAX, EBX, ECX, and EDX cannot be used directly when working with floating-point numbers. Instead, we have eight data registers, each 80 bits long. Their names are ST or ST(0), ST(1), ST(2), ST(3), ST(4), ST(5), ST(6), ST(7). These eight registers are shown stacked vertically top down and should be visualized as follows.

ST
ST(1)
ST(2)
ST(3)
ST(4)
ST(5)
ST(6)
ST(7)

Exercise:

    1. What is the largest value (base 10) that can be stored in ST(k)?

The operands of all floating-point instructions begin with the letter f. The following will give the most important floating-point instructions according to their general functions. Additional floating-point instructions will be discussed in a later chapter of this book.

Storing data from memory to the registers

For demonstration purposes, we will assume the registers have the following numbers.

ST	10.0
ST(1)	15.0
ST(2)	20.0
ST(3)	25.0
ST(4)	
ST(5)	
ST(6)	
ST(7)	

The following are the floating-point instructions that will store data from memory to a given register.

    • **fld**

MNEMONIC	OPERAND	ACTION
Fld	memory variable (real)	The real number from memory is stored in ST.

Example

    .DATA

    x REAL4   30.0

    fld x ; stores the content of x in register ST and pushes the other values down.

REGISTER	BEFORE EXECUTION	AFTER EXECUTION
ST	10.0	**30.0**
ST(1)	15.0	10.0
ST(2)	20.0	15.0
ST(3)	25.0	20.0
ST(4)		25.0
ST(5)		
ST(6)		
ST(7)		

- **fild**

MNEMONIC	OPERAND	ACTION
fild	variable memory (integer)	The integer number from memory is stored in ST, converted to floating point, and data is pushed down.

Example:

.DATA

x   DWORD 50

fild x ; stores the content of x (integer value) in register ST and pushes the other values down.

REGISTER	BEFORE EXECUTION	AFTER EXECUTION
ST	10.0	**50.0**
ST(1)	15.0	10.0
ST(2)	20.0	15.0
ST(3)	25.0	20.0
ST(4)		25.0
ST(5)		
ST(6)		
ST(7)		

- **fld**

MNEMONIC	OPERAND	ACTION
fld	st(k)	The number in st(k) is stored in ST, and data is pushed down.

Example:

fld st(2) ; stores the contents of register st(2) in register ST and pushes the other values down.

REGISTER	BEFORE EXECUTION	AFTER EXECUTION
ST	10.0	**20.0**
ST(1)	15.0	10.0
ST(2)	20.0	15.0
ST(3)	25.0	20.0

ST(4)		25.0
ST(5)		
ST(6)		
ST(7)		

Important: Once the stack is full, additional stored data will cause the bottom values to be lost. Also the *finit* instruction will clear all the values in the register.

Copying data from the stack

We will assume the registers have the following numbers.

ST	10.0
ST(1)	15.0
ST(2)	20.0
ST(3)	25.0
ST(4)	
ST(5)	
ST(6)	
ST(7)	

The following are the floating-point instructions that will copy data from stack.

- **fst**

MNEMONIC	OPERAND	ACTION
Fst	st(k)	Makes a copy of ST and stores the value in ST(k)

Example:

fst ST(2) ; stores the content of ST in ST(2).

REGISTER	BEFORE EXECUTION	AFTER EXECUTION
ST	10.0	10.0
ST(1)	15.0	15.0
ST(2)	20.0	**10.0**
ST(3)	25.0	25.0
ST(4)		
ST(5)		
ST(6)		
ST(7)		

• **fst**

MNEMONIC	OPERAND	ACTION
fst	memory variable (real)	Makes a copy of ST and stores the value in a real memory location

Example:

.DATA

x   real4 ?

fst x ; stores the content of ST in x. The stack is not affected.

REGISTER	BEFORE EXECUTION	AFTER EXECUTION
ST	10.0	10.0
ST(1)	15.0	15.0
ST(2)	20.0	20.0
ST(3)	25.0	25.0
ST(4)		
ST(5)		
ST(6)		
ST(7)		

- **fist**

MNEMONIC	OPERAND	ACTION
fist	memory variable (integer)	Converts to integer a copy of ST and stores the rounded value in an integer memory location

Example:

.DATA

x   DWORD?

fist x ; stores the content of ST as an integer number in x.

REGISTER	BEFORE EXECUTION	AFTER EXECUTION
ST	10.0	10.0
ST(1)	15.0	15.0
ST(2)	20.0	20.0
ST(3)	25.0	25.0
ST(4)		
ST(5)		
ST(6)		
ST(7)		

Exchanging the contents of the two floating-point registers

We will assume the registers have the following numbers.

ST	10.0
ST(1)	15.0
ST(2)	20.0
ST(3)	25.0
ST(4)	
ST(5)	
ST(6)	
ST(7)	

The following are the floating-point instructions that will exchange the contents of two float- ing- point registers.

- **fxch**

MNEMONIC	OPERAND	ACTION
fxch	None	Exchanges the content of ST and ST(1)

Example:

fxch ; exchanges the content of ST and ST(1).

REGISTER	BEFORE EXECUTION	AFTER EXECUTION
ST	10.0	**15.0**
ST(1)	15.0	**10.0**
ST(2)	20.0	20.0
ST(3)	25.0	25.0
ST(4)		
ST(5)		
ST(6)		
ST(7)		

- **fxch**

MNEMONIC	OPERAND	ACTION
fxch	st(k)	Exchanges the content of ST and ST(k)

Example:

fxch st(3) ; exchanges the content of ST and ST(3).

REGISTER	BEFORE EXECUTION	AFTER EXECUTION
ST	10.0	**25.0**
ST(1)	15.0	15.0
ST(2)	20.0	20.0
ST(3)	25.0	**10.0**
ST(4)		
ST(5)		
ST(6)		
ST(7)		

Adding contents of the two floating-point registers

We will assume the registers have the following numbers.

ST	10.0
ST(1)	15.0
ST(2)	20.0
ST(3)	25.0
ST(4)	
ST(5)	
ST(6)	
ST(7)	

The following are the floating-point instructions that will add the contents of two floating-point registers.

- **fadd**

MNEMONIC	OPERAND	ACTION
fadd	st(k), st	Adds ST(k) and ST; then ST(k) is replaced by the sum

Example

fadd st(3), st ; adds ST(3) and ST; then ST(3) is replaced by the sum.

REGISTER	BEFORE EXECUTION	AFTER EXECUTION
ST	10.0	10.0
ST(1)	15.0	15.0
ST(2)	20.0	20.0
ST(3)	25.0	**35.0**
ST(4)		
ST(5)		
ST(6)		
ST(7)		

- **fadd**

MNEMONIC	OPERAND	ACTION
fadd	st, st(k)	Adds ST and ST(k); then ST is replaced by the sum

Example:

fadd st, st(3) ; adds the content of ST and ST(3); then ST is replaced by the sum.

REGISTER	BEFORE EXECUTION	AFTER EXECUTION
ST	10.0	**35.0**
ST(1)	15.0	15.0
ST(2)	20.0	20.0
ST(3)	25.0	25.0
ST(4)		
ST(5)		
ST(6)		
ST(7)		

- **fadd**

MNEMONIC	OPERAND	ACTION
fadd	memory variable (real)	Adds ST and the contents of a real variable; then ST is replaced by the sum

Example:

x REAL4 12.0

fadd x ; adds the content of ST and x; then ST is replaced by the sum.

REGISTER	BEFORE EXECUTION	AFTER EXECUTION
ST	10.0	**22.0**
ST(1)	15.0	15.0
ST(2)	20.0	20.0

ST(3)	25.0	25.0
ST(4)		
ST(5)		
ST(6)		
ST(7)		

- **fiadd**

MNEMONIC	OPERAND	ACTION
fiadd	memory variable (integer)	Adds ST and the contents of an integer variable; then ST is replaced by the sum.

Example

x DWORD   70

fadd x ; adds the content of ST and x; then ST is replaced by the sum.

REGISTER	BEFORE EXECUTION	AFTER EXECUTION
ST	10.0	**80.0**
ST(1)	15.0	15.0
ST(2)	20.0	20.0
ST(3)	25.0	25.0
ST(4)		
ST(5)		
ST(6)		
ST(7)		

Subtracting the contents of the two floating-point registers

The following are the floating-point instructions that will subtract the contents of two float-ing- point registers.

- **fsub**

- **fsbur**

MNEMONIC	OPERAND	ACTION
fsub	st(k), st	Computes ST(k)–ST; then ST(k) is replaced by the difference.
fsbur	st(k), st	Computes ST–ST(k); then ST(k) is replaced by the difference.

Example

fsub st(3), st ; computes ST(3)–ST; then ST(3) is replaced by the difference.

REGISTER	BEFORE EXECUTION	AFTER EXECUTION
ST	10.0	10.0
ST(1)	15.0	15.0
ST(2)	20.0	20.0
ST(3)	25.0	**15.0**
ST(4)		
ST(5)		
ST(6)		
ST(7)		

- **fsub**

- **fsubr**

MNEMONIC	OPERAND	ACTION
Fsub	st, st(k)	Computes ST–ST(k); then ST is replaced by the difference
Fsubr	st, st(k)	Computes ST(k)–ST; then ST is replaced by the difference

Example:

fsub st, st(1) ; computes st–st(1); then st is replaced by the difference.

REGISTER	BEFORE EXECUTION	AFTER EXECUTION
ST	10.0	**- 5.0**
ST(1)	15.0	15.0
ST(2)	20.0	20.0
ST(3)	25.0	25.0
ST(4)		
ST(5)		
ST(6)		
ST(7)		

- **fsub**

- **fsubr**

MNEMONIC	OPERAND	ACTION
fsub	memory (real)	Calculates ST–real number; then ST is replaced by the difference
fsubr	memory (real)	Calculates real number–ST; then ST is replaced by the difference

Example:

x REAL412.0

fsub x ; calculates st–x; then st is replaced by the difference.

REGISTER	BEFORE EXECUTION	AFTER EXECUTION
ST	10.0	**- 2.0**
ST(1)	15.0	15.0
ST(2)	20.0	20.0
ST(3)	25.0	25.0
ST(4)		
ST(5)		
ST(6)		
ST(7)		

- **fisub**

- **fisubr**

MNEMONIC	OPERAND	ACTION
fisub	memory (integer)	Calculates ST–integer number; then ST is replaced by the difference
fisubr	memory (integer)	Calculates integer number–ST; then ST is replaced by the difference

Example:

x DWORD 70

fisub x ; calculates st–x; then st is replaced by the difference.

REGISTER	BEFORE EXECUTION	AFTER EXECUTION
ST	10.0	**- 60.0**
ST(1)	15.0	15.0
ST(2)	20.0	20.0
ST(3)	25.0	25.0
ST(4)		
ST(5)		
ST(6)		
ST(7)		

Multiplying the contents of the two floating-point registers

The following are the floating-point instructions that will multiply the contents of two floating- point registers.

- **fmul**

MNEMONIC	OPERAND	ACTION
Fmul	st(k), st	Multiplies ST(k) and ST; then ST(k) is replaced by the product

Example:

fmul st(3), st ; multiplies st(3) and st; then st(3) is replaced by the product.

REGISTER	BEFORE EXECUTION	AFTER EXECUTION
ST	10.0	10.0
ST(1)	15.0	15.0
ST(2)	20.0	20.0

ST(3)	25.0	**250.0**
ST(4)		
ST(5)		
ST(6)		
ST(7)		

- **fmul**

MNEMONIC	OPERAND	ACTION
fmul	st, st(k)	Multiplies ST(k) and ST; then ST is replaced by the product

Example:

fmul st, st(3) ; multiplies st(3) and st; then st is replaced by the product.

REGISTER	BEFORE EXECUTION	AFTER EXECUTION
ST	10.0	**250.0**
ST(1)	15.0	15.0
ST(2)	20.0	20.0
ST(3)	25.0	25.0
ST(4)		
ST(5)		
ST(6)		
ST(7)		

- **fmul**

MNEMONIC	OPERAND	ACTION
fmul	memory variable (real)	Multiplies ST and real variable; then ST is replaced by the product

Example:

    x REAL4   35.0

fmul x ; multiplies x and st; then st is replaced by the product.

REGISTER	BEFORE EXECUTION	AFTER EXECUTION
ST	10.0	**350.0**
ST(1)	15.0	15.0
ST(2)	20.0	20.0
ST(3)	25.0	25.0
ST(4)		
ST(5)		
ST(6)		
ST(7)		

- **fmul**

MNEMONIC	OPERAND	ACTION
fmul	memory variable (integer)	Multiplies integer variable and ST; then ST is replaced by the product

Example

x DWORD 45

fmul x ; multiplies x and st; then st is replaced by the product.

REGISTER	BEFORE EXECUTION	AFTER EXECUTION
ST	10.0	**450.0**
ST(1)	15.0	15.0
ST(2)	20.0	20.0
ST(3)	25.0	25.0
ST(4)		
ST(5)		
ST(6)		
ST(7)		

Dividing the contents of floating-point registers

The following are the floating-point instructions that will divide the contents of floating-point registers.

- **fdiv**
- **fdivr**

MNEMONIC	OPERAND	ACTION
fdiv	st(k), st	Computes ST(k)/ ST; then ST(k) is replaced by the quotient
fdivr	st(k), st	Computes ST/ ST(k); then ST(k) is replaced by the quotient

Example:

fdiv st(1), st ; computes st(1)/st; then st(1) is replaced by the quotient.

REGISTER	BEFORE EXECUTION	AFTER EXECUTION
ST	5.0	5.0
ST(1)	15.0	**3.0**
ST(2)	20.0	20.0
ST(3)	25.0	25.0
ST(4)		
ST(5)		
ST(6)		
ST(7)		

- **fdiv**

- **fdivr**

MNEMONIC	OPERAND	ACTION
fdiv	st, st(k)	Computes ST/ ST(k); then ST is replaced by the quotient
fdivr	st, st(k)	Computes ST(k)/ ST; then ST is replaced by the quotient

Example

fdiv st, st(2) ; computes st/ st(2); then st is replaced by the quotient.

REGISTER	BEFORE EXECUTION	AFTER EXECUTION
ST	5.0	**0.25**
ST(1)	15.0	15.0
ST(2)	20.0	20.0
ST(3)	25.0	25.0
ST(4)		
ST(5)		
ST(6)		
ST(7)		

- **fdiv**

- **fdivr**

MNEMONIC	OPERAND	ACTION
fdiv	memory variable (real)	Computes ST/ real variable; then ST is replaced by the quotient
fdivr	memory variable (real)	Computes real variable/ST; then ST is replaced by the quotient

Example:

x real4   10.0

fdiv x ; computes st/ x; then st is replaced by the quotient.

REGISTER	BEFORE EXECUTION	AFTER EXECUTION
ST	5.0	**0.5**
ST(1)	15.0	15.0
ST(2)	20.0	20.0
ST(3)	25.0	25.0

ST(4)		
ST(5)		
ST(6)		
ST(7)		

- **fidv**

- **fidvr**

MNEMONIC	OPERAND	ACTION
fidiv	memory (integer)	Computes ST/ integer variable; then ST is replaced by the quotient
fidivr	memory (integer)	Computes integer variable /ST; then ST is replaced by the quotient

Example

x DWORD   5

fdiv x ; computes st/ x; then st is replaced by the quotient.

REGISTER	BEFORE EXECUTION	AFTER EXECUTION
ST	5.0	**1.0**
ST(1)	15.0	15.0
ST(2)	20.0	20.0
ST(3)	25.0	25.0
ST(4)		
ST(5)		
ST(6)		
ST(7)		

Summary tables of floating-point arithmetic operations

Store data from memory to a given register

MNEMONIC	OPERAND	ACTION
fld	variable memory (real)	The real number from memory is stored in ST, and data is pushed down
fild	variable memory (integer)	The integer number from memory is stored in ST, converted to floating-point, and data is pushed down
fld	st(k)	The number in st(k) is stored in ST, and data is pushed down

Copy data from the stack

MNEMONIC	OPERAND	ACTION
Fst	st(k)	Makes a copy of ST and stores the value in ST(k)
Fst	memory variable (real)	Makes a copy of ST and stores the value in a real memory location
fist	memory (integer)	Converts to integer a copy of ST and stores the rounded value in an integer memory location

Exchange the contents of the two floating-point registers

MNEMONIC	OPERAND	ACTION
Fxch	(none)	Exchanges the content of ST and ST(1)
Fxch	st(k)	Exchanges the content of ST and ST(k)

Add contents of the two floating-point registers

MNEMONIC	OPERAND	ACTION
Fadd	st(k), st	Adds ST(k) and ST; then ST(k) is replaced by the sum
Fadd	st, st(k)	Adds ST and ST(k); then ST is replaced by the sum
Fadd	memory variable (real)	Adds ST and the contents of a real variable; then ST is replaced by the sum
Fiadd	memory variable (integer)	Adds ST and the contents of an integer variable; then ST is replaced by the sum

Subtract the contents of the two floating-point registers

MNEMONIC	OPERAND	ACTION
Fisub	memory (integer)	Calculates ST−integer number; then ST is replaced by the difference
Fisubr	memory (integer)	Calculates integer number−ST; then ST is replaced by the difference
Fsbur	st(k), st	Computes ST−ST(k); then ST(k) is replaced by the difference
Fsub	memory (real)	Calculates ST−real number; then ST is replaced by the difference
Fsub	st, st(k)	Computes ST−ST(k); then ST is replaced by the difference
Fsub	st(k), st	Computes ST(k)−ST; then ST(k) is replaced by the difference
Fsubr	st, st(k)	Computes ST(k)−ST; then ST is replaced by the difference
fsubr	memory (real)	Calculates real number−ST; then ST is replaced by the difference

Multiply the contents of the two floating-point registers

MNEMONIC	OPERAND	ACTION
fmul	st, st(k)	Multiplies ST(k) and ST; then ST is replaced by the product
fmul	st(k), st	Multiplies ST(k) and ST; then ST(k) is replaced by the product
fmul	memory variable (real)	Multiplies ST and real variable; then ST is replaced by the product
fmul	memory variable (integer)	Multiplies integer variable and ST; then ST is replaced by the product

Divide the contents of floating-point registers

MNEMONIC	OPERAND	ACTION
fdiv	st(k), st	Computes ST(k) / ST; then ST(k) is replaced by the quotient
fdiv	st, st(k)	Computes ST / ST(k); then ST is replaced by the quotient
fdiv	memory variable (real)	Computes ST / real variable; then ST is replaced by the quotient
fdivr	st(k), st	Computes ST / ST(k); then ST(k) is replaced by the quotient
fdivr	st, st(k)	Computes ST(k) / ST; then ST is replaced by the quotient
fdivr	memory variable (real)	Computes real variable / ST; then ST is replaced by the quotient
fidiv	memory variable (integer)	Computes ST / integer variable; then ST is replaced by the quotient
fidivr	memory variable (integer)	Computes integer variable / ST; then ST is replaced by the quotient

Miscellaneous floating-point instructions

1.

MNEMONIC	OPERAND	ACTION
fabs	(none)	Replaces the contents of ST with it absolute value

Example:

REGISTER	BEFORE EXECUTION	AFTER EXECUTION
ST	- 10.0	**10.0**

2.

MNEMONIC	OPERAND	ACTION
fchs	(none)	Replaces the contents of ST with–ST

Example:

REGISTER	BEFORE EXECUTION	AFTER EXECUTION
ST	10.0	**- 10.0**

3.

MNEMONIC	OPERAND	ACTION
frndint	(none)	Rounds ST to an integer value

Example:

REGISTER	BEFORE EXECUTION	AFTER EXECUTION
ST	12.424	**12.0**

Example:

A harmonic sum is defined by the sum $1 + 1/2 + 1/3 + ... + ... + 1/n$.

The following pseudocode programs will compute $1 + 1/2 + 1/3 + 1/4 + 1/5 + 1/6$.

PSEUDOCODE	CYCLE OF INSTRUCTIONS	SUM	N	ONE
SUM := 0.0	SUM:= 0.0	**0.0**	1	
N := 1	N := 1	0.0	1	
ONE:= 1	ONE:= 1	**0.0**	1	1
WHILE N <= 6	WHILE N <= 6	0.0	1	1
BEGIN	**BEGIN**	0.0	1	1
SUM := SUM + 1/N	SUM:= SUM+1/ N	**1**	1	1
N := N + 1	N := N + 1	1	2	1
	SUM:= SUM+1/ N	**1.5**	2	1
	N := N + 1	1.5	3	1
	SUM:= SUM+ 1/N	**1.8333...33333**	3	1
	N := N + 1	1.833...33333	4	1
	SUM:= SUM+ 1/N	**2.0833....33333**	4	1
	N := N + 1	2.0833....33333	5	1
	SUM:= SUM+ 1/N	**2.2833...33333**	5	1
	N := N + 1	2.2833...33333	6	1
	SUM:= SUM+ 1/N	**2.45**	6	1
	N := N + 1	2.45	7	1
END	**END**	2.45	7	1

PSEUDOCODE	AL PSEUDO CODE	ASSEMBLY CODE
SUM := 0.0	SUM := 0.0	sum real4 0.0
N := 1	N := 1	n byte 1
ONE:= 1	ONE:= 1	one byte 1
WHILE N <= 6	WHILE N ≤ 6	While1: cmp n, 6 jg end1
SUM := SUM + 1/N N:= N + 1	ST := ONE	fld one
	ST:= ST/N	fidiv n
	ST:= SUM + ST	fadd sum
	SUM:= ST	fst sum
	EAX := N	mov eax, n
	EAX := EAX + 1	add eax, 1
	N:= EAX	mov n, eax
	END	jmp while1
		end1:

Exercises

1. Write an assembly program to compute the sum:

   $1^2 + 1/2^2 + 1/3^2 + 1/4^2 + 1/5^2 + 1/6^2$.

2. It can be shown that $2 = 1 + 1/2 + 1/2^2 + 1/2^3 + \ldots$

   (a) Write an AL algorithm to compute $S_n = 1 + 1/2 + 1/2^2 + 1/2^3 + \ldots + 1/2^n$.

   (b) Write an AL algorithm to find for a given n The error $= 2 - S_n$.

3. It can be shown that $1/4 = 1/3 - 1/3^2 + 1/3^3 - 1/3^4 + \ldots$.

   Write an AL algorithm to find for a given n the sum $= 1/3 - 1/3^2 + 1/3^3 - 1/3^4 + \ldots \pm 1/3^n$.

4. The determinate of a square table plays a major rule in mathematics.
   The following is a definition of a 2-by-2 determinate:

$$\Delta = \begin{vmatrix} a_{11} & a_{12} \\ a_{21} & a_{22} \end{vmatrix} = a_{11}a_{22} - a_{21}a_{12}$$

Write an algorithm that will compute an arbitrary 2-by-2 determinate.

Interchanging integer and floating-point numbers

The following table demonstrates how integer numbers and floating-point numbers are interchanged (all numbers are decimal).

AS CODE	N	X	Y	Z	ST(0)
n dword ?					
x real4 2.0		2.0			
y real4 23.7		2.0	23.7		
z real4 55.4		2.0	23.7	55.4	
fld x		2.0	23.7	55.4	2.0
fist n	2	2.0	23.7	55.4	2.0
fld y	2	2.0	23.7	55.4	23.7
fist n	24	2.0	23.7	55.4	23.7
fld z	24	20	23.7	55.4	55.4
fist n	55	20	23.7	55.4	55.4

Model program

```
;This program will compute the harmonic sum
;1 + 1/2 + 1/3 + 1/4 + 1/5 + 1/6
.386
.model flat
.stack 4096
.data
sum real4 0.0
n byte 1
one byte 1
.code
_start:
;start assembly language code
while1 cmp n, 6
jg end1
fild one
fidiv n
fadd sum
fst sum
mov eax, n
add eax, 1
mov n, eax
jmp while1
end:
;end of assembly language code
public _start
end
```

PROJECTS

1. It can be shown that

$$\pi \approx 4 - \frac{4}{3} + \frac{4}{5} - \frac{4}{7} + \frac{4}{9} - \frac{4}{11} + \ldots \pm \frac{4}{2n+1}$$

    (a) Write an assembly language algorithm to approximate π.

    (b) Write an assembly language program to approximate π for $n = 10$.

2. The solution of a 2-by-2 system of equations:

The determinate of a square table plays a major rule in mathematics. The following is a definition of a 2-by-2 determinate:

$$\Delta = \begin{vmatrix} a_{11} & a_{12} \\ a_{21} & a_{22} \end{vmatrix} = a_{11}a_{22} - a_{21}a_{12}$$

Write an algorithm that will compute an arbitrary 2-by-2 determinate.

Cramer's rules

Assume we wish to solve the following 2-by-2 system of equations:

$$a_{11}x + a_{12}y = b_1$$

$$a_{21}x + a_{22}y = b_2$$

The following Cramer's rules give us a solution of the above system of equations, where

$$x = \frac{\begin{vmatrix} b_1 & a_{12} \\ b_2 & a_{22} \end{vmatrix}}{\Delta}$$

$$y = \frac{\begin{vmatrix} a_{11} & b_1 \\ a_{21} & b_2 \end{vmatrix}}{\Delta}$$

Write an algorithm that solves any 3 a 2-by-2 system of equations. Make sure that Δ does not equal zero.

CHAPTER NINETEEN

COMPARING AND ROUNDING
FLOATING-POINT NUMBERS

INTRODUCTION

19.1 INSTRUCTIONS THAT COMPARE FLOATING-POINT NUMBERS

When we are comparing floating-point numbers, we cannot directly use the instruction *cmp*. Instead, we have the following instructions that allow us to compare the register ST to a second operand.

MNEMONIC	OPERAND	ACTION
fcom	(none)	Compares ST and ST(1)
fcom	st(k)	Compares ST and ST(k)
fcom	variable memory (real)	Compares ST and a real number in memory
ficom	variable memory (integer)	Compares ST and an integer number in memory
ftst	(none)	Compares ST and 0.0

The status word register

When one of the comparison instructions is made, the contents of a special 16-bit register, called the *status word* register, is modified. The comparison instruction will assign bits (0 or 1) to the bits 9, 11, and 15 of the status word.

The status word register cannot be directly accessed. In order to evaluate the bits in the status word, we can, with the following two instructions, copy the contents of the status word to a memory variable or the AX register:

MNEMONIC	OPERAND	ACTION
fstsw	variable (word) memory (integer)	Copies the status register into memory
fstsw	AX	Copies the status register into AX

Examples:

> x dword ?
>
> fcom
>
> fstsw x
>
> fstsw ax

Interpretation of the contents of the status word

When a comparison is made, the table below gives the bit values that are assigned to the status word by the comparison instructions.

COMPARISON	STATUS WORD															
BIT POSITION	16	15	14	13	12	11	10	9	8	7	6	5	4	3	2	1
ST > second operand	x	0	x	x	x	0	x	0	x	x	x	x	x	x	x	x
ST < second operand	x	0	x	x	x	0	x	1	x	x	x	x	x	x	x	x
ST = second operand	x	1	x	x	x	0	x	0	x	x	x	x	x	x	x	x

Where the values x are 0 or 1.

Since we are not sure what the other bits are in the status word, we need to create a mask that will convert the bits represented above by x's to the bit 0. By doing this, we can make correct comparisons. The following mask will be used.

BIT POSITION	16	15	14	13	12	11	10	9	8	7	6	5	4	3	2	1
MASK (binary)	0	1	0	0	0	1	0	1	0	0	0	0	0	0	0	0

The following codes show the effect of the mask on the possible contents of the status word resulting from a comparison instruction.

ST > second operand

AL CODE	AX	MASK
mov mask,01000101000000000b		01000101000000000b
fstsw ax; stores the contents of the status word in ax	x0xxx0x0xxxxxxxxb	01000101000000000b
and ax, mask	00000000000000000b	01000101000000000b

ST < second operand

AL CODE	AX	MASK
mov mask, 01000101000000000b		01000101000000000b
fstsw ax; stores the contents of the status word in ax	x0xxx0x1xxxxxxxxb	01000101000000000b
and ax, mask	00000001000000000b	01000101000000000b

ST = second operand

AL CODE	AX	MASK
mov mask,01000101000000000b		01000101000000000b
fstsw ax; stores the contents of the status word in ax	x1xxx0x0xxxxxxxxb	01000101000000000b
and ax, mask	01000000000000000b	01000101000000000b

Performing jumps

From above, we see that comparison instructions only set the status word. Therefore, to make our jump instructions from chapter 12 work, we need to check the contents of the status word. In order to make the comparison, we must first store the status word in a variable (word) or the ax register and then use the above mask, as shown above. The following examples should give us a clear idea of how this is done.

Examples:

1. Assume each of the registers in the stack have been previously assigned values. The following pseudocode and AL pseudocode will perform the following tasks:

    Task 1: If y is larger than x, then assign the contents of y to the memory location z.

    Task 2: If y is smaller than x, then assign contents of x to the memory location z.

    Task 3: If y is equal to x, then assign zero to the memory location z.

PSEUDOCODE	AL PSEUDOCODE
mov mask, 0100010100000000b	mov MASK, 0100010100000000b
IF Y > X THEN	ST:= Y
	; COMPARE ST, X
	AX:= STATUS- WORD
	AX:= AX .AND. MASK
	IF AX = 0000000000000000b THEN
BEGIN	BEGIN
Z:= Y	EAX:= Y
	Z:= EAX
END	END
IF Y < X THEN	IF AX = 0000000100000000b THEN
BEGIN	BEGIN
Z:= X	EAX:= X
	Z:= EAX
END	END
IF Y = X THEN	IF AX:= 0100000000000000b THEN
BEGIN	BEGIN
Z:= 0	Z:= 0
END	END

Using the above pseudocode and AL pseudocode, the below partial assembly language program will find the larger of two positive x and y where x = 7 and y = 2.

AL PSEUDOCODE	AL CODE	Z	ST	AX
m= 010001010000000 b	mov m, 010001010000000 b			
X:= 7	mov x, 7			
Y:= 2	mov y, 2			
ST:= Y	fild y		2	
COMPARE ST, X	fcom x		2	
AX:= STATUS- WORD	fstsw ax		2	**x0xxx0x1xxxxxxxxb**
AX:= AX .AND. M	and ax,m		2	0000000100000000b
IF X = ST THEN	cmp ax, 0100000000000000b		2	0000000100000000b
	jne L1		2	0000000100000000b
BEGIN	begin:		2	0000000100000000b
Z := 0	mov z, 0		2	0000000100000000b
END	end: jmp end2		2	0000000100000000b
IF X < ST THEN	L1: cmp ax, 0000000000000000b		2	0000000100000000b
	jne begin2		2	0000000100000000b
BEGIN	begin:		2	0000000100000000b
EAX:= X	mov eax, x		2	0000000100000000b
Z:= EAX	mov z, eax		2	0000000100000000b
END	end: jmp end2		2	0000000100000000b
IF X > ST THEN			2	0000000100000000b
BEGIN	begin2:		2	0000000100000000b
EAX := X	mov eax, x		2	0000000100000000b
Z:= EAX	mov z, eax	7	2	0000000100000000b
END	end2:	7	2	0000000100000000b

2. The following program will compute the harmonic sum

$$1 + 1/2 + 1/3 + ... + 1/n \quad \text{until } 1/n < e, \text{ where } 0 < e < 1.$$

Assume e = 0.00001.

Note: See model program below.

PSEUDOCODE	AL PSEUDO CODE	ASSEMBLY CODE
E:= 0.00001	E:= 0.00001	e real4 0.00001
F:= 1.0	F:= 1.0	f real4 1.0
SUM := 0.0	SUM:= 0.0	sum real4 0.0
N := 1	N:= 1.0	n real4 1.0
ONE:= 1	ONE:= 1.0	one real4, 1.0
MASK:= 0010001010000000b	MASK:= 0100010100000000b	mov mask, 0100010100000000b
WHILE F ≥ E	WHILE: ST ≥ F	while1: fld f
	FCOM E	fcom e
	AX:= STATUS WORD	fstsw ax
	AX:= AX .AND. MASK	and ax, mask
	IF AX = 100h THEN	comp ax, 0000000100000000b
	JUMP END	je end1
BEGIN	**BEGIN**	**BEGIN**
SUM:= SUM + F	ST:= SUM	fld sum
	ST:= ST + F	fadd f
	SUM:= ST	fst sum
N:= N + ONE	ST:= N	fld n
	ST:= ST + ONE	fadd one
	N:= S	fst n
F:= ONE/N	ST:= ONE	fld one
	ST:= ST/N	fdiv n
	F:= ST	fst f
	JUMP WHILE	jmp while1
END	**END**	end:

19.2 ROUNDING FLOATING-POINT NUMBERS

In order to write such programs, we need to be able to truncate decimal values. The contents of the control register (see below) determine how data is to be rounded when data in the ST register is transferred to an integer variable. There are four types of rounding:

- **Normal** rounding of the number to an integer

- **Rounding** the number **up** to the nearest integer

- **Rounding** the number **down** to the nearest integer

- **Truncating** the number to its integer value

The following table gives the hexadecimal representation of the contents of the control register that is needed to perform rounding in ST.

BYTE POSITION	2	1
Round the number to the nearest integer.	00	00
Round the number up to the nearest integer.	08	00
Round the number down to the nearest integer.	04	00
Truncate the number to its integer value.	06	00

Examples:

1. 23.678 => 24, normal rounding to an integer

2. 23.678 => 24, rounded up to the nearest integer

3. 23.678 => 23, rounded down to the nearest integer

4. 23.678 => 23, truncated to its integer value

The control register

The control register is a 16-bit register that determines the kind of rounding that is to take place. When copying a value from the ST register to an integer variable, the 11th and 12th bits of the control register have to be modified to determine what type of rounding is to take place. This can be accomplished by transferring to the control register one of the bytes in the table above.

The table below contains the instructions that will copy the contents of an integer variable from and to the control register.

MNEMONIC	OPERAND	ACTION
fstcw	memory variable (integer)	Copies the contents of the control register to a memory variable
fldcw	memory variable (integer)	Copies the contents of the memory variable to the control register

To round a number to the desired type, the following order has to be followed:

1. Copy the desired byte, from the table above, to the control register.

2. Copy the contents of ST to a given integer variable.

Examples:

1. Normal rounding

```
; 2.9 => 3
.data
n word ?
x real4 2.9
round word 0h
.code

_start :

fld x ;          2.9 => st(0)
fldcw round;  0h => control register
fist n;          3 => n
public _start

end
```

2. Rounding down

```
; 2.9 => 2
.data
n word ?
x real4 2.9
round word 0400h
.code

_start :

fld x ;          2.9 => st(0)
fldcw round;  0400h => control register
fist n;          2 => n
public _start

end
```

3. Rounding up

```
; 2.1 => 3
.data
n word ?
x real4 2.1
round word 0800h
.code

_start :

fld x ;          2.1 => st(0)
fldcw round;  0800h => control register
fist n;          3 => n
public _start

end
```

4. Truncating

```
; 2.9 => 2
.data
n word ?
x real4 2.9
round word 0600h
.code

_start :

fld x ;          2.9 => st(0)
fldcw round;  0600h => control register
fist n;          2 => n
public _start

end
```

Exercises:

1. Write an AL program that will perform the following:

   (a) Store in a variable the decimal representation of the number 1/7.

   (b) Round the number to 10 places of accuracy.

2. It can be shown that $2 = 1 + 1/2 + 1/2^2 + 1/2^3 + ...$

   Write an AL program to compute the $S_n = 1 + 1/2 + 1/2^2 + ... + 1/2^n$ where the error $= 2 - Sn < 10^{-n}$ is for a given value of n.

3. It can be shown that $1 + 2 + ... + N = N(N + 1)/2$

   Write an AL algorithm that will compute and store the number:
   $1.0 + 2.0 + ... + N.0$ and compute, if any, the error
   $|(1.0 + 2.0 + ... + N.0) - N.0(N.0 + 1.0)/2.0|$.

4. The determinate of a square table plays a major role in mathematics. The following is a definition of a 2-by-2 determinate:

   $$\Delta = \begin{vmatrix} a_{11} & a_{12} \\ a_{21} & a_{22} \end{vmatrix} = a_{11}a_{22} - a_{21}a_{12}$$

   Write an algorithm that will compute an arbitrary 2-by-2 determinate and check that $|\Delta| > E > 0$, for a given E.

Model program

```
;This program will compute the harmonic sum

;1 + 1/2 + 1/3 + ... + 1/n
;until
;1/n < e,
;where 0 < e < 1


;Assume e = 0.00001


.386
.MODEL FLAT


.STACK 4096


.DATA


.CODE
e real4 0.00001
f real4 1.0
sum real4 0.0
n real4 1.0
one real4, 1.0

_start:
;start assembly language code
```

```
mov mask ,010001010000000 b


whil1: fld f

fcom e

fstsw ax

and ax, mask

comp ax, 0000000010000000b

je end

begin:

fld sum

fadd f

fst sum

fld n

fadd one

fst n

fld one

fdiv n

fst f

jmpwhil1

end:


;end of assembly language code


PUBLIC_start


END
```

PROJECT

1. It can be shown that $4 \approx 3 + \dfrac{3}{4} + \dfrac{3}{4^2} + \dfrac{3}{4^3} + \dfrac{3}{4^4} + \dfrac{3}{4^5} + \ldots + \dfrac{3}{4^n}$

   To approximate 4, we compute the above sum untill $\dfrac{3}{4^M} < 10^{-M}$

   for a positive value of M

   (a) Write an assembly language algorithm to approximate 4.

   (a) Write an assembly language program to approximate 4 for M = 10.

2. It can be shown that $\pi \approx 4 - \dfrac{4}{3} + \dfrac{4}{5} - \dfrac{4}{7} + \dfrac{4}{9} - \dfrac{4}{11} + \ldots \pm \dfrac{4}{2n+1} \pm \ldots$

   Let $\pi \approx 4 - \dfrac{4}{3} + \dfrac{4}{5} - \dfrac{4}{7} + \dfrac{4}{9} - \dfrac{4}{11} + \ldots \pm \dfrac{4}{2n+1} + R_n$

   where

   $$R_n = \pm \frac{4}{2n+1} \pm \frac{4}{2n+3} \pm \frac{4}{2n+5} + \ldots \pm \frac{4}{4n-1}$$

   Write an AL program that will for a value of n_0, will make $\left| R_n \right| < 1/10^M$, for M > 0

   and will approximate $\pi = 4 - \dfrac{4}{3} + \dfrac{4}{5} - \dfrac{4}{7} + \dfrac{4}{9} - \dfrac{4}{11} + \ldots \pm \dfrac{4}{4n_0-1}$.

CHAPTER TWENTY

DYNAMIC STORAGE FOR DECIMAL NUMBERS: STACKS

INTRODUCTION

Chapter 15 demonstrated how arrays in assembly language allow the programmer to store a large amount of integer numeric data sequentially in memory locations. This chapter will show two other types of instructions in assembly language that perform dynamic storage for decimal numbers: the push and pop instructions.

Definition of push instructions:

Push instructions will insert data into registers or memory locations.

Definition of pop instructions:

Pop instructions may remove data from registers or memory locations and insert data into registers or memory locations.

20.1 FLOATING-POINT PUSH AND POP INSTRUCTIONS

The following instructions will bring about pushes and pops that are used in floating-point programming. They are part of the instruction sets that were first introduced in chapter 18.

As you will recall, the operands of all floating-point instructions begin with the letter f. When storing or changing data in the registers, the following floating-point instructions will cause the data that is replaced in the register to be pushed down to the registers below or up to the registers above.

Storing data from memory to the registers

We will assume the registers have the following numbers.

ST	10.0
ST(1)	15.0
ST(2)	20.0
ST(3)	25.0
ST(4)	
ST(5)	
ST(6)	
ST(7)	

The following are the floating-point instructions that will store data from memory to a given register.

MNEMONIC	OPERAND	ACTION
fld	memory (real)	The real number from memory is stored in ST, and *data is pushed down.*

Example:

> .DATA
>
> x REAL4 30.0
>
> fld x; stores the content of x (real) into register ST and pushes the other values down.

REGISTER	BEFORE EXECUTION	AFTER EXECUTION
ST	10.0	**30.0**
ST(1)	15.0	10.0
ST(2)	20.0	15.0
ST(3)	25.0	20.0
ST(4)		25.0
ST(5)		
ST(6)		
ST(7)		

MNEMONIC	OPERAND	ACTION
fild	memory (integer)	The integer number from memory is stored in ST, converted to floating-point, and *data is pushed down.*

Example:

.DATA

x   DWORD   50

fild x; stores the content of x (integer) in register ST and pushes the other values down.

REGISTER	BEFORE EXECUTION	AFTER EXECUTION
ST	10.0	**50.0**
ST(1)	15.0	10.0
ST(2)	20.0	15.0
ST(3)	25.0	20.0
ST(4)		25.0
ST(5)		
ST(6)		
ST(7)		

MNEMONIC	OPERAND	ACTION
fld	st(k)	The number in st(k) is stored in ST, and *data is pushed down.*

Example:

fld st(2); stores the number 20.0 into register ST and pushes the other values down.

REGISTER	BEFORE EXECUTION	AFTER EXECUTION
ST	10.0	**20.0**
ST(1)	15.0	10.0
ST(2)	20.0	15.0
ST(3)	25.0	20.0
ST(4)		25.0
ST(5)		
ST(6)		
ST(7)		

Important: Once the stack is full, additional stored data will cause the bottom values to be lost. Also, the *finit* instruction will clear all the values in the register.

Copying data from the stack

We will assume the registers have the following numbers.

ST	10.0
ST(1)	15.0
ST(2)	20.0
ST(3)	25.0
ST(4)	
ST(5)	
ST(6)	
ST(7)	

MNEMONIC	OPERAND	ACTION
fstp	st(k)	Makes a copy of ST and stores the value in ST(k). *ST is popped off the stack by moving the data up.*

Example:

fstp ST(2); stores the content of ST in ST(2) and then pops ST off the stack by moving the data up.

REGISTER	BEFORE EXECUTION	AFTER EXECUTION
ST	10.0	15.0
ST(1)	15.0	**10.0**
ST(2)	20.0	25.0
ST(3)	25.0	
ST(4)		
ST(5)		
ST(6)		
ST(7)		

MNEMONIC	OPERAND	ACTION
fstp	memory (real)	Makes a copy of ST and stores the value in a real memory location. *ST is popped off the stack.*

Example:

.DATA

x   real 4   ?

fstp x; stores the content of ST in x. ST is popped off the stack.

REGISTER	BEFORE EXECUTION	AFTER EXECUTION
ST	10.0	15.0
ST(1)	15.0	20.0
ST(2)	20.0	25.0
ST(3)	25.0	
ST(4)		
ST(5)		
ST(6)		
ST(7)		

MNEMONIC	OPERAND	ACTION
fstp	memory (integer)	Converts to integer a copy of ST and stores the value in an integer memory location. *ST is popped off the stack.*

Example

```
.DATA
x   DWORD   ?
fstp x; stores the content of ST as an integer number in x.
```

REGISTER	BEFORE EXECUTION	AFTER EXECUTION
ST	10.0	15.0
ST(1)	15.0	20.0
ST(2)	20.0	25.0
ST(3)	25.0	
ST(4)		
ST(5)		
ST(6)		
ST(7)		

Adding contents of the two floating-point registers

We will assume the registers have the following numbers.

ST	10.0
ST(1)	15.0
ST(2)	20.0
ST(3)	25.0
ST(4)	
ST(5)	
ST(6)	
ST(7)	

The following are the floating-point instructions that will add the contents of two floating-point registers.

MNEMONIC	OPERAND	ACTION
fadd	none	First it *pops both ST and ST(1)*; next it adds ST and ST(1); finally *the sum is pushed onto the stack.*

Example:

> fadd; first it pops both st and st(1); next it adds st and st(1); finally the sum is pushed onto the stack.

REGISTER	BEFORE EXECUTION	AFTER EXECUTION
ST	10.0	**45.0**
ST(1)	15.0	20.0

ST(2)	20.0	25.0
ST(3)	25.0	
ST(4)		
ST(5)		
ST(6)		
ST(7)		

MNEMONIC	OPERAND	ACTION
faddp	st(k), st	Adds ST(k) and ST; ST(k) is replaced by the sum and *ST is popped from the stack.*

Example:

faddp st(2), st; adds ST(2) and ST; ST(2) is replaced by the sum, and ST is popped from the stack.

REGISTER	BEFORE EXECUTION	AFTER EXECUTION
ST	10.0	15.0
ST(1)	15.0	**30.0**
ST(2)	20.0	25.0
ST(3)	25.0	
ST(4)		
ST(5)		
ST(6)		
ST(7)		

Subtracting the contents of the two floating-point registers

The following are the floating-point instructions that will subtract the contents of two floating-point registers.

MNEMONIC	OPERAND	ACTION
fsub	none	First it pops ST and ST(1); next it calculates ST(1)–ST; next it pushes the difference into ST.
fsubr	none	First it pops ST and ST(1); next it calculates ST–ST(1); next it pushes the difference into ST.

Example:

fsub; first it pops st and st(1); next it calculates st(1)–st; next it pushes the difference into st.

REGISTER	BEFORE EXECUTION	AFTER EXECUTION
ST	10.0	**- 2.0**
ST(1)	15.0	27.0
ST(2)	27.0	25.0
ST(3)	25.0	
ST(4)		
ST(5)		
ST(6)		
ST(7)		

MNEMONIC	OPERAND	ACTION
fsubp	st(k), st	Computes ST(k)–ST; replaces ST(k) by the difference; finally *pops ST from the stack*
fsubpr	st(k), st	Computes ST–ST(k); replaces ST(k) by the difference; finally *pops ST from the stack*

Example:

fsubp st(1), st; computes st(1)–st; replaces st(1) by the difference; finally pops ST from the stack.

REGISTER	BEFORE EXECUTION	AFTER EXECUTION
ST	10.0	**5.0**
ST(1)	15.0	20.0
ST(2)	20.0	25.0
ST(3)	25.0	
ST(4)		
ST(5)		
ST(6)		
ST(7)		

Multiplying the contents of the two floating-point registers

The following are the floating-point instructions that will multiply the contents of two floating-point registers.

MNEMONIC	OPERAND	ACTION
fmul	none	First it *pops both ST and ST(1)*; next it multiplies ST and ST(1); finally the *product is pushed onto the stack.*

Example:

fmul; first it pops both st and st(1); next it multiplies st and st(1); finally the product is pushed onto the stack.

REGISTER	BEFORE EXECUTION	AFTER EXECUTION
ST	10.0	**500.0**
ST(1)	15.0	20.0
ST(2)	20.0	25.0
ST(3)	25.0	
ST(4)		
ST(5)		
ST(6)		
ST(7)		

MNEMONIC	OPERAND	ACTION
fmulp	st(k), st	Multiplies ST(k) and ST; ST(k) is replaced by the product, and *ST is popped from the stack.*

Example:

fmulp st(3), st; multiplies st(3) and st; then st(k) is replaced by the product and st is popped from the stack.

REGISTER	BEFORE EXECUTION	AFTER EXECUTION
ST	10.0	15.0
ST(1)	15.0	20.0
ST(2)	20.0	**250.0**
ST(3)	25.0	
ST(4)		

ST(5)		
ST(6)		
ST(7)		

Dividing the contents of floating-point registers

The following are the floating-point instructions that will divide the contents of floating-point registers.

MNEMONIC	OPERAND	ACTION
fdiv	none	First it *pops both ST and ST(1)*; next it computes ST(1)/ ST; finally *the quotient is pushed onto the stack.*
fdivr	none	*First it pops both ST and ST(1)*; next it computes ST/ ST(1); finally *the quotient is pushed onto the stack.*

Example:

fdiv; first it pops both st and st(1); next it computes ST(1)/ ST; finally the quotient is pushed onto the stack.

REGISTER	BEFORE EXECUTION	AFTER EXECUTION
ST	5.0	**1.25**
ST(1)	15.0	20.0
ST(2)	20.0	25.0
ST(3)	25.0	
ST(4)		
ST(5)		
ST(6)		
ST(7)		

MNEMONIC	OPERAND	ACTION
fdivp	st(k), st	Computes ST(k) /ST; then ST(k) is replaced by the quotient. Next *ST is popped from the stack.*
fdivpr	st(k), st	Computes ST /ST(k); then ST(k) is replaced by the quotient. Next *ST is popped from the stack.*

Example:

fidivp st(2); computes st(2) /st; then st(2) is replaced by the quotient, and ST is popped from the stack.

REGISTER	BEFORE EXECUTION	AFTER EXECUTION
ST	5.0	15.0
ST(1)	15.0	**4.0**
ST(2)	20.0	25.0
ST(3)	25.0	
ST(4)		
ST(5)		
ST(6)		
ST(7)		

Instructions that compare floating-point numbers

MNEMONIC	OPERAND	ACTION
fcomp	(none)	Compares ST and ST(1); then *pops the stack*
fcomp	st(k)	Compares ST and ST(k); then *pops the stack*
fcomp	memory (real)	Compares ST and a real number in memory; then *pops the stack*
fcomp	memory (integer)	Compares ST and an integer number in memory; then *pops the stack*
fcompp	(none)	Compares ST and ST(1); then *pops the stack twice*

20.2 THE 80X86 STACK

The directive

.STACK 4096

in the assembly language has the assembler reserve of 4096 bytes of storage. This will allow the programmer to temporarily store integer data in this location. The instruction to store data sequentially is the push instruction.

The push instruction

The syntax of the push instruction is push *source* where the source can be any of the following:

- 16-bit register (AX, BX, CX, DX)

- 32-bit register (EAX, EBX, EDX, EDX)

- A declared word or double word variable

- A numeric byte, word or double word

The push instruction will sequentially store data in the stack starting at the initial location.

Note: For simplicity, we will only push 32-bit registers or numeric values.

Example:

AL CODE	EAX	STACK											
mov eax, 52B6h	**52B6**												
push eax	52B6	**00**	**00**	**52**	**B6**								
mov eax, 23A7h	**23A7**	00	00	52	B6								
push eax	23A7	**00**	**00**	**23**	**A7**	00	00	52	B6				
mov eax, 72346711h	**72346711**	00	00	23	A7	00	00	52	B6				
push eax	72346711	**72**	**34**	**67**	**11**	00	00	23	A7	0	0	52	B6

Exercises

1. Complete the table. Use only hexadecimal numbers.

AL CODE	AX	STACK											
mov ax, 23deh													
push ax													
mov ax, 3425													
push ax													
mov ax, 7f7ah													
push eax													

2. Complete the table. Use only hexadecimal numbers.

AL CODE	EAX	STACK											
mov eax, 0													
push eax													
mov eax, 243544h													
push eax													
mov eax, 1001111b													
push eax													

Other push instructions

pushw

When a numeric integer is to be pushed into the stack, to prevent confusion, the assembler needs to be informed as to its data type. The following push instructions perform this task:

- pushw *source* where source is a numeric value.

  This push instruction will identify the numeric value to be stored as a word.

- pushd *source* where source is a numeric value.

  This push instruction will identify the numeric value to be stored as a doubleword.

The pop instruction

The pop instruction will copy data from the stack, using the rule "last in first copied," and store the data at the designated destination. The data copied will be popped from the stack, and the remaining data will be pushed up the stack.

The syntax of the pop instruction is pop *destination* where the destination can be any of the following:

- 16-bit register (AX, BX, CX, DX)

- 32-bit register (EAX, EBX, EDX, EDX)

- A declared word or double word variable

Examples:

1.

AL CODE	EAX	EBX	STACK							
mov eax, 52B6h	**52B6**									
push eax	52B6		**00**	**00**	**52**	**B6**				
mov eax, 23A7h	**23A7**		00	00	52	B6				
push eax	23A7		**00**	**00**	**23**	**A7**	00	00	52	B6
pop ebx	23A7	**000023A7**	00	00	52	B6				
pop ebx	23A7	**000052B6**								

2.

AL CODE	EAX	EBX	STACK							
mov eax, 52B6h	**52B6**									
push eax	52B6		00	00	52	B6				
pushw 3AB4h	52B6		3A	B4	00	00	52	B6		
pushd 636AD9h	52B6		00	63	6A	D9	3A	B4	00	00
pop ebx	52B6	**00636AD9**	3A	B4	00	00				
pop ebx	52B6	**3AB40000**								

Note: Perhaps the best use of the push and pop instructions is to give the programmer additional temporary storage.

Exercises:

1. Store in a stack the sequence 1, 2, ..., 100.

2. In exercise 1 take the numbers from the stack and compute the number $12 + 22 + 32 + ... + 100^2$.

PROJECT

Write an assembly language program that will find and store in the stack all positive integer numbers between 1 and N that are prime.

III. WORKING WITH STRINGS

CHAPTER TWENTY-ONE

DYNAMIC STORAGE: STRINGS

INTRODUCTION

So far in this book, we have only been working with numeric data. In this chapter, we will define and work with string data. Strings are very important in that they can be used to communicate with the programmer and user.

We start with the definition of a string and its numeric representation: the ASCII code.

21.1 THE ASCII CODE

Definition of a string:

A string is a sequence of printable characters such as numbers, letters, spaces, and special symbols : $, *, and so on enclosed in single quotation marks: ' '.

Examples:

'Hello!' ,   'Sam lives here' ,   'To be or not to be' ,   'x = 2y + 3z.'

All data entered must be represented as numeric values. In assembly language, as well as many computer languages, the numeric representation of the ASCII code is used.

ASCII (American Standard Code for Information Interchange) is a character encoding based on the English alphabet. ASCII codes represent text in computers, communications equipment, and other devices that work with text. Most modern character encoding systems have a historical basis in ASCII.

ASCII was first published as a standard in 1967 and was last updated in 1986. It currently defines codes for 33 nonprinting, mostly obsolete control characters that affect how text is processed, plus 95 printable characters (starting with the space character).

ASCII is strictly a 7-bit code; meaning that it uses the bit patterns representable with seven binary digits (a range of 0 to 127 decimal) to represent character information. For example, three important codes are the null code (00), carriage return (0D), and line feed (0A).

The following is a table of the ASCII code along with each string's symbol associated with its hexadecimal number value.

ASCII table

ASCII SYMBOL	HEX	DEC	NAME	ASCII SYMBOL	HEX	DEC	NAME
	00	0	Null	@	40	64	At
SOH	01	1	Start of header	A	41	65	
STX	02	2	Start of text	B	42	66	
ETX	03	3	End of text	C	43	67	
EOT	04	4	End of transmission	D	44	68	
ENG	05	5	Enquire	E	45	69	
ACK	06	6	Acknowledge	F	46	70	
BEL	07	7	Bell	G	47	71	
BS	08	8	Backspace	H	48	72	
HT	09	9	Horizontal tab	I	49	73	
LF	0A	10	Line feed	J	4A	74	
VT	0B	11	Vertical tab	K	4B	75	
FF	0C	12	Form feed	L	4C	76	
CR	0D	13	Carriage return	M	4D	77	
SO	0E	14	Shift out	N	4E	78	
SI	0F	15	Shift in	O	4F	79	
DLE	10	16	Data link escape	P	50	80	
DC1	11	17	Device control 1	Q	51	81	
DC2	12	18	Device control 2	R	52	82	
DC3	13	19	Device Control 3	S	53	83	
DC4	14	20	Device control 4	T	54	84	

NAK	15	21	Negative acknowledge	U	55	85	
SYN	16	22	Synchronous idle	V	56	86	
ETB	17	23	End of transmission block	W	57	87	
CAN	18	24	Cancel	X	58	88	
EM	19	25	End of medium	Y	59	89	
SUB	1A	26	Substitute	Z	5A	90	
ESC	1B	27	Escape	[	5B	91	Open square bracket
FS	1C	28	File separator	\	5C	92	Backslash
GS	1D	29	Group separator	]	5D	93	Close square bracket
RS	1E	30	Record separator	^	5E	94	Circumflex
US	1F	31	Unit separator	_	5F	95	Underscore
SP	20	32	Space or blank	`	60	96	Single quote
!	21	33	Exclamation point	a	61	97	
"	22	34	Quotation mark	b	62	98	
#	23	35	Number sign (pound sign)	c	63	99	
$	24	36	Dollar sign	d	64	100	
%	25	37	Percent sign	e	65	101	
&	26	38	Ampersand	f	66	102	
'	27	39	Apostrophe (single quote)	g	67	103	
(	28	40	Opening parenthesis	h	68	104	
)	29	41	Close parenthesis	i	69	105	

*	2A	42	Asterisk (star sign)	j	6A	106	
+	2B	43	Plus sign	k	6B	107	
,	2C	44	Comma	l	6C	108	
-	2D	45	Hyphen (minus)	m	6D	109	
.	2E	46	Dot (period)	n	6E	110	
/	2F	47	Forward slash	o	6F	111	
0	30	48	Zero	p	70	112	
1	31	49		q	71	113	
2	32	50		r	72	114	
3	33	51		s	73	115	
4	34	52		t	74	116	
5	35	53		u	75	117	
6	36	54		v	76	118	
7	37	55		w	77	119	
8	38	56		x	78	120	
9	39	57		y	79	121	
:	3A	58	Colon	z	7A	122	
;	3B	59	Semicolon	{	7B	123	Open curly bracket
<	3C	60	Less than	|	7C	124	OR (pipe)
=	3D	61	Equality	}	7D	125	Close curly bracket
>	3E	62	Greater than	~	7E	126	Equivalence (tilde)
?	3F	63	Question mark	DEL	7F	127	Delete

Note: The associated ASCII codes are always in hexadecimal.

21.2 STORING STRINGS

In this chapter, we will find that there are several instructions to store strings in registers as well as defined variables.

- mov register, string

- mov variable, string

The register and the variable can be of any data type.

When a string is stored, each character of the string is converted to its hexadecimal ASCII code. For example, the string '- x3' is made up of four characters (counting the space but not the single quotation marks). The assembler will convert the four characters into the corresponding ASII code:

Examples:

ASSEMBLY CODE	EAX			
mov eax, '- x3'	2D	20	78	33

ASSEMBLY CODE	X
x byte ?	
mov x , '/ '	2F

Exercise:

Convert the following strings to ASCII code.

ASSEMBLY CODE	EAX			
mov eax, '+ YZ '				
mov eax, '/'				
mov eax, '* %'				

The string variables

Since all strings are converted by the assembler into integer bytes, we use the normal directives to define the variables as bytes, words, or double words.

Examples

1.

x BYTE 20 DUP (?); This directive will assign 20 blank bytes to the variable x.																			

2. Hamlet BYTE 'To be or not to be'; The assembler will set aside 18 bytes containing the ASCII codes.

54	6F	60	62	65	60	65	72	60	6E	65	54	60	54	65	60	62	65

3.

array_x DWORD 4 DUP '- 23'; The assembler will set aside dwords containing the ASCII code '- 23'.															
2D	60	32	33	2D	60	32	33	2D	60	32	33	2D	60	32	33

Exercise:

1. Complete the following tables.

Hamlet BYTE 'Brevity is the soul of wit'																							

A natural question should be raised: How does the programmer assign strings to registers and variables without using directly the above type of directives? For example, the above x variable has 20 blank bytes assigned to it for storage. Therefore, we should be able to assign any string of 20 characters' length or less to the variable x.

Since string data are changed to ASCII code by the assembler, we can use, as shown above, the *mov* instruction to assign a string to a register or a variable. However, there are times when we want to copy strings stored in one variable to another variable. We should note that transferring some strings through a register may not be possible, due to the size of the string. The following sections will give the necessary instructions to perform such tasks.

The movs instructions

To move strings from one variable to another variable, we define the following three movs instructions:

Definition of movsb:

The movsb will move the bytes of a variable, byte by byte, to another variable. The movsb instruction has no operands.

Definition of movsw:

The movsw will move the words of a variable, word by word, to another variable. The movsw instruction has no operands.

Definition of movsd:

The movsd will move the dwords of a variable, dword by dword, to another variable. The movsd instruction has no operands.

Since the three movs instructions have no operands, the assembler has to know which variable is the source of the string and which variable is the destination. The location of these variables is to be stored in the ESI and the EDI registers.

The ESI and EDI registers

Definition ESI:

The ESI register must contain the location of the source variable.

Definition EDI:

The EDI register must contain the location of the destination variable.

The lea instruction

In order to store the locations in these two registers, we use the *lea* instruction:

Definition of lea:

The form of the lea instruction is lea register, variable name

where, for this application, the registers are esi or edi.

Once the esi and edi are initialized, the movs instructions will increment these registers under the following rules:

1. The movsb will cause the esi and edi to be incremented to the next byte.

2. The movsw will cause the esi and edi to be incremented to the next word.

3. The movsd will cause the esi and edi to be incremented to the next dword.

Example:

ASSEMBLY CODE	X				Y			
x dword '- x3'	2D	20	78	33				
y dword ?	2D	20	78	33				
lea esi, x	2D	20	78	33				
lea edi, y	2D	20	78	33				
Movsb	2D	20	78	33	33			
Movsb	2D	20	78	33	78	33		
Movsb	2D	20	78	33	20	78	33	
Movsb	2D	20	78	33	2D	20	78	33

Exercises:

1. Hamlet DWORD 'To be or not to be'

Write an AL program that will move the string in variable Hamlet to the variable Shakespeare DWORD ?

21.3 MORE STRING INSTRUCTIONS

The following are additional string instructions that can be very useful when working with strings.

The stos instruction

There are three stos instructions:

Definition: stosb copies a byte stored in the AL register to the destination variable.

Example:

AL CODE	AL (Byte is in ASCII symbols)	X (Byte is in ASCII symbols)
x byte ?		
mov al, '&'	&	
lea edi, x	&	
stosb	&	&

Definition: stosw copies a word stored in the AX register to the destination variable.

Example:

AL CODE	AX (Word is in ASCII symbols)	X (Word is in ASCII symbols)
x word ?		
mov ax, '-9'	-9	
lea edi, x	-9	
stosw	-9	-9

Definition: stosd copies a word stored in the EAX register to the destination variable.

Example:

AL CODE	EAX (DWord is in ASCII symbols)	X (DWord is in ASCII symbols)
x dword ?		
mov eax, 'home'	**home**	
lea edi, x	home	
Stosd	home	**Home**

The lods instruction

There are three lods instruction:

Definition: lodsb copies a source stored in the byte variable to the AL register.

Example:

AL CODE	AL (Byte is in ASCII symbols)	X (Byte is in ASCII symbols)
x byte '#'		#
lea esi, x		#
Lodsb	#	#

Definition: lodsw copies a source stored in the word variable to the AX register.

Example:

AL CODE	AX (Word is in ASCII symbols)	X (Word is in ASCII symbols)
x word '$7 '		$7
lea esi, x		$7
Lodsw	$7	

Definition: lodsd copies a source stored in the word variable to the EAX register.

Example:

AL CODE	EAX (Word is in ASCII symbols)	X (DWord is in ASCII symbols)
xdword 'Bach '		**Bach**
lea esi, x		Bach
Lodsd	**Bach**	

The rep instruction

Definition: The rep instruction is a prefix to several other instructions to perform a given repetitive task. The number of repetitions is a given number stored in the ECX register. When completed, the ECX register will contain zero (0).

Examples:

   1.

AL CODE	ECX	AL (Byte is in ASCII symbols)	X (Dword is in ASCII symbols)			
x dword ?						
mov al, '^'		^				
lea edi, x		^				
mov ecx, 4	4	^				
rep stosb	0	^	^	^	^	^

2.

AL CODE	ECX	AX (Words in ASCII symbols)	X (Words in ASCII symbols)				
x word 5 dup (?)							
mov ax, 'WA'		WA					
lea edi, x		WA					
mov ecx, 5	5	WA					
rep stosw	0	WA	WA	WA	WA	WA	WA

3.

AL CODE	ECX	EAX (Words in ASCII symbols)	X (DWords in ASCII symbols)			
x dword 4 dup (?)						
mov eax, '1234'		1234				
lea edi, x		1234				
mov ecx, 4	4	1234				
rep stosd	0	1234	1234	123	123	123

Exercise:

1. Complete the table below:

AL CODE	ECX	Y (DWords in ASCIIsymbols)	X			
x dword 4 dup (?)						
Y dword '1234'						
mov ecx, 4						

lea esi, y						
lea edi, x						
rep movsd						

Other repeat instructions

Depending on the suffix, the following are additional versions of the rep instruction:

- *Definition:* the repe prefix is to repeat while ECX > 0 and the suffix operation compute a value equal to 0.

- *Definition:* the repz prefix is to repeat while ECX > 0 and the suffix operation compute a value equal to 0.

- *Definition:* the repne prefix is to repeat while ECX > 0 and the suffix operation compute a value not equal to 0.

- *Definition:* the repnz prefix is to repeat while ECX > 0 and the suffix operation compute a value not equal to 0.

Note: repz/repe and repnz/repne pairs are equivalent instructions. Also, all repeat instructions can be used in conjunction with procedures. In this way multiple instructions can be repeated.

The cmps instruction

There are three cmps instructions:

- *Definition:* cmpsb compares the binary source and binary designation strings. It does not have operands.

- *Definition:* cmpsw compares the word source and word designation strings. It does not have operands.

- *Definition:* cmpsd compares the double word and double word designation strings. It does not have operands.

Note: The cmps instructions should be used in conjunction with the jump instructions of chapter 11.

The following is a table of the conditional jumps for the signed order of rings in assembly language.

Mnemonic	Description
Je	jump to the label if *source* = *destination*; *jump if equal to*
Jne	jump to the label if *source* ≠ *destination*; *jump if not equal to*
Jnge	jump to the label if *source* < *destination*; *jump if not greater or equal to*
Jnle	jump to the label if *source* > *destination*; *jump if not less than or equal*
Jge	jump to the label if *source* ≥ *destination*; *jump if greater than or equal*
Jle	jump to the label if *source* ≤ *destination*; *jump if less than or equal*
Jl	jump to the label if *source* < *destination*; *jump if less than*
Jnl	jump to the label if *source* ≥ *destination*; *jump if not less than*
Jg	jump to the label if *source* > *destination*; *jump if greater than*
Jng	jump to the label if *source* ≤ *destination*; *jump if not greater than*

Note: Remember that the string comparisons are actually the comparisons of the numeric values associated with the strings.

The scas instruction

The scan string instruction, scas, is used to scan a string for the presence of a given string element. The scan string is the designation string, and the element that is being searched for is in a given register.

There are three scas instructions:

- *Definition:* The scasb requires that the element being searched for is in the AL register.

- *Definition:* The scasw requires that the element being searched for is in the AX register.

- *Definition:* The scasd requires that the element being search for is in the EAX register.

Note: To scan the entire string for the given elements, the repne *prefix* is used with the scas instruction.

Algorithm: Checks to see if a string has a given element of a byte size.

ASSEMBLY LANGUAGE CODE	COMMENTS
string location byte 'string'	
mov al, 'byte element'	
lea edi,stringlocation	'string' is the string to check if it contains the byte element.
mov ecx, n	The number of bytes containing string
mov eax, ecx	Will contain the location of the element
repne scasb	Checks byte by byte. Will stop checking if the byte is found.
sub eax, ecx	Location of the element if it exists in the string.

Example:

    x dword   'Bach'

    mov al, 'c'

    lea edi, x

    mov ecx, 4

    mov eax, ecx

    repne scasb

    sub eax, ecx

Exercise:

1. Write a program that will find the position location of "f" in the string 'I live in California'.

PROJECT

1. Write an assembly language program that will convert an arbitrary string "$a_1a_2a_3 \ldots a_n$" to it number value $a_1a_2a_3 \ldots a_n$.

2. Write an assembly language program that will convert an arbitrary integer number $a_1a_2a_3 \ldots a_n$ to the string "$a_1a_2a_3 \ldots a_n$".

CHAPTER TWENTY-TWO

STRING ARRAYS

INTRODUCTION

In chapter 15, we created one-dimensional integer arrays. In this chapter, we will create arrays that contain strings. We will see that the string arrays and integer arrays share many of the same rules.

The following are the ways string(s) can be stored using the directive in the data portion of the program. We can use the following directives:

- *variable name data type ?*

- *variable name data type string*

- *variable name data type string_1, string_2, ..., string_n*

- *variable name data type dimension dup(?)*

Examples:

variable name data type ?

1. x byte ?

   will allow a one-character string to be stored in x.

2. x word ?

   will allow a two-character string to be stored in x.

3. x dword ?

   will allow a four-character string to be stored in x.

variable name data type string

1. x byte *a string of any length*

   will allow any size string to be stored in an array starting in location x.
   x byte 'abcde'.

2. x word *string*

   will allow a string of two characters to be stored in x.
   x word 'ab'

3. x dword *string*

   will allow a string of four characters to be stored in x.
   x dword 'abcd'

variable name data type string_1, string_2, ..., string_n

1. x byte *string_1, string_2, ..., string_n*

   will allow a list of strings of any length starting in location x. x byte 'a', 'b', 'c', 'd'.

2. x word *string_1, string_2, ..., string_n*

   will allow a list of strings of two characters each starting in location x. x word 'ab', 'cd', 'ef', 'gh'.

3. x dword *string_1, string_2, ..., string_n*

   will allow a list of strings of four characters each starting in location x. x dword 'abcd', 'efgh', 'ijkl', 'mnop'.

variable name data type dimension dup(?)

will create a string array with a given dimension and data type.

Note: As in chapter 14, the lea instruction will still be used to determine the first byte position of the array.

22.1 RETRIEVING STRINGS STORED IN THE VARIABLE

The following examples will demonstrate how strings are retrieved from the variables.

Examples:

1.

AL CODE	AL	BYTE 1	BYTE 2	BYTE 3
x byte 'abc'		**a**	**b**	**c**
lea ebx, x		a	b	c
mov al, [ebx]	**a**	a	b	c
add ebx, 1	a	a	b	c
mov al, [ebx]	**b**	a	b	c
add ebx, 1	b	a	b	c
mov al, [ebx]	**c**	a	b	c

2.

AL CODE	AL	BYTE 1	BYTE 2	BYTE 3
x byte 'a', 'b', 'c'		**a**	**b**	**c**
lea ebx, x		a	b	c
mov al, [ebx]	**a**	a	b	c
add ebx, 1	a	a	b	c
mov al, [ebx]	**b**	a	b	c
add ebx, 1	b	a	b	c
mov al, [ebx]	**c**	a	b	c

3.

AL CODE	AX	WORD 1	WORD 2	WORD 3
x word 'ab', 'cd','ef'		**ab**	**cd**	**ef**
lea ebx, x		ab	cd	ef
mov ax, [ebx]	**ab**	ab	cd	ef
add ebx, 2	ab	ab	cd	ef
mov ax, [ebx]	**cd**	ab	cd	ef
add ebx, 2	cd	ab	cd	ef
mov ax, [ebx]	**ef**	ab	cd	ef

4.

AL CODE	EAX	DWORD 1	DWORD 2	DWORD 3
x dword 'abcd','ef','ghi'		**abcd**	**ef**	**ghi**
lea ebx, x		abcd	ef	ghi
mov eax, [ebx]	**abcd**	abcd	ef	ghi
add ebx, 4	abcd	abcd	ef	ghi
mov eax, [ebx]	**ef**	abcd	ef	ghi
add ebx, 4	ef	abcd	ef	ghi
mov eax, [ebx]	**ghi**	Abcd	ef	Ghi

Exercises:

1. Write an AL program that will retrieve the string: "Brevity is the soul of wit" from the variable SHAKESPEARE word "Brevity is the soul of wit".

2. Rewrite the above exercise so that the repetitive instructions are carried out in a loop.

22.2 CREATING AND STORING A ONE-DIMENSIONAL STRING ARRAY IN THE DUP(?) DIRECTIVE

The following steps will define and set up the array.

Step 1: Define the directive *variable name data type dimension* dup(?)

Step 2: Using the lea instruction, store the first byte location in a 32-bit register.

Example

x byte 10 (?)

lea ebx, x

Storing data in a string array

In the assembler, we can use any of the registers EAX, EBX, ECX, and EDX. The following definition is the assignment statement that will allow us to perform data assignments to and from memory cells:

mov [register], source instruction

Definition: mov [register], source where the following rules apply:

> **Rule 1:** The registers must be EAX, EBX, ECX, or EDX.
>
> **Rule 2:** The source can be any register or variable.
>
> **Rule 3:** The *[register]* indicates the cell locations where the bytes are to be located.
>
> *The [register]* is called the indirect register.
>
> **Rule 4:** The lea instruction will establish the first byte location.

The mov [register], source instruction will store the string in the source register or variable in the memory location indicated by the contents of the register.

Examples:

The following examples show how string arrays are created and stored.

1. The following program will store the strings a, b, and c in the array of type BYTE.

PSEUDOCODE	AL CODE	AL	X		
Array X	x byte 100 dup(?) lea ebx, x		**Byte 1**	**Byte 2**	**Byte 3**
X(1) := 'a'	mov al, 'a'	**a**			
	mov [ebx], al	a	**a**		
	add ebx, 1	a	a		
X(2):= 'b'	mov al, 'b'	**b**	a		
	mov [ebx], al	b	a	**a**	
	add ebx, 1	b	a	b	

| X(3):= 'c' | mov al, 'c' | **c** | a | b | |
| | mov [ebx], al | c | a | b | **c** |

Important: Since we are storing into individual bytes, we increment by 1.

2. The following program will store numbers ab, cd, and ef in the array of type WORD.

PSEUDOCODE	AL CODE	AX	X		
Array X	x word ? lea ebx,x		**Word 1**	**Word 2**	**Word 3**
X(1) := 'ab'	mov ax, 'ab'	**ab**			
	mov [ebx], ax	ab	**ab**		
	add ebx,2	ab	ab		
X(2):= 'cd'	mov ax, 'cd'	**cd**	ab		
	mov [ebx], ax	cd	ab	**cd**	
	add ebx,2	cd	ab	cd	
X(3):= 'ef'	mov ax, 'ef''	**ef**	ab	cd	
	mov [ebx],ax	ef	ab	cd	**ef**

Important: Since we are storing in individual bytes for each word, we increment by 2.

3. The following program will store numbers 'abcd', 'efgh', and 'ijk' in the array of type DWORD.

PSEUDO	AL CODE	EAX	X		
			Dword I	Dword 2	Dword 3
Array X	x dword ? lea ebx,x				
X(1) := abcd'	mov eax, 'abcd'	**abcd**			
	mov [ebx], eax	abcd	**abcd**		
	add ebx, 4	abcd	abcd		
X(2):= 'efgh'	mov eax, 'efgh'	**efgh**	abcd		
	mov [ebx], eax	efgh	abcd	**efgh**	
	add ebx, 4	efgh	abcd	efgh	
X(3):= 'ijk'	mov eax, 'ijk'	**ijk**	abcd	efgh	
	mov [ebx], eax	ijk	abcd	efgh	**Ijk**

Important: Since we are storing in individual bytes for each dword, we increment by 4.

Exercises

1. Write an AL program that will retrieve the string "Brevity is the soul of wit" from the variable

2. SHAKESPEARE byte "Brevity is the soul of wit"

   and copy it into the variable:

   HAMLET byte 100 dup(?)

3. Rewrite the above exercise so that the repetitive instructions are carried out in a loop.

PROJECT

Assume we have two string variables:

   Shakespeare byte 'Brevity is the soul of wit' and

   Poet byte 'The problem is not in the stars but within ourselves'

Write an AL program that will interchange the contents of the two variables.

CHAPTER TWENTY-THREE

INPUT/OUTPUT

INTRODUCTION

The 80x86 MASM assembler provides the Kernel32 library of program utilities, which includes input/out instructions. In this chapter, we will examine programs that will perform the following functions:

- Output strings to the monitor

- Input strings from the keyboard

23.1 OUTPUTTING STRINGS TO THE MONITOR

The following is a complete program that will output to the screen the message: "Good morning America!"

The following directives are used to input and output string data:

- ExitProcess PROTO NEAR32 stdcall, dwExitCode:WORD where

  PROTO is a directive that prototypes the function ExitProcess and

  ExitProcess is a directive that is used to terminate a program.

- GetStdHandle

  The *GetStdHandle* returns in EAX a handle for the I/O device.

Examples:

Program

```
;A complete program that will output to the screen the message:"Good morning
America!"


.386

.MODEL FLAT
```

```
;Setup for Writing to the Monitor

GetStdHandle PROTO NEAR32 stdcall, nStdHandle:DWORD
  WriteFile PROTO NEAR32 stdcall,

    hFile:DWORD, lpBuffer:NEAR32, nNumberOfCharsToWrite:DWORD,
lpNumberOfBytesWritten:NEAR32, lpOverlapped:NEAR32

STD_OUTPUT EQU -11

cr       EQU 0dh        ; carriage return character

lf       EQU 0ah        ; line feed
```

```
.STACK 4096

.DATA

message BYTE    'Good morning America!';This is the message that will be displayed on
the monitor

size DWORD 21;                    Number of characters in message
written DWORD ?

message_out     DWORD ?
```

```
.CODE
;The following instructions will print the message "Good morning America!"
_start:

INVOKE GetStdHandle,          ;       Prepare output

  STD_OUTPUT                  ;           — to screen

    mov message_out, eax;

  INVOKE WriteFile,           ;           Initial output

    message_out,              ;               screen hardware location

      NEAR32 PTR message, size,  ;     size of message

      NEAR32 PTR written,      ;      bytes written

      0        ;                      overlapped mode

INVOKE ExitProcess, o         ;    exit with return code o

PUBLIC _start

END
```

23.2 INPUTTING STRINGS FROM THE KEYBOARD

The following complete program will perform the following tasks.

Task 1: A message to the monitor will prompt the user to enter a message.

Task 2: Allow the user to enter a message.

Example:

```
;A complete program that will allow the user to enter a message and enter data from
the keyboard.

.386

.MODEL FLAT
```

```
ExitProcess PROTO NEAR32 stdcall, dwExitCode:DWORD

GetStdHandle PROTO NEAR32 stdcall,
  nStdHandle:DWORD

ReadFile PROTO NEAR32 stdcall,

  hFile:DWORD, lpBuffer:NEAR32, nNumberOFCharsToRead:DWORD,
lpNumberOfBytesRead:NEAR32, lpOverlapped:NEAR32

WriteFile PROTO NEAR32 stdcall,

  hFile:DWORD, lpBuffer:NEAR32, nNumberOFCharsToWrite:DWORD,
lpNumberOfBytesWritten:NEAR32, lpOverlapped:NEAR32

STD_INPUT EQU -10

STD_OUTPUT EQU -11
```

```
.STACK 4096

.DATA

request BYTE "Please enter a message ?"
CrLf     BYTE 0ah, 0dh

Enter_message BYTE 80 DUP (?)
read_in DWORD ?

written_out DWORD ?
handle_Out DWORD ?
handle_In DWORD ?
```

```
.code
;The following instructions will print the message "Please enter a message"
_start:
;WRITE REQUEST
INVOKE GetStdHandle,      ; get handle for console output
STD_OUTPUT
mov handle_In, eax
   INVOKE WriteFile,
   handle_In,
   NEAR32 PTR request, 80,
   NEAR32 PTR written_out,
   0
```

```
;The following instructions will allow a message to be entered from the keyboard.
; INPUT DATA
INVOKE GetStdHandle,   ; get handle for console output
STD_INPUT
mov handle_In, eax
INVOKE ReadFile,
handle_In,
NEAR32 PTR Enter_message,
80,
NEAR32 PTR read_in ,
0
INVOKE ExitProcess, 0
INVOKE ExitProcess, o      ;      exit with return code o
PUBLIC_start
END
```

PROJECT

Write a program that will perform the following two tasks:

- An arbitrary number of hexadecimal numbers can be entered from the keyboard and stored in an array.

- The numbers can be retrieved from the array, converted to decimal, and displayed on the monitor.

CHAPTER TWENTY-FOUR

NUMERIC APPROXIMATIONS (OPTIONAL)

INTRODUCTION

Numeric approximations play an important role in assembly language programming. The assembler that you use will provide some numeric algorithms, but in most cases the programmer will have to program several necessary numeric algorithms. For example, at this point we cannot even approximate the square root of a number. Unless the assembler provides a square root approximation algorithm, the programmer will have to write such an algorithm usually in the form of a procedure. At this point, in passing, we should note the following additional floating-point instructions that are provided by the 80x86 Assembly Language.

24.1 ASSEMBLER FLOATING-POINT NUMERIC APPROXIMATIONS

The following floating-point instructions are provided by the assembler to compute approximations for specific functions.

1.

MNEMONIC	OPERAND	ACTION
fsin	(none)	Replaces the contents of ST by sin(ST)

2.

MNEMONIC	OPERAND	ACTION
fcos	**(none)**	**Replaces the contents of ST by cos(ST)**

3.

MNEMONIC	OPERAND	ACTION
fsincos	(none)	Replaces the contents of ST by sin(ST), pushes the stack down, and then replaces the contents of ST by cos(ST)

4.

MNEMONIC	OPERAND	ACTION
fptan	(none)	Replaces the contents of ST by tan(ST)

5.

MNEMONIC	OPERAND	ACTION
fldpi	(none)	Replaces the contents of ST by π

6.

MNEMONIC	OPERAND	ACTION
fldl2e	(none)	Replaces the contents of ST by $\log_2 (e)$.

7.

MNEMONIC	OPERAND	ACTION
fldl2t	(none)	Replaces the contents of ST by $\log_2 (10)$.

8.

MNEMONIC	OPERAND	ACTION
fldlog2	(none)	Replaces the contents of ST by $\log_{10} (2)$.

9.

MNEMONIC	OPERAND	ACTION
fldln2	(none)	Replaces the contents of ST by $\log_e (2)$.

10.

MNEMONIC	OPERAND	ACTION
fsqrt	(none)	Replaces the contents of ST by its square root

24.2 SPECIAL APPROXIMATIONS

Although the above are useful, we will need more powerful algorithms that we can call as procedures in our assembly language. We begin with the Newton interpolation method.

Newton interpolation method

The Newton interpolation method is a powerful method for approximation-solving solutions of equations. First we will show how it can be used to write an algorithm f or compute an approximation of the square root of any nonnegative number. Then we will apply Newton's method to approximate the nth root of any appropriate number.

Roots of an equation

Assume you have an equation $y = f(x)$, represented by the graph below. The root(s) of the equation is (are) the value(s) of x where the graph crosses the x-axis ($f(x) = 0$) . First, we start with an initial value x_0. Next, we compute the tangent line of the curve at x_0. We next find the point x_1 where the tangent line crosses the x-axis. Continuing, we compute the tangent line of the curve at x_1, and we find the point x_2 where the tangent line crosses the x-axis. From the graph we see that this will lead to a sequence of numbers $x_0, x_1, x_2, ..., x_n, ...$ that will converge at one of the roots of the equation.

The Newton interpolation method gives us the following sequential formulas:

$$x_1 = x_0 - \frac{f(x_0)}{f'(x_0)}$$

$$x_{k+1} = x_k - \frac{f(x_k)}{f'(x_k)}$$

where $f'(x_k)$ are the slopes of the tangent lines.

Using the Newton interpolation method to approximate $\sqrt[n]{a}$ of a number where a > 0

Assume we wish to approximate the nth root of a number a, $\sqrt[n]{a}$, using Newton's interpolation method. We start by defining f(x) as

$$f(x) = x^n - a$$

which has a root $\sqrt[n]{a}$

It can be shown that $f'(x) = n\,x^{n-1}$, which gives use a formula for the slopes of the tangent lines. We therefore have:

$$f(x_k) = x_k^n - a$$

$$f'(x_k) = nx_k^{n-1}$$

$$x_{k+1} = x_k - \frac{x_k^n - a}{nx_k^{n-1}}$$

Example:

Assume we wish to approximate $\sqrt{5}$ using Newton's approximation method.

Step 1: $f(x)\ x^2 - 5$

Step 2: $f'(x_k) = 2x$

Step 3: $x_{k+1} = x_k - \dfrac{x_k^2 - 5}{2x_k}$; $k = 0, 1, 2, \ldots$

Step 4: First we set $x_0 = 3$

$$x_1 = x_0 - \frac{x_0^2 - 5}{2x_0} = 3 - \frac{3^2 - 5}{2(3)} = 3 - 2/3 = 7/3 = 2.333\ldots$$

$$x_2 = x_1 - \frac{x_1^2 - 5}{2x_1} = 2.\overline{3} - \frac{2.\overline{3}^2 - 5}{2(2.\overline{3})} = 2.236067978\ldots$$

Since $\sqrt{5} \approx 2.236067978$ is accurate to 8 places we see that if we let $x_2 = 2.236067978\ldots$

will give us at least 8 places of accuracy.

A pseudo-code algorithm for approximating the square root $\sqrt{a}$, where a ≥ 0.

INSTRUCTIONS	EXPLANATION
X := A + 1	X IS LARGER THAN ROOT OF A.
WHILE N > 0	N IS THE POSITIVE INTEGER
BEGIN	
$X := X - \dfrac{X^2 - A}{2*X}$	$x_{k+1} = x_k - \dfrac{x_k^2 - a}{2x_k}$
N := N − 1	
END	

PROJECTS

1. Using the above pseudo-code algorithm for approximating the square root $\sqrt{a}$. where a ≥ 0, write an assembly language program that will approximate the square root.

2. Modify the above pseudo-code algorithm by replacing the number a by its absolute value.

3. We say that two numbers x, y are at least equal to the nth place if $|x - y| < 1/10^0$

   For example, the 2 numbers 7.12567890435656 and 7.12567890438905 are at least equal to the 10th place since

   $|7.12567890435656 - 7.12567890438905| = 0.00000000003249 < 1/10^{10}$

4. Modify the above pseudo-code algorithm that will terminate the computation x_{n+1} when $|x_{n+1} - x_n| < 1/10^n$.

   Explain why this would be the better way of estimating the square root $\sqrt{a}$.

5. For problem 4, write an assembly language program.

6. Write a pseudo-code algorithm that will approximate the nth root $\sqrt[n]{a}$.

7. From problem 6, write an assembly language program.

8. Write an assembly language program that will approximate $a^{m/n}$, where m, n are positive integers.

Using polynomials to approximate transcendental functions and numbers

As you may recall, real polynomials are of the form $a_n x^n + a_{n-1} x^{n-1} \ldots + a_1 x + a_0$, where a_k are real numbers (k = 0, 1, ..., n).

The following transcendental functions and numbers can often play an important part in any assembly language program:

Transcendental functions: e^x, $\ln(x)$, $\sin(x)$, $\cos(x)$, $\tan^{-1}(x)$.

Transcendental numbers: e, π.

The following are polynomial approximations of transcendental functions:

$$e^x \approx 1 + \frac{x}{1!} + \frac{x^2}{2!} + \ldots + \frac{x^n}{n!}, \quad -\infty < x < \infty; \; n = 0, 1, 2, \ldots$$

$$\sin(x) \approx x - \frac{x^3}{3!} + \frac{x^5}{5!} - \frac{x^7}{7!} + \ldots + (-1)^n \frac{x^{2n+1}}{(2n+1)!}, \quad -\infty < x < \infty; \; n = 0, 1, 2, \ldots$$

$$\cos(x) \approx 1 - \frac{x^2}{2!} + \frac{x^4}{4!} - \frac{x^6}{6!} + \ldots + (-1)^n \frac{x^{2n}}{(2n)!}, \quad -\infty < x < \infty; \; n = 0, 1, 2, \ldots$$

$$\tan^{-1}(x) \approx x - \frac{x^3}{3} + \frac{x^5}{5} - \frac{x^7}{7} + \ldots + (-1)^n \frac{x^{2n+1}}{2n+1}, \quad -1 \leq x \leq 1; \; n = 0, 1, 2, \ldots$$

$$\ln(x) \approx -\left\{ 1 - x + \frac{(1-x)^2}{2} + \frac{(1-x)^3}{3} + \ldots + \frac{(1-x)^n}{n} \right\}; \; 0 < x < 1; \; n = 1, 2, \ldots$$

$$\ln(x) \approx \left(1 - \frac{1}{x}\right) + \frac{1}{2}\left(1 - \frac{1}{x}\right)^2 + \frac{1}{3}\left(1 - \frac{1}{x}\right)^3 + \ldots + \frac{1}{n}\left(1 - \frac{1}{x}\right)^n \quad 1 \leq x; \; n = 1, 2, \ldots$$

Using the above approximations, the following transcendental numbers e and π can be approximated:

$$e = e^1 \approx 1 + \frac{1}{1!} + \frac{1}{2!} + \ldots + \frac{1}{n!}; \; n = 0, 1, 2, \ldots$$

$$\frac{\pi}{4} = \tan(1) \approx 1 - \frac{1}{3} + \frac{1}{5} - \frac{1}{7} + \ldots + (-1)^n \frac{1}{2n + 1} \; ; n = 0, 1, 2, \ldots$$

Therefore,

$$\pi \approx 4\{1 - \frac{1}{3} + \frac{1}{5} - \frac{1}{7} + \ldots + (-1)^n \frac{1}{2n + 1}\}$$

Pseudocode algorithms for approximating transcendental functions and numbers

The following pseudocode algorithm will estimate:

$$e^x \approx 1 + \frac{x}{1!} + \frac{x^2}{2!} + \ldots + \frac{x^n}{n!} :$$

INSTRUCTIONS	EXPLANATION
K := 0	COUNTER
SUM_EX := 0	WILL SUM POLYNOMIAL
WHILE K ≤ N	WILL COMPUTE N TIMES
BEGIN	
SUM_EX := SUM_EX + X^K/K!	X^K WRITTEN AS A PROCEDURE K! WRITTEN AS A PROCEDURE
K := K + 1	
END	

The following pseudocode algorithm will estimate:

$$\sin(x) \approx x - \frac{x^3}{3!} + \frac{x^5}{5!} - \frac{x^7}{7!} + \ldots + (-1)^n \frac{x^{2n+1}}{(2n+1)!}$$

INSTRUCTIONS	EXPLANATION
K := 0	COUNTER
SUM_SIN := 0	WILL SUM POLYNOMIAL
WHILE K ≤ N	WILL COMPUTE N TIMES
BEGIN	
SUM_SIN := SUM_SIN + $(-1)^K * X^{2K+1}/(2K + 1)!$	X^K WRITTEN AS A PROCEDURE K! WRITTEN AS A PROCEDURE
K := K + 1	
END	

The following pseudocode algorithm will estimate:

$$\cos(x) \approx 1 - \frac{x^2}{2!} + \frac{x^4}{4!} - \frac{x^6}{6!} + \ldots + (-1)^n \frac{x^{2n}}{(2n)!}$$

INSTRUCTIONS	EXPLANATION
K := 0	COUNTER
SUM_COS := 0	WILL SUM POLYNOMIAL
WHILE K ≤ N	WILL COMPUTE N TIMES
BEGIN	
SUM_COS := SUM_COS + $(-1)^K * X^{2K}/(2K)!$	X^K WRITTEN AS A PROCEDURE K! WRITTEN AS A PROCEDURE
K := K + 1	
END	

The following pseudocode algorithm will estimate:

$$\tan^{-1}(x) \approx x - \frac{x^3}{3} + \frac{x^5}{5} - \frac{x^7}{7} + \ldots + (-1)^n \frac{x^{2n+1}}{2n+1}$$

INSTRUCTIONS	EXPLANATION
K := 0	COUNTER
SUM_INTAN := 0	WILL SUM POLYNOMIAL
WHILE K ≤ N	WILL COMPUTE N TIMES
BEGIN	
SUM_INTAN := SUM_INTAN + $(-1)^K * X^{2K+1} /(2K+1)!$	X^K WRITTEN AS A PROCEDURE
K := K + 1	
END	

The following pseudocode algorithm will estimate:

$$\ln(x) \approx - \left\{ (1 - x) + \frac{(1 - x)^2}{2} + \frac{(1 - x)^3}{3} + \ldots + \frac{(1 - x)^n}{n} \right\}; 0 < x < 1; n = 1, 2, \ldots$$

$$\ln(x) \approx (1 - \frac{1}{x}) + \frac{1}{2}(1 - \frac{1}{x})^2 + \frac{1}{3}(1 - \frac{1}{x})^3 + \ldots + \frac{1}{n}(1 - \frac{1}{x})^n \; 1 \le x; n=1, 2, \ldots$$

INSTRUCTIONS	EXPLANATION
IF 0 < X < 1 THEN	
BEGIN	
K := 1	COUNTER
SUM_LN := 0	WILL SUM POLYNOMIAL
WHILE K ≤ N	WILL COMPUTE N TIMES

BEGIN	
SUM_LN := SUM_LN–$(1–X)^K$ /K	X^K WRITTEN AS A PROCEDURE
K := K + 1	
END	
ELSE	
BEGIN	
SUM_LN := 0	WILL SUM POLYNOMIAL
WHILE K ≤ N	WILL COMPUTE N TIMES
BEGIN	
SUM_LN := SUM_LN + $(1–1/X)^K$ /K	X^K WRITTEN AS A PROCEDURE
K := K + 1	
END	
END	

PROJECTS

1. Using the above algorithm, write a pseudocode to estimate the number e.

2. Using the above algorithm, write a pseudocode to estimate the number π.

3. For each of the above algorithms, write an assembly language program.

4. The error created by using the above polynomial approximation is written as E(x) = transcendental function–polynomial for the sin(x), cos(x), $\tan^{-1}(x)$ functions,

$$|E(x)| \leq \frac{|X|^{n+1}}{n!}$$

5. Modify the above algorithms so that the program terminates when $|E(x)| \leq 1/10^n$. Also, write an assembly language program for each of these algorithms.

Monte Carlo simulations

Monte Carlo simulations solve certain types of problems through the use of random numbers. These problems can be broken down into sampling models, which will give us an approximation of the solution of the given problem. In order apply these simulation techniques, we need to develop algorithms that will generate random numbers. In most cases these generated random numbers will have a uniform distribution.

Definition: A uniform distribution of random numbers is a sequence of numbers in which each has equal probability of occurring and the numbers are generated independently of each other.

Example

If we toss a die 100 times, we will generate a sequence of 100 numbers, and each number (1, 2, 3, 4, 5, 6) has a 1/6 probability of appearing.

Since we have to generate the random sequence internally in the assembler, we cannot independently generate the numbers. The best we can do is generate sequences that correlate very closely to independent uniform distributions. These types of generated sequences are called pseudo-random number generators (PRNG).

For our Monte Carlo simulation problems, we will use two types of PRNGs:

- John von Neumann's middle square method
- D.H. Lehmer's linear congruence method

John von Neumann's middle square method

Description: This method is very simple. Take any given number, square it, and remove the middle digits of the resulting number as your "random" number, then use it as the seed for the next iteration. For example, assume we start with the "seed" number 1111. Squaring the number 1111 would result in 1234321, which we can write as 01234321, an eight-digit number. From this number, we extract the middle four digits, 2343, as the "random" number. Repeating this process again would give $2343^2 = 05489649$. Again, extract the middle four digits, which will yield 4896. Repeating this process will give a sequence of PRNGs.

To write an assembly language program, use the following steps:

Step 1: Store a four-digit decimal number into EAX.

Step 2: Square this number.

Step 3: Integer divide the number in EAX by 1000.

Step 4: Integer divide the number in EAX by 100000.

Step 5: Move the remainder in EDX to EAX.

Step 6: Repeat steps 2–5.

The following partial assembly language program will perform these steps an undetermined number of times.

ASSEMBLY LANGUAGE	EAX	EDX
mov eax, 6511	6511	
mul eax	42393121	
div 100	423931	21
div 10000	42	3931
mov eax, edx	3931	3931
(Repeat above instructions.)		

Example:

The following pseudocode will simulate the tossing of a die 100 times.

INSTRUCTIONS	EXPLANATION
N:= 100	NUMBER OF TOSSES
EAX := 6511	SEED
LABEL: EAX := EAX* EAX	SQUARE SEED
EAX := EAX/100	
EDX := EAX/10000	SEED
SEED := EDX	
DIE := EDX / 6 + 1	
N := N − 1	COUNT
EAX := SEED	
IF N <> 0 THEN	
BEGIN	
JUMP LABEL	
END	

PROJECTS

1. Write a partial assembly language program from the die pseudocode program.

2. Write a partial assembly language program that will perform the following tasks:

   Task 1: Toss a die 100 times.

   Task 2: Compute the number of times the number 6 occurs.

3. Write a partial assembly language program that will perform the following tasks:

   Task 1: Toss a pair of dice 100 times.

   Task 2: Sum the resulting numbers for each toss.

   Task 3: Compute the number of times the number 7 occurs.

4. Write a partial assembly language program that will perform the following tasks:

   Task 1: Toss a coin 100 times.

   Task 2: Count the number of times "heads" appears.

5. Write a partial assembly language program that will compute 100 random numbers x where $0 \le x \le 1$.

1. D.H. Lehmer's linear congruence method

The linear congruence method for generating PRNGs uses the linear recurrence relation:

$$x_{n+1} = ax_n + b \pmod{m} \text{ where } n = 0, 1, 2, \ldots$$

Lehmer proposed the following values:

$m = 10^8 + 1$

$a = 23$

$b = 0$

$x_0 = 47594118$

These values will result a repetition period of 5,882,352.

Using these values, the following partial program will compute an undermined number of random numbers x where $0 \le x \le 10^8 + 1$.

ASSEMBLY LANGUAGE CODE
mov m, 100000001; number m = 10^8 + 1
mov x, 47594118
mov a, 23
mov eax, x
mul a
div m; remainder stored in edx
mov eax, edx
mul a
div m
::::::::::::::
(Repeat the above in bold.)

2. Monte Carlo approximations

Random sampling from a population can be applied in solving simple and complex mathematics and scientific problems. This type of application is known as a Monte Carlo approximation. To best illustrate this method, assume we wish to approximate by random sampling the number π. One method is to use a unit square that contains a circle of radius 1.

We know that the area of a circle of radius 1 is π. However, for simplicity, we will only examine one quadrant, as shown in the figure below, where r = 1 and the area is $\pi/4$.

The following steps will approximate π.

Step 1: Generate a pair of random numbers (x, y) where $0 \le x, y \le 1$. To generate these numbers, we will use linear congruence method in the following form:

$$x_{n+1} = a_1 x_n + b_1 \pmod{m_1} \text{ where } n = 0, 1, 2, \ldots$$

$$y_{n+1} = a_2 y_n + b_2 \pmod{m_2} \text{ where } n = 0, 1, 2, \ldots$$

$$x = x_{n+1}/m_1$$

$$y = y_{n+1}/m_2$$

Step 2: If $x^2 + y^2 \leq 1$ then (x, y) lies in the circle of the first quadrant, and we will assume success.

Step 3: Generating N pairs (x, y), the law of large number states that #successes/N $\to \pi/4$, for large values of N.

The following pseudocode algorithm will perform this sampling and approximate π.

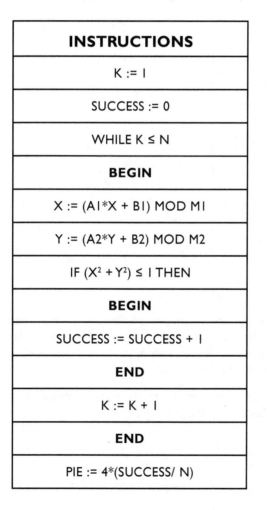

INSTRUCTIONS
K := 1
SUCCESS := 0
WHILE K ≤ N
BEGIN
X := (A1*X + B1) MOD M1
Y := (A2*Y + B2) MOD M2
IF (X² + Y²) ≤ 1 THEN
BEGIN
SUCCESS := SUCCESS + 1
END
K := K + 1
END
PIE := 4*(SUCCESS/ N)

PROJECTS

1. From the above pseudocode algorithm, write a assembly language algorithm.

2. To test the above assembly language algorithm, write an assembly language program for different values of m, a, and b.

3. The Gambler's Ruin

Assume a gambler with initial capital of n dollars plays a game against a casino. Assume the following rules of the game:

- For each bet, he bets one dollar.

- The gambler will play until he wins m dollars, where m > n or goes broke.

- For each bet, the gambler's chance of winning is p, where 0 < p < 1.

For different values of p, write an assembly language program that will compute the number of times he bets.

PROJECTS

Bose-Einstein Statistics

In physics, the Bose-Einstein statistics deal with the number of ways to place m indistinguishable particles into n distinguishable cells. This is analogous to placing m indistinguishable balls into n distinguishable urns.

The number of distinguishable arrangement is

$\binom{n + m - 1}{m}$, where each distinguishable arrangement has equal probability.

Assume that m < n. Write an assembly language program, using Monte Carlo approximations, that will approximate the probability that each cell has at most one particle.

Note: $\binom{n}{k} = \dfrac{n!}{k!(n - k)!}$,

APPENDIX A

SIGNED NUMBERS AND THE EFLAG SIGNALS

INTRODUCTION

It is important to keep in mind that when working with integer numbers, the numbers are contained in a ring of a given data type. When we preform arithmetic operations, it is possible that the resulting computations do not always return the expected values as they would appear in the ordinary integer number system. For example, we would expect the simple expression 2–3 to return a value of -1. But if our number system is an 8-bit ring, we will obtain the result 255, which is the additive inverse of -1. Let us assume for further discussion that the register we will work with in this chapter is the register AL, which is an 8-bit ring. Further, we will assume the following table is a signed order representation of this ring in decimal (see chapter 8):

128	129	...	253	254	255	0	1	2	3	...	126	127
128	127	...	3	2	1	0	255	254	253	...	130	129

where the bottom row represents the additive inverse of the above values.

If we wish to write a program that will print out the true value -1, how is this done when the instructions

>   move al, 2
>
>   sub al, 3

will return the value 255 in the register AL?

To print the correct -1, we need to write AL instructions that will perform the following tasks:

>   Task 1: Test what value resulted in the subtraction: 255.
>
>   Task 2: Convert 255 into its additive inverse: 1.
>
>   Task 3: Store in a variable the ASCII code for -1: 2D31 (see chapter 23).
>
>   Task 4: Print this ASCII code (see chapter 25).

Performing operations such as task 1 is the main emphasis of this chapter.

THE EFLAGS

The EFLAG is a 32-bit register where some of its 32 bits indicate three important types of flag signals resulting from arithmetic or logical operations:

- The sign flag

- The carry flag

- The overflow flag

The EFLAG is of the form:

32 31 30 29 28 27 26 25 24 23 22 21 20 19 18 17 16 15 14 13 12 11 10 9 8 7 6 5 4 3 2 1

x	x	x	x	x	x	x	x	x	x	x	x	x	x	x	x	x	x	x	x	x	x	x	x	x	x	x	x	x	x	x	x

Before defining these important flags, we make the following observation: When performing arithmetic or logical operations, we first assign a numeric integer to a byte register that has a 0 or 1 bit at its left-most bit position. If, after the operation, the resulting binary value will have a 0 or 1 in its left-most bit position. If this bit is the same or different than the left-most bit of the original value, a change may occur in the various flags listed above.

Definition of the sign flag:

After an arithmetic or logical operation on an integer value in a byte register, if the resulting binary number has at its left-most position a 1, then the sign flag will be assigned a value 1 to its 8th bit; otherwise a value 0.

Depending on the result of the operation, the Eflag is of the form:

32 ::: 8 7 6 5 4 3 2 1

x	x	x	x	x	x	x	x	x	x	x	x	x	x	x	x	x	x	x	x	x	x	x	x	x	1	x	x	x	x	x	x

or

32 ::: 8 7 6 5 4 3 2 1

x	x	x	x	x	x	x	x	x	x	x	x	x	x	x	x	x	x	x	x	x	x	x	x	x	0	x	x	x	x	x	x

Definition of the overflow flag:

The overflow flag (OF) tells whether a carry flipped the sign of the most significant bit in the result so that it is different from the most significant bits of the arguments. If numbers are interpreted as unsigned, the overflow flag is irrelevant, but if they are interpreted as signed, OF means the result was negative.

Depending on the result of the overflow flag, the Eflag is of the form:

or

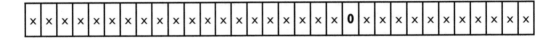

Definition of the carry flag:

The carry flag becomes 1 if an addition, multiplication, AND, OR, and so on results in a value larger than the register meant for the result.

Depending on the result of the carry flag, the Eflag is of the form:

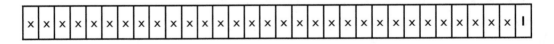

or

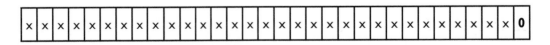

EFLAG JUMP INSTRUCTIONS

The eflag bits cannot be directly accessed. However, the following jump instructions can be used to jump to a designated instruction:

JUMP INSTRUCTION	RESULT
js	Jump if sign bit is turned on.
jns	Jump if sign bit is turned off.
jc	Jump if carry bit is turned on.
jnc	Jump if carry bit is turned off.
jo	Jump if overflow bit is turned on.
jno	Jump if overflow bit is turned off.

Multiplication

There are two types of multiplication operations: mul and imul (see chapter 10). The mul instruction is when the numbers are considered as unsigned (natural order), and the imul instruction is when the numbers are considered as signed. The mul instruction will set the carry and overflow flags depending on the value of the left-most bit.

The imul instruction will set the carry if the resulting number is too large. This will result in the edx register not equal to zero.

REFERENCES

Intel 80x86 Assembly Language OpCodes:

      www.mathemainzel.info/files/x86asmref.html

Visual Studio Express 2015 (free) :

      https://www.visualstudio.com/en-us/products/visual-studio-express-vs.aspx

Kernal32 Library

ANSWERS TO SELECTED EXERCISES

1.1   Definition of Integers

Exercises

1. Write the following integers in expanded form:

   (a) 56   (b) 26,578   (c) 23,556,891,010

Solution:

(a) $5*10 + 6$ (b) $2*10^4 + 6*10^3 + 5*10^2 + 7*10 + 8$

(c) $2*10^{10} + 3*10^9 + 5*10^8 + 5*10^7 + 6*10^6 + 8*10^5 + 9*10^4 + 1*10^3 + 1*10$

1.2   Numbers in Other Bases

Exercises

1. Write the octal number 2370123_8 in expanded form.

Solution:

$2,370,123_8 = 2*10^6 + 3*10^5 + 7*10^4 + 0*10^3 + 1 10^2 + 2*10 + 3*10^0$

3. In the octal number system, simplify the following expressions:

   (a) $2361_8 + 4_8$ (b) $33_8 - 2_8$ (c) $777_8 + 3_8$

Solutions:

(a) 2365_8 (b) 31_8 (c) 1002_8

DECIMAL NUMBERS	OCTAL NUMBERS (Base 8)
0	0_8
1	1_8
2	2_8
3	3_8
4	4_8

5	5_8
6	6_8
7	7_8
8	10_8
9	11_8
10	12_8
11	13_8
12	14_8
13	15_8
14	16_8
15	17_8
16	20_8
17	21_8
18	22_8
19	23_8
20	24_8
....	....

DECIMAL NUMBERS	OCTAL NUMBERS (Base 8)
0	0_8
1	1_8
2	2_8
3	3_8
4	4_8
5	5_8
6	6_8
7	7_8
8	10_8
9	11_8
10	12_8
11	13_8
12	14_8
13	15_8
14	16_8
15	17_8
16	20_8
17	21_8
18	22_8
19	23_8
20	24_8
....	....

5. Add on 10 more rows to the above table

Solution:

DECIMAL NUMBERS	OCTAL NUMBERS (Base 8)
0	0_8
1	1_8
2	2_8
3	3_8
4	4_8
5	5_8
6	6_8
7	7_8
8	10_8
9	11_8
10	12_8
11	13_8
12	14_8
13	15_8
14	16_8
15	17_8
16	20_8
17	21_8

18	22_8
19	23_8
20	24_8
21	25_8
22	26_8
23	27_8
24	30_8
25	31_8
26	32_8
27	33_8
28	34_8
29	35_8
30	36_8

7. Add on 10 more rows to the above table the second column will consists of the corresponding numbers in the base 5, starting with the digit 0.

Solution:

DECIMAL NUMBERS	NUMBERS (Base 5)
0	0_5
1	1_5
2	2_5
3	3_5

4	4_5
5	10_5
6	11_5
7	12_5
8	13_5
9	14_5
10	20_5
11	21_5
12	22_5
13	23_5
14	24_5
15	30_5
16	31_5
17	32_5
18	33_5
19	34_5
20	40_5

9. In the base 5 number system simplify the following expressions:

   (a) $22212_5 + 3_5$ (b) $23333_5 + 2_5$ (c) $12011_5 - 2_5$

Solution:

   (a) 22220_5 (b) 23340_5 (c) 12004_5

11. Extend the above table for the integer numbers 21–30.

Solution

DECIMAL NUMBERS	BINARY NUMBERS
21	10101_2
22	10110_2
23	10111_2
24	11000_2
25	11001_2
26	11010_2
27	11011_2
28	11100_2
29	11101_2
30	11110_2

13. Complete the following table:

OCTAL NUMBERS	BINARY NUMBERS
0_8	
1_8	
2_8	
3_8	
....	....
16_8	

Solution:

OCTAL NUMBERS	BINARY NUMBERS
0_8	0_2
1_8	1_2
2_8	10_2
3_8	11_2
4_8	100_2
5_8	101_2
6_8	110_2
7_8	111_2
10_8	1000_2
11_8	1001_2
12_8	1010_2
13_8	1011_2
14_8	1100_2
15_8	1101_2
16_8	1110_2

15. Write the hexadecimal number $4E0AC1_{16}$ in expanded form.

Solution:

$$4E0AC1_{16} = 4*10^5 + E*10^4 + 0*10^3 + A*10^2 + C*10^1 + 1*10^0$$

17. Simplify $n_{16} =$ (a) $A_{16} + 6_{16}$ (b) $FFFF_{16} + 1_{16}$ (c) $100_{16} + E_{16}$

Solutions:

(a) 10_{16} (b) 10000_{16} (c) $10E_{16}$

19. Complete the followingtable:

Solution:

HEXADECIMAL NUMBERS	BINARY NUMBERS
0_{16}	0_2
1_{16}	1_2
2_{16}	10_2
3_{16}	11_2
4_{16}	100_2
5_{16}	101_2
6_{16}	110_2
7_{16}	111_2
8_{16}	1000_2
9_{16}	1001_2
A_{16}	1010_2
B_{16}	1011_2
C_{16}	1100_2
D_{16}	1101_2

E_{16}	1110_2
F_{16}	1111_2
10_{16}	$1\ 0000_2$
11_{16}	$1\ 0001_2$
12_{16}	$1\ 0010_2$
13_{16}	$1\ 0011_2$
14_{16}	$1\ 0100_2$
15_{16}	$1\ 0101_2$
16_{16}	$1\ 0110_2$
17_{16}	$1\ 0111_2$
18_{16}	$1\ 1000_2$
19_{16}	$1\ 1001_2$
$1A_{16}$	$1\ 1010_2$
$1B_{16}$	$1\ 1011_2$
$1C_{16}$	$1\ 1100_2$
$1D_{16}$	$1\ 1101_2$
$1E_{16}$	$1\ 1110_2$
$1F_{16}$	11111_2
20_{16}	$10\ 0000_2$
21_{16}	$10\ 0001_2$
22_{16}	$10\ 0010_2$

23_{16}	$10\ 0011_2$
24_{16}	$10\ 0100_2$
25_{16}	$10\ 0101_2$
26_{16}	$10\ 0110_2$
27_{16}	$10\ 0111_2$
28_{16}	$10\ 1000_2$
29_{16}	$10\ 1001_2$
$2A_{16}$	$10\ 1010_2$
$2B_{16}$	$10\ 1011_2$
$2C_{16}$	$10\ 1100_2$
$2D_{16}$	$10\ 1101_2$
$2E_{16}$	$10\ 1110_2$
$2F_{16}$	$10\ 1111_2$

2.1 Sets

Exercises:

1. For the following bases, write out the first 10 numbers as a set in natural order:

   (a) N_3 (b) N_4 (c) N_5 (d) N_6 (e) N_7

Solution:

   (a) $N_3 = \{0,1,2,10,11,12,20,21,22,30\}$

   (b) $N_4 = \{0,1,2,3,10,11,12,13,20,21,22\}$

   (c) $N_5 = \{0,1,2,3,4,10,11,12,13,14\}$

   (d) $N_6 = \{0,1,2,3,4,5,10,11,12,13\}$

   (e) $N_7 = \{0,1,2,3,4,5,6,10,11,12\}$

2.2 One to One Correspondence Between Sets

Exercises:

1. If $D = \{2,4,6,8,10, ...\}$ and $R = \{1,3,5,7,9,...\}$, show that $D \Leftrightarrow R$.

Solution

   $2k \Rightarrow 2k - 1$

   for $k = 1,2,3,4,...$

2.3 Expanding Numbers in the Base b (N_b).

1. Find the expansions for the following numbers in their give bases:

   (a) 4312322_5 (b) $ABCDEF_{16}$ (c) 12322_4 (d) 111101101_2

Solutions:

   (a) $4 \star 10_5^6 + 3 \star 10_5^5 + 1 \star 10_5^4 + 2 \star 10_5^3 + 3 \star 10_5^2 + 2 \star 10_5 + 2$

   (b) $A \star 10_{16}^5 + B \star 10_{16}^4 + C \star 10_{16}^3 + D \star 10_{16}^2 + E \star 10_{16} + F$

   (c) $1 \star 10_4^4 + 2 \star 10_4^3 + 3 \star 10_4^2 + 2 \star 10_4 + 2$

   (d) $1 \star 10_2^8 + 1 \star 10_2^7 + 1 \star 10_2^6 + 1 \star 10_2^5 + 0 \star 10_2^4 + 1 \star 10_2^3 + 1 \star 10_2^2 + 0 \star 10_2 + 1$

2.4 Converting numbers in any base b to its corresponding number in the base 10

Exercises:

1. Convert the following numbers to the base 10.

   (a) 2022301_6 (b) 66061_9 (c) 11101101_2 (d) 756402_8 (e) $A0CD8_{16}$

Solutions:

   (a) 96445_{10} (b) 43795_{10} (c) 237_{10} (d) 253186_{10} (e) 658648_{10}

2.5 Converting numbers in the base 10 to its corresponding number in any base b

Exercises:

1. Convert the following:

   (a) $2545601_{10} \Leftrightarrow$ base 2

   (b) $16523823_{10} \Leftrightarrow$ base 16

   (c) $5321_{10} \Leftrightarrow$ base 3

   (d) $81401_{10} \Leftrightarrow$ base 8.

Solutions:

   (a) 1001101101011111000001_2 (b) $\mathbf{FC222F}_{16}$ (c) 21022002_3

   (d) 236771_8

2.6 A Quick Method of Converting Between Binary and Hexadecimal numbers

Exercises:

1. Complete the table below that matching the digits of the octal number system with its corresponding binary numbers:

OCTAL DIGITS	CORRESPONDING BINARY NUMBERS
0	000
1	001

Solution:

1.

OCTAL DIGITS	CORRESPONDING BINARY NUMBERS
0	000
1	001
2	010
3	011
4	100
5	101
6	110
7	111

2.

BASE 4	BASE 2
0	00
1	01
2	10
3	11

Create a similar table to convert numbers of the base 4 to the base 2.

Solution:

BASE 4	BASE 2
0	00
1	01
2	10
3	11

2.7   Performing Arithmetic For Different Number Bases

Exercise:

1. Perform the following:

   (a) $(212_3 + 2222_3)*101_3$ (b) $(101101_2 - 1101_2)*11101_2$

   (c) $AB2F_{16}*23D_{16} + 2F5_{16}$ (d) $2_{16}{}^{A}{}_{16}$

Solution:

1.

   (a) 11201010221_3 (b) 1110100000_2 (c) $D53E24_{16}$ (d) 400

   (e) $EF156_{16} \Rightarrow 222314121_5$ (f) 47D6

3.1   The Assignment Statement

Exercises:

1. Complete the following table:

ASSIGNMENT STATEMENTS	T	YZ2	TABLE	FORM	TAB
YZ2 :=3					
TABLE:=YZ2					
YZ2 :=1123					
FORM:=TABLE					
YZ2 :=FORM					

Solution:

ASSIGNMENT STATEMENTS	T	YZ2	TABLE	FORM	TAB
YZ2 :=3		**3**			
TABLE:=YZ2		3	**3**		
YZ2 :=1123		**1123**	3		
FORM:=TABLE		1123	3	**3**	
YZ2 :=FORM		1123	3	**1123**	

Exercises:

3. Assume we have the following assignments:

A	B	C	D
10	20	30	40

Write a series of assignment statements which will rotate the values of A, B, C, D as show in the table below:

A	B	C	D
40	10	20	30

Solution:

ASSIGNMENT STATEMENTS	A	B	C	D	TEMP
TEMP :=A	10	20	30	40	10
A:=D	40	20	30	40	10
D :=TEMP	40	20	30	10	10
TEMP:=B	40	20	30	10	20
B:=D	40	10	30	10	20
D:=TEMP	40	10	30	20	20
TEMP :=C	40	10	30	20	30
C:=D	40	10	20	20	30
D:=TEMP	40	10	20	30	30

5. The following instructions

A :=2
B :=3
Z :=A
A :=B
B :=Z

will exchange the contents of the variables A and B. (a). True   (b).False

Solution:

true

3.2 Mathematical Expressions

Exercises:

1. Complete the table:

ASSIGNMENT STATEMENTS	X
X :=2	
X :=X*X	
X := X + X	
X :=X*X	

Solution:

ASSIGNMENT STATEMENTS	X
X :=2	2
X :=X*X	4
X := X + X	8
X :=X*X	64

3. Complete the table below.

ASSIGNMENT STATEMENTS	X	TI	Z
X:=3			
Z :=15			
TI:=10			
X:=Z+X*X			
Z:=X+Z+I			
TI:=TI + Z÷TI +TI			

Solution:

ASSIGNMENT STATEMENTS	X	T1	Z
X:=3	3		
Z :=15	3		15
T1:=10	3	10	15
X:=Z+X*X	24	10	15
Z:=X+Z+1	24	10	40
T1:=T1 + Z÷T1 +T1	40	24	40

5. Set up a table for evaluating the following sequence of instructions.

NUM1 :=0

NUM2 :=20

NUM3 :=30

SUM1 := NUM1 +NUM2

SUM2 := NUM2 +NUM3

TOTAL := NUM1 + NUM2 +NUM3

AVG1 := SUM1 ÷2

AVG2 := SUM2 ÷2

AVG := TOTAL÷3

Solution:

NUM1	NUM2	NUM3	SUM1	SUM2	TOTAL	AVG1	AVG2	AVG
0								
0	20							
0	20	30						
0	20	30	20					
0	20	30	20	50				

0	20	30	20	50	70			
0	20	30	20	50	70	10		
0	20	30	20	50	70	10	25	
0	20	30	20	50	70	10	25	11

3.3 Algorithms and Programs

Exercises:

1. Write a program that computes 10!

Solution:

```
N :=10
NFACTORIAL :=10
N:=N-1
NFACTORIAL:=NFACTORIAL*N
N:=N-1
NFACTORIAL:=NFACTORIAL*N
N:=N-1
NFACTORIAL:=NFACTORIAL*N
N:=N-1
NFACTORIAL:=NFACTORIAL*N
N:=N-1
NFACTORIAL:=NFACTORIAL*N
N:=N-1
NFACTORIAL:=NFACTORIAL*N
N:=N-1
NFACTORIAL:=NFACTORIAL*N
N:=N-1
NFACTORIAL:=NFACTORIAL*N
N:=N-1
NFACTORIAL:=NFACTORIAL*N
```

4.1 An Algorithm to Convert any Positive Integer Number In any Base b < 10 To Its Corresponding Number in the Base 10.

Exercises:

PSEUDO-CODE INSTRUCTIONS	N8	P	A	N10	BASE
N10:=0				0	
N8 :=267	267			0	
BASE :=8	267			0	8
P :=1	267	1		0	8
A := N8 MOD 10	267	1	7	0	8
N10 := N10+A*P	267	1	7	7	8
N8 := N8 ÷10	26	1	7	7	8
P :=P*BASE	26	8	7	7	8
A := N8 MOD 10	26	8	6	7	8
N10 := N10 +A*P	26	8	6	55	8
N8 := N8 ÷10	2	8	6	55	8
P :=P*BASE	2	64	6	55	8
A := N8 MOD 10	2	8	2	55	8
N10 := N10+A*P	2	8	2	183	8
N8 := N8 ÷10	0	8	2	183	8

Modify the above program to convert the number 56328 to the corresponding number in the base 10.

Solution:

PSEUDO-CODE INSTRUCTIONS
N10:=0
N8 :=5632
BASE :=8
P :=1
A := N8 MOD 10
N10 := N10+A*P
N8 := N8 ÷10
P :=P*BASE
A := N8 MOD 10
N10 := N10 +A*P
N8 := N8 ÷10
P :=P(BASE
A := N8 MOD 10
N10 := N10+A*P
N8 := N8 ÷10
P:=P*BASE
A := N8 MOD 10
N10 := N10 +A*P

4.2 An Algorithm to Convert any Integer Number in the Base 10 to a Corresponding Number in the Base b <10.

Program

Task: Convert the integer number 1625 to the base 8.

PSEUDO-CODE	N10	Q	N8	R	BA	P	TEN
N10 :=1625	1625						
BASE :=8	1625				8		
TEN :=10	1625				8		10
P :=10	1625				8	10	10
N8 :=0	1625		0		8	10	10
R := N10 MOD BASE	1625		0	1	8	10	10
Q:= (N10 - R) ÷BASE	1625	203	0	1	8	10	10
N8:= N8 +R	1625	203	1	1	8	10	10
N10 :=Q	203	203	1	1	8	10	10
R := N10 MOD BASE	203	203	1	3	8	10	10
N8 := N8 +R*P	203	25	31	3	8	10	10
P :=P*TEN	203	25	31	3	8	100	10
N10 :=Q	25	25	31	3	8	100	10
R := N10 MOD BASE	25	25	31	1	8	100	10
Q:= (N10 - R)÷BASE	25	3	31	1	8	100	10
N8 := N8 +R(P	25	3	131	1	8	100	10
P :=P(TEN	25	3	131	1	8	1000	10
N10 :=Q	3	3	131	1	8	1000	10
R := N10 MOD BASE	3	3	131	3	8	1000	10
Q:= (N10 -R)÷BASE	3	0	131	3	8	1000	10
N8:= N8 +R(P	3	0	3131	3	8	1000	10
N10 :=Q	0	0	3131	3	8	1000	10

1. Use the above algorithm to write a program to convert the decimal number 2543_{10} to octal.

Solution:

PSEUDO-CODE INSTRUCTIONS
N10 :=2543
BASE :=8
TEN :=10
P :=10
N8 :=0
R := N10 MOD BASE
Q:= (N10 - R) ÷ BASE
N8:= N8 +R
N10 :=Q
R := N10 MOD BASE
N8 := N8 +R*P
P :=P*TEN
N10 :=Q
R := N10 MOD BASE
Q:= (N10 - R)÷BASE
N8 := N8 +R*P
P :=P*TEN
N10 :=Q
R := N10 MOD BASE
Q:= (N10 -R)÷BASE
N8:= N8 +R*P
N10 :=Q

5.1   Conditional Expressions

Exercises:

1. Evaluate the following conditional expressions:

   (a) 3 + 3 =6   (b) 8 >=10   (c) 7 <>7

Solutions:

   (a) TRUE   (b) FALSE   (c) FALSE

5.2   The If-Then Statement

Exercises:

1. Modify the above program so that it performs the following tasks:

   Task 1: Assign 4 numbers.

   Task 2: Counts the number of positive numbers entered.

   Task 3: Add the positive numbers.

Solution:

PSEUDO-CODE INSTRUCTIONS
X1 :=6
X2 :=-5
X3 :=-25
X4:=100
COUNT :=0

IF X1 > 0 THEN
BEGIN
COUNT := COUNT +1
END

```
IF X2 > 0 THEN
    BEGIN
COUNT := COUNT +1
    END
```

```
IF X3 > 0 THEN
    BEGIN
COUNT := COUNT +1
    END
```

```
IF X4 > 0 THEN
    BEGIN
COUNT := COUNT +1
    END
```

```
SUM:=0
```

```
IF X1 > 0 THEN
    BEGIN
SUM := SUM +X1
    END
```

```
IF X2 > 0 THEN
    BEGIN
SUM:= SUM +X2
    END
```

```
IF X3 > 0 THEN
    BEGIN
SUM := SUM +X3
    END
```

```
IF X4> 0 THEN
    BEGIN
SUM := SUM +X4
    END
```

3. Complete the table below

PSEUDO-CODE INSTRUCTIONS	X	Y	Z
X :=2	2		
Y :=5	2	5	
Z :=-4	2	5	-4
IF (X + Y + Z) <> X*Y THEN	2	5	-4
BEGIN	2	5	-4
X : = (X -Y)÷X	-1	5	-4
Y := X +2(Y	-1	9	-4
Z : = X -2	-1	9	-3
END	-1	9	-3
IF (X - Y + Z) <> X +Y THEN	-1	9	-3
BEGIN	-1	9	-3
X : = 2*(X -Y)÷X	20	9	-3
Y := X -3*Z	20	29	-3
Z : = X +2	20	29	22
END	20	29	22

Solution

PSEUDO-CODE INSTRUCTIONS	X	Y	Z
X :=2	**2**		
Y :=5	2	**5**	
Z :=-4	2	5	**-4**
IF (X + Y + Z) <> X*Y THEN	2	5	-4
BEGIN	2	5	-4
X := (X -Y)÷X	**-1**	5	-4
Y := X +2(Y	-1	**9**	-4
Z := X -2	-1	9	**-3**
END	-1	9	-3
IF (X - Y + Z) <> X +Y THEN	-1	9	-3
BEGIN	-1	9	-3
X := 2*(X -Y)÷X	**20**	9	-3
Y := X -3*Z	20	**29**	-3
Z := X +2	20	29	**22**
END	20	29	22

5. Write an algorithm to find the second largest number amongst 4 numbers. Assume all the numbers are positive and different.

Solution

PSEUDO-CODE INSTRUCTIONS

```
LARGEST :=X1
IF X2 > LARGEST   THEN
BEGIN
LARGEST :=X2
END
IF X3 > LARGEST   THEN
BEGIN
LARGEST :=X3
END
IF X4 > LARGEST   THEN
BEGIN
LARGEST :=X4
IF LARGEST = X1   THEN
BEGIN
X1 :=0
END
IF LARGEST = X2   THEN
BEGIN
X2 :=0
END
IF LARGEST = X3   THEN
BEGIN
X3 :=0
END
IF LARGEST = X4   THEN
BEGIN
X4 :=0
END
SECOND_LARGEST :=X1
IF X2 > SECOND_LARGEST   THEN
BEGIN
SECOND_LARGEST :=X2
END
IF X3 > SECOND_LARGEST   THEN
BEGIN
SECOND_LARGEST :=X3
END
IF X4 > LARGEST   THEN
BEGIN
SECOND_ LARGEST :=X4
END
```

6.1   The While Statement

Exercises:

1. Write an algorithm that performs the following tasks:

   Task 1: Finds the proper divisors of a positive integer N >2,

   Task 2: Sum the proper divisors.

Solution:

PSEUDO-CODE INSTRUCTIONS
SUM_DIVISORS :=0
DIVIDE :=2
WHILE N <>DIVIDE
BEGIN
R := N MODDIVIDE
IF R = 0 THEN
BEGIN
SUM_DIVISORS := SUM_DIVISORS +DIVIDE
END
DIVIDE := DIVIDE +1
END

3. A factorial number, written as N!, is defined as

   N! = N(N - 1)(N–2)...(2)(1)

   where N is a positive integer >1.

   Write an algorithm that will compute N!

Solution

FACTORIAL := I
K := I
WHILE K < N
BEGIN
K := K + I
FACTORIAL := K*FACTORIAL
END

5.

PSEUDO-CODE INSTRUCTIONS
X := 0
DIVIDE := 2
WHILE N <> DIVIDE
BEGIN
R := N MOD DIVIDE
IF R = 0 THEN
BEGIN
DIVIDE := N - I
END
DIVIDE := DIVIDE + I
END

7. For the following program below, what is the final value X:

   K :=1
   X : =2
   WHILE K <=6
   BEGIN
   X := X +3
   K : = K +1
   END

Solution:

   24

7.1 Writing a Program and Algorithm to Convert numbers in the Base b < 10 to the Base 10:

Exercise:

1. Write a program and complete the table that will convert the number 231_4 to the base 10 and complete a table as above.

Solution:

```
INSTRUCTIONS
N4:=231
P :=1
N10 :=0
WHILE N4 <>0
BEGIN
R := N4 MOD10
N4 := N4 -R
N4:=N4÷10
N10 := N10+R*P
P :=4*P
END
```

7.2 Writing an Algorithm to Convert Numbers in the base 10 to its Corresponding Number in the Base b<10.

Exercises:

1. Write a program and complete the table that converts the decimal number 25 to base 2.

Solution:

INSTRUCTIONS
N10 :=25
K : =1
N2 :=0
WHILE N10 <>0
BEGIN
A := N10 MOD 2
N2 := N2 +A*K
N10 :=N10÷2
K :=10*K
END

8.1   Rings

Exercises:

1. Assume R is clock time. Simplify the following:

   (a) $7 \oplus 8 \oplus {\sim}7 \oplus 11 \oplus {\sim}4$

   (b) $2 \otimes (6 \oplus {\sim}10)$

   (c) ${\sim}11 \otimes [(2 \otimes {\sim}11) \otimes (11 \oplus {\sim}9)]$

Solutions:

   (a) 3

   (b) 4

   (c) 4

3. Show that the set $R = \{0, 1, -1, 2, -2, 4, -4, 6, -6, \ldots \pm 2n, \ldots\}$ is not ring.

Solution

R has no odd numbers greater than 1 . Since 1 + 2 = 3 and 3 is not in R, the set R is not a ring.

5. Assume $R = \{0, 1, -1, 2, -2, 3, -3, 4, -4, \ldots\}$. Define $\oplus$ and $\otimes$ are defined under the following rules:

   R1.: $n \oplus m = n + (m + 2)$.

   R2: $n \otimes m = n$

   (a) Find Θ.

   (b) For n in R, find ${\sim}n$, the additive inverse of n.

   (c) Show R is a ring.

Solution:

(a)

$$n \oplus \Theta = n + \Theta + 2n \oplus \Theta = n + \Theta + 2$$

Therefore $\Theta = -2$

(b)

$$n \; r \sim \mathbf{n} = n + -\mathbf{n} + 2 = \Theta = -2 \text{ Therefore } \sim\mathbf{n} = -n - 4$$

$$n \; r \sim \mathbf{n} = n + -\mathbf{n} + 2 = n + (-n + -4) + 2 = -2 = \Theta$$

(c)

Since the five rules hold is a ring.

8.2   The Finite Ring R

Exercises:

1. For $R = \{0, 1, 2, 3, 4\}$, simplify:

   (a) $4 \otimes 4$

Solution

$$4 \otimes 4 = (4*4) \bmod (5) = 1$$

(b) $[(4 \oplus 2) \otimes 4 \oplus 4] \otimes 3$

Solution

$$(4 \oplus 2) = 6 \bmod (5) = 1$$

$$(4 \oplus 2) \otimes 4 = \mathbf{24} \bmod (5) = 4$$

$$(4 \oplus 2) \otimes 4 \oplus 4 = 4 \oplus 4 = \bmod(5) = 3$$

$$[(4 \oplus 2) \otimes 4 \oplus 4] \otimes 3 = [3] \otimes 3 = 9 \bmod 5 = 4$$

(c) $3 \otimes (3 \oplus 4)$

Solution

$$3 \otimes (3 \oplus 4) = 3 \otimes ((3 + 4) \bmod 5)) = 3 \otimes (2) = 1$$

3. For the following finite rings, find the additive inverse of each number in the ring:

Solutions

(a) R_{10}

n	0	1	2	3	4	5	6	7	8	9
~n	0	9	8	7	6	5	4	3	2	1

(b) R_2

n	0	1
~n	0	1

(c) R_8

N	0	1	2	3	4	5	6	7
~n	0	7	6	5	4	3	2	1

(d) R_{16}

d. n	0	1	2	3	4	5	6	7	8	9	10	11	12	13	14	15
~n	0	15	14	13	12	11	10	9	8	7	6	5	4	3	2	1

(e) R_{Hex}

n	0	1	2	3	4	5	6	7	8	9	A	B	C	D	E	F
~n	0	F	E	D	C	B	A	9	8	7	6	5	4	3	2	1

8.3 Subtraction for *R*

Exercises:

1. Assume a byte ring. If n < 256, and ~n = n, find all solutions.

Solution:

(n + ~n)mod 256 = (n + n)mod(256) = (2n)mod(256) = 0. Therefore, 2n = 256 or 0.

Hence n = 128, or 0.

8.4 Rings in Different Bases

Exercises:

1. For the finite ring R_{16} = {0,1,2,3,4,5,6,7,8,9,A,B,C,D,E,F} find:

   (a) $9 \oplus 8$

   (b) $5 \otimes B$

Solution:

   (a) $9_{16} \oplus 8_{16} = (9_{16} + 8_{16})mod(10_{16}) => (9_{10} + 8_{10})mod\ 16_{10} = 17\ mod\ 16_{10} = 1_{10} => 1_{16}$

   (b) $5 \otimes B = (5_{16} * 11_{16})mod(10_{16}) => (5_{10} * 17_{10})mod(16_{10}) = 85_{10}\ mod(16_{10}) = 5_{10} => 5_{16}$

Modular arithmetic in the base b.

Exercises:

1. If Assume a byte ring. If $a \oplus b$ = 0 does b = ~a and a = ~b?

Solution:

   Yes. $a \oplus b = (a + b)mod\ 256 = 0$

8.5 The Additive Inverse of Numbers for the Rings $R_b = \{0...0, 0...1, 0...2, ..., \beta_1\beta_2 ..., \beta_n\}$

Exercises:

1. Assume a word ring. For each of the following binary numbers, find their additive inverses:

   (a) 10011100110   (b) 11011011   (c) 10101010

Solutions:

(a) $\sim$10011100110 = $\sim$00000100110011 0 = 1111101100011010

(b) $\sim$11011011 = $\sim$0000000011011011 = 1111111100100100

(c) $\sim$10101010 = $\sim$0000000010101010 = 1111111101010110

3. Assume we have the hexadecimal ring:

   R_{16} = {0,1,2,3,4,5,6,7,8,9,A,B,C,D,E,F,10,...,FF}. Find the following:

   (a) $\sim$ AC   (b) A9$\ominus\sim$55   (c) $\sim$10$\ominus$5E   (d) $\sim$10$\ominus\sim$5E

Solutions:

(a) $\sim$ AC $\Rightarrow \sim$ 10101100_2 = $01010100_2 \Rightarrow 54_{16}$

(b) A9$\ominus\sim$55 = .A9 + 55 $\Rightarrow 11111110_2 \Rightarrow$ FE

(c) $\sim$10$\ominus$5E = $\sim$(10 + FE) = $\sim$ E $\Rightarrow \sim 1110_2 = 0010_2 \Rightarrow 2_{16}$

(d) $\sim$10$\ominus\sim$5E = $\sim$10 + 5E $\Rightarrow (\sim 00010000_2$) + 01011110_2 = 11110000_2 + 01011110_2 = $11001110_2 \Rightarrow$ CE

(a) $\sim$ AC $\Rightarrow \sim$ 10101100_2 = $01010100_2 \Rightarrow 54_{16}$

(b) A9$\ominus\sim$55 = .A9 + 55 $\Rightarrow 11111110_2 \Rightarrow$ FE

(c) $\sim$10$\ominus$5E = $\sim$(10 + FE) = $\sim$ E $\Rightarrow \sim 1110_2 = 0010_2 \Rightarrow 2_{16}$

(d) $\sim$10$\ominus\sim$5E = $\sim$10 + 5E $\Rightarrow (\sim 00010000_2$) + 01011110_2 = 11110000_2 + 01011110_2 = $11001110_2 \Rightarrow$ CE

8.6 Special Binary Rings For Assembly Language

THE BYTE RING (8 bits)	THE WORD RING (16 bits)	THE DWORD (32 bits)
00000000	0000000000000000	00000000000000000000000000000000
00000001	0000000000000001	00000000000000000000000000000001
00000010	0000000000000010	00000000000000000000000000000010
00000011	0000000000000011	00000000000000000000000000000011
00000100	0000000000000100	00000000000000000000000000000100
00000101	0000000000000101	00000000000000000000000000000101
00000110	0000000000000110	00000000000000000000000000000110
00000111	0000000000000111	00000000000000000000000000000111
00001000	0000000000001000	00000000000000000000000000001000
::::::::::::::	::::::::::::::::::::::::	::
11111111	1111111111111111	11111111111111111111111111111111

Exercises:

1. Convert the above binary tables to hexadecimal.

Solution:

THE BYTE RING (8 bits)	THE WORD RING (16 bits)	THE DWORD (32 bits)
00	00 00	00 00 00
01	00 01	00 00 00 01

02	00 02	00 00 00 02
03	.00 03	.00 00 00 03
.	.0004	00 00 00 04
.	00 05	00 00 00 05
.	.	.
.		.
09	00 09.	00 00 00 09
0A	00 0A	00 00 00 0A
0B	00 0B	00 00 00 0B
0C	00 0C	00 00 00 0C
0D	00 0D	00 00 00 0D
0E	00 0E	00 00 00 0E
0F	00 0F	00 00 00 0F
10	00 10	00 00 00 10
11	00 11	00 00 00 11
.	.	.
	.	.
	.	.
	.	.
	.	.
FF	FF FF	FF FF FF FF

3. Using exercise 2 , show that

(a) the largest decimal number in the byte ring is 255.

(b) the largest decimal number in the word ring is 65,535.

(c) the largest decimal number in the dword ring is 4,294,967,295.

Solution:

(a) $2^8 - 1 = 256 - 1 = 255$

(b) $2^{16} - 1 = 65536 - 1 = 65,535$

(c) $2^{32} - 1 = 4294967296 - 1 = 4,294,967,295$

Modular arithmetic for the byte ring (in decimal)

Exercises:

1. Compute:

(a) $122 \oplus 122$ (b) $162 \otimes 31$ (c) $175 \otimes 222 \otimes 13$ (d) $(175 \oplus 222) \otimes 13$

Solution:

(a) $122 \oplus 122 = 244$

(b) $162 \otimes 31 = (162*31) \mod 256 = (5022) \mod 256 = 158$

(c) $175 \otimes 222 \otimes 13 = (175*222*13 \mod 256 = 505050 \mod 256 = 218$

(d) $(175 \oplus 222) \otimes 13 = [(175 + 222)*13] \mod 256 = 5161 \mod 256 = 41$

Modular arithmetic for the word ring (in decimal)

Exercises:

1. Find the additive inverse for the following:

(a) 214   (b) 0   (c) 60000

Solutions:

(a) $[214 + (65536 - 214)] \mod 65536 = (214 + 65322) \mod 65536 = 0$.
Therefore, ~214 = 65322

(b) $[0 + (65536 - 0)] \bmod 65536 = (0 + 65536) \bmod 65536 = 0$.
Therefore, ~0 = 65536

(c) $[60000 + (65536 - 60000)] \bmod 65536 = (60000 + 5536) \bmod 65536 = 0$.
Therefore, ~60000 = 5536

Modular arithmetic for the dword ring (in decimal).

Exercises:

1. Find the additive inverse for the following:

   (a) 214   (b) 0   (c) 60000

Solution:

(a) $[214 + (4294967296 - 214)] \bmod 4294967296 = (214 + 4294967082)$
$\bmod 4294967296 = 0$. Therefore, ~214 = 4294967082

(b) $[0 + (4294967296 - 0)] \bmod 4294967296 = (0 + 4294967296) \bmod$
$4294967296 = 0$. Therefore, ~0 = 4294967296

(c) $[60000 + (4294967296 - 60000)] \bmod 4294967296 = (60000$
$+ 4294907296) \bmod 4294967296 = 0$. Therefore, ~60000 =
4294907296

3. Convert the decimal number $- 202_{10}$ to a binary number in a

   (a) byte ring   (b) word ring   (c) dword ring.

Solution:

(a) $(202 + 256 - 202) \bmod 256 = (202 + 54) \bmod 256 = 0$, Therefore,
$-202 = \sim 54 \Rightarrow 1101\ 10_2$

(b) $(202 + 65536 - 202) \bmod 65536 = (202 + 65334) \bmod 65536 = 0$,
Therefore, $-202 = \sim 65334 \Rightarrow 1111111100110110^2$

(c) $(202 + 4294967296 - 202) \bmod 4294967296 = (202 + 4294967094)$
$\bmod 4294967296 = 0$, Therefore,

$-202 = \sim 4294967094 \Rightarrow 11111111111111111111111100110110_2$

8.7   Ordered Relations of Rings 2

Exercises:

1. For the ring R = {0,1,2,3,4}, using the special symbols, write out the relations of the ordered pair:

{(0,0), (1,1), (1,0), (2,2), (2,1), (2,0), (3,3), (3,2), (3,1), (3,0), (4,4), (4,3),(4,2), (4,1),(4,0)}

Solution:

0 = 0, 1=1, 1< 0, 2=2, 2<1, 2<0, 3=3, 3<2, 3<1, 3 < 0, 4=4,4 < 3, 4 < 2, 4 < 1, 4<0

8.8   Special Ordering of Rings For Assembly Language

Exercises:

1. Construct a natural order table for the values the word ring.

Solution:

0	1	2	3	4	5	6	----	65531	65532	65533	6553	65535

3. Construct a natural order table for the values the dword ring.

Solution:

0	1	2	3	4	..	4294967293	4294967294	4294967295

9.1   Data Types of Integer Binary Numbers

Exercises:

For the examples above of bytes,

1. find the binary complements.

Solutions:

(a) 10010001

(b) 11111010

3. find the equivalent numbers in the hexadecimal base.

Solution:

(a) 9AE7AB73

(b) B6

9.2   Other Integers

Examples:

(a) e239ch   (b) 101101b   (c) 23771o   (d) 3499h

Exercises:

1. For the examples above, convert each to decimal.

Solution:

(a) 926620   (b) 45   (c) 10233   (d) 13465

9.3   Variables

Exercises:

Which of the following are legal variable names:

1.

(a) _apple_of_my_eye   (b) S_23x   (c) $money2&

(d) hdachslager@ivc.edu   (e) 1XorX2

Solution:

All but e.

9.5 Registers

Exercises:

1. Explain why the follow instructions will cause an error:

   (a) mov eax, D2h

   (b) x byte ?

      mov eax, x

   (c) mov eax, 3ABDD12E1h

Solutions:

   (a) Hexadecimal must begin with a number value 0,...,9

   (b) eax and x are of different data types.

   (c) The number is too large.

3. Complete the following table, using only binary numbers in EAX:

ASSEMBLY CODE	EAX							
mov eax, 2D3Fh	0000	0000	0000	0000	0010	1101	0011	1111
mov eax, 3h	0000	0000	0000	0000	0000	0000	0000	0011
mov eax, 10101101b	0000	0000	0000	0000	0000	0000	0101	0101
mov eax, 434789	0000	0000	0000	0110	1010	0010	0110	0101
mov eax, 4DFA1101h	0100	1101	1111	1010	0001	0001	0000	0001
mov eax 2675411o	0000	0000	0000	10 11	0 111	101 1	00 00	1 001

Exercises:

1. Complete the following:

   (a) mov eax , 278901

Solutions:

EAX

BASE 2:	00 00	00 00	00 00	01 00	01 00	00 01	01 11	01 01
BASE 16:	0	0	0	4	4	1	7	5
BASE 10:	2789 01							

(b) mov eax , 3ABCD10Fh

EAX

BASE 2:	011	1010	1011	1100	1101	0001	0000	1111
BASE 16:	3	A	B	C	D	1	0	F
BASE 10:	985452 815							

(c) mov edx , 27721010

EDX

BASE 2:	0000	0000	1011	1111	0100	0100	0100	0001
BASE 16:	0	0	0	B	F	4	4	1
BASE 10:	783425							

(d) mov eax , 278901

EAX

BASE 2:	0000	000 0	0000	0100	0100	0001	0111	0101
BASE 8:	0	1	0	4	F0	5	6	5
BASE 16:	0	0	0	4	4	1	7	5

(e) mov ecx , 3ABCD10Fh

EAX

BASE 2:	0011	1010	1011	1100	1101	0001	0000	1111
BASE 8:	0	0	07	25	71	15	04	17
BASE 10:	985452815							

(f) mov edx , 2772101o

EDX

BASE 2:	0000	0000	0000	1011	1111	0100	0100	0001
BASE 16:	0	0	0	B	F	4	4	1
BASE 10:	783425							

Mixing Registers

Exercise:

1. Complete the following tables using hexadecimal numbers only :

INSTRUCTIONS	32	25	24	17	16	9	8	1
mov eax, 293567h								
mov ax, 9BCh								
mov ax, 3D32h								
mov ax, 5h								
mov ax, 3h								
mov eax, 1267								
mov ax, 3AF4h								
mov ah, 27h								
mov al, 25								

Solution:

1. Complete the following tables using hexadecimal numbers only :

INSTRUCTIONS	32	25	24	17	16	9	8	1
mov eax, 293567h	0	0	2	9	3	5	6	7
mov ax, 9BCh	0	0	2	9	0	9	B	C
mov ax, 3D32h	0	0	2	9	3	D	3	2
mov ah, 5Ch	0	0	2	9	5	C	3	2
mov ax, 3h	0	0	2	9	0	0	0	3
mov eax, 1267	0	0	0	0	0	4	F	3
mov ax, 3AF4h	0	0	0	0	3	A	F	4
mov ah, 27h	0	0	0	0	2	7	F	4
mov al, 25	0	0	0	0	2	7	1	9

9.6 Transferring data between registers and variables

Exercises:

1. Modify the above program by initializing the values in x, y without using the *mov* instruction.

Solution:

AL PSEUDO CODE	ASSEMBLY LANGUAGE CODE
X := 23	X BYE 23
Y := 59	Y BYTE 59
EAX := X	mov eax, x
Y := EAX	mov y,eax

3. In exercise 1, what does the code accomplish ?

Solution:

Replace Y with the contents of X.

9.7   Assembly Language Statements

Exercises:

1. What is the largest integer number base 10 that can be store in a variable of type BYTE.

Solution:

255

3. What is the largest integer number base 10 that can be store in a variable of type DWORD.

Solution:

4294967295

5. What is the largest integer number base 16 that can be store in a variable of type WORD.

Solution:

FF FF

7. What is the largest integer number base 8 that can be store in a variable of type BYTE.

Solution:

9. What is the largest integer number base 8 that can be store in a variable of type DWORD.

Solution:

37777777777

Exercise:

1. Assume the above program is run. For the table below, fill as hexadecimal numbers, the final values stored.

EAX	EBX	A	B	C	D	E	F

Solution:

EAX	EBX	A	B	C	D	E	F
00000E0F	00000015	28	1E		0000000A	32	0014

Introduction

10.1 Ring Registers

Additive Inverses

The 8 bit ring as unsigned binary and integer numbers.

Exercises:

1. Find the additive inverse of the following numbers in binary as well as the number system given:

   (a) 100101b   (b) 2E h   (c) 222 d

Solution:

   (a) 11011011b   (b) D2 h   (c) 34 d

The 16 bit rings

Exercises:

1. Assuming the following numbers are words. Find their additive inverse.

   (a) 100101b   (b) 2E h   (c) 222 d

Solutions:

   (a) 1111111111011011b   (b) FFD2h   (c) 65314d

The 32 bit rings

Note: in the above table, the hexadecimal numbers in each of the columns are additive inverses of each other.

Exercises:

1. Find the additive inverse of the following numbers in binary as well as the number system given:

   (a) 100101b   (b) 2E h   (c) 222 d

Solutions:

   (a) 11111111111111111111111111011011b   (b) FFFFFFD2 h

   (c) 4,294,967,296 - 222

10.2 Working with Modular Arithmetic for Addition and Subtraction

Exercises:

1. Find N_2 for byte rings, word rings, and dword rings.

Solution:

100000000_2, 10000000000000000_2, $100000000000000000000000000000000_2$

Addition on finite rings

Addition on byte rings:

Exercises:

1. Add over a byte ring: $N = 11011101_2 + 01001111_2$

Solution:

$(11011101_2 + 01001111_2)$ mod 100000000_2 => $(221 + 79)$mod $256 =$
300 mod $256 = 4$ => 100_2

Addition on word rings:

Exercises:

3. Add over a word ring: $N = 1100\ 1111\ 1101\ 1101_2 + 1010\ 1110\ 1001\ 1111_2$

Solution:

$1100\ 1111\ 1101\ 1101_2 + 1010\ 1110\ 1001\ 1111_2$ => $(53213 + 44703)$ mod $65536 =$
97916mod $65536 = 32380$ => 111111001111100_2

Addition on dword rings:

Exercises:

5. Add over a dword ring: $N = 1100\ 1111\ 1101\ 1101_2 + 111\ 1110\ 1001\ 1111_2$

Solution:

$1100\ 1111\ 1101\ 1101_2 + 111\ 1110\ 1001\ 1111_2$ => $(53213 + 32415)$mod $4294967296 =$
85628 => 10100111001111100_2

Subtraction on finite rings

Subtraction on byte rings:

Exercises:

Assume a byte ring:

Find:

      7. ~ 201_{10}

Solution:

      $256 - 201 = 55 = $ ~ 201_{10}

      9. ~277_8

Solution:

      ~277_8 => ~$191_{10} = 256 - 191 = 65$ => 101_8

      11. (~250_{10})$\ominus 252_{10}$

Solution

      (~250_{10})$\ominus 25210 = (6)\ominus(252_{10}) = (6 + $~$252)$mod $256 = (6 + 4)$mod $256 = 10$

      13. $772_8 \ominus$ ~1427_8

Solution:

      $772_8 \ominus$ ~$1427_8 = (772_8 + $~~$1427_8)$ mod $400_8 = (772_8 + 1427_8)$ mod $400_8 = $
      (2421_8)mod 400_8
      =>1297mod $256 = 17$ => 21_8

Assume a word ring:

Find:

      15. ~6780

Solution:

      ~$6780 = 65536 - 6780 = 58756$

      17. ~175673_8

Solution:

      ~175673_8 => ~$64443 = 65536 - 64443 = 1093$ => 2105_8

19. $(\sim6550_{10})\ominus22221_{10}$

Solution:

$(\sim6550_{10})\ominus22221_{10} = \{(65536 - 6550) + \sim22221]\bmod (65536) =$

$[58986 + (65536 - 22221)]\bmod 65536 = [58986 + 43315]\bmod 65536 = 102301$

$\bmod 65536 = \ = 102301$

21. $110772_8 \ominus \sim12642_8$

Solution:

$110772_8 \ominus \sim12642_8 => 37370\ominus \sim5538 = > 37370\ominus(65535 - 5538) = 37370 \ominus59997$

$= (37370 + \sim59997)\bmod 65536 = (37370 + 65536 - 59997)\bmod 65536 =$

$(37370 + 5539)\bmod 65536 = 42909 \bmod 65536 = 42909 =>123635_8$

Assume a dword ring

Find:

23. $\sim99456780_{10}$

Solution:

$\sim99456780 = 4294967296 - 99456780 = 4195510516$

25. $\sim11124767565_8$

Solution:

$\sim 11124767565 = 40000000000_8 - 11124767565_8 = 11124767565_8$

27. $\sim[43465756_{10})\ominus(\sim45754_{10})]$

Solution:

$\sim[43465756)\ominus(\sim45754)] = \sim[43465756)\ominus(4294967296 - 45754)] =$

$\sim[43465756)\ominus(4294921542)] =$

$\sim\{(43465756 + (4294967296 - 4294921542)\bmod 4294967296 \} =$

$= \sim\{[43465756)+ 45754]\}\bmod 4294967296 = \sim43511510\bmod 4294967296 =$

$(4294967296 - 43511510) \bmod 4294967296 = 4251455786$

29. $700772_8 \ominus (\sim 54533_8)$

Solution:

$700772_8 \ominus (\sim 54533_8) \Rightarrow 229882_{10} \ominus (\sim 22875_{10}) =$

$229882_{10} \ominus (4294967296 - 22875_{10})$

$= 229882_{10} \ominus 4294944421_{10} = [229882_{10} + (4294967296 - 4294944421_{10})] \bmod$

$4294967296 = [229882_{10} + 22875)] \bmod 4294967296 = [252757] \bmod$

$4294967296 = 252757$

10.3 Assembly Language Arithmetic Operations For Integers

Addition (+):

Exercises:

1. Complete the following tables:

   Complete the table with hexadecimal numbers.

Solutions:

ASSEMBLY CODE	EAX	AX	AH	AL	X
x dword 2					2h
mov eax, 12345	00 00 30 39h	30 39h	30h	39h	2h
add eax, x	00 00 30 3Bh	30 3Bh	30h	3Bh	2h

ASSEMBLY CODE	EAX	AX	AH	AL	X
x dword 100					64h
mov eax, 54321	00 00 D4 31h	D4 31h	D4h	31h	64h
add eax, x	00 00 D495h	D495h	D4h	95h	64h

ASSEMBLY CODE	EAX	AX	AH	AL
mov eax,9fffffffh	9f ff ff ffh	ff ffh	ffh	ffh
add ah, I	9f ff 00 ffh	00 ffh	00h	ffh

Subtraction (-):

Exercises:

1. **Complete the following table in hexadecimal:**

PSEUDO-CODE	AL PSEUDO-CODE	AL CODE	EAX	X	Y
		x dword ? y dword ? z dword ?			
X := 0CD2h - 2h	EAX := 0CD2h	mov eax, 0CD2h	0CD2		
	EAX := EAX - 2h	sub eax, 2h	0CD0		
	X := EAX	mov x, eax	0CD0	0CD0	
X := 421h	**X := 421h**	mov x, 421h	0CD0	421	
Y := 4E75h	Y := 4E75h	mov y, 421h	0CD0	421	4E75
	EAX := X	mov eax, x	421	421	4E75
Z:= X - Y	EAX := EAX - Y	sub eax, y	FFFFB5AC	421	4E75
	Z := EAX	mov z,eax	FFFFB5AC	421	4E75

Z
FFFFB5AC

3.

ASSEMBLY CODE	EAX	AX	AH	AL	X
x word 0ab9h					0AB9
mov eax, 0cca18h	000CCA18	CA18	CA	18	0AB9
sub ax, x	000C BF5F	BF5F	BF	5F	0AB9

Multiplication

(*): Exercises:

    1. Complete the following tables:

ASSEMBLY CODE	EAX	AX	AH	AL	EDX	X
x byte 0EDh						ED
mov al, 9Fh	00 00 00 9F	00 9F	00	9F		ED
mul x	00 00 93 33	93 33	93	33		ED

ASSEMBLY CODE	EAX	AX	AL	EDX	X
x word 2EF2h					2EF2
mov ax, 26DCh	00 00 26 DC	26 DC	DC		2EF2
mul x	EF F8	EF F8	F8	08 39	2EF2

ASSEMBLY CODE	EAX	EDX	X
x dword 46A577DEh			46 A5 77 DE
mov eax, 7EA769Fh	7 EA76 9F		46 A5 77 DE
mul x	C8 F1 C6 E2	02 2F 3A 42	46 A5 77 DE

Division (÷):

Exercises:

1. For the following integer division, find the division form: n = q + m + r:

   (a) 143÷3   (b) 3,457÷55   (c) 579÷2   (d) 23÷ 40

Solutions:

(a) 143 = 47*3 + 2   (b) 3457 = 62*55 + 47   (c) 579 =289*2+1

(d) 23 =0*40 + 23

Exercises:

Complete the following table:

1. complete the following tables in hexadecimal :

ASSEMBLY CODE	EAX	EDX	X
x dword E722Ch			E722C
mov edx, 0		0	**E722C**
mov eax, 5670F3AAh	**56 70 F3 AA**	**0**	E722C
div x	**00 00 05 FB**	**00 0C 26 86**	E722C

ASSEMBLY CODE	EAX	AX	EDX	X
x word 2567h = m				2567
mov edx,0	0		0	2567
mov ax, 9D37h= n	00 00 9D 57	9D57	0	2567
div x	00 00 00 04	00 04	00 00 07 9B	2567

ASSEMBLY CODE	EAX	AX	AH	AL
x byte 0FDh				
mov ax, 0ABB6h	00 00 AB B6	AB B6		
div x	00 00 AB B6	AB B6	BD	AD

X	
FD	
FD	
FD	

11.1 An Assembly Language Program to Convert a Positive Integer Number In any Base b < 10 to its Corresponding Number in the Base 10.

Exercise

1. Use the manual method to linearize the number 230451_6 that will convert it to its corresponding number in the base 10.

Solution:

$$230451_6 => N_{10} = (((((2*8 + 3)*6 + 0)*6) + 4)*6 + 5)*6 + 1 = 19615$$

11.2 An Algorithm to Convert any Integer Number in the Base 10 to a Corresponding Number in the Base b < 10.

Exercise:

1. Use the above algorithm to write a program to convert the decimal number 2543_{10} to octal.

Solution:

PSEUDO-CODE	AL PSEUDO-CODE	AL CODE
B := 8	B := 8	mov b, 8
N := 2543	N := 2543	mov n, 2543
S:= 0	S:= 0	mov s, 0
M:= 1	M:= 1	mov m, 1
T:= 10	T:= 10	mov t, 10
R := N MOD B	EAX:= N	mov eax, n
	EAX:= EAX÷B EDX:= EAX MOD B	mov edx,0 div b
	R:= EDX	mov r, edx

N:= N÷B	N:= EAX	mov n, eax
R := R* M	EAX:= R	mov eax, r
	EAX:= EAX(M	mul m
	R:= EAX	mov r, eax
S:= S + R	EAX:= S	mov eax, s
	EAX:= EAX + R	add eax, r
	S:= EAX	mov s, eax
M:= M*T	EAX:= M	mov eax, m
	EAX:= EAX*T	mul t
	M:= EAX	mov m eax
R := N MOD B	EAX:= N	mov eax, n
	EAX:= EAX÷B EDX:= EAX MOD B	mov edx,0 div b
	R:= EDX	mov r, edx
N:= N÷B	N:= EAX	mov n, eax
R := R*M	EAX:= R	mov eax, r
	EAX:= EAX*M	mul m
	R:= EAX	mov r, eax
S:= S + R	EAX:= S	mov eax, s
	EAX:= EAX + R	add eax, r
	S:= EAX	mov s, eax
M:= M*T	EAX:= M	mov eax, m
	EAX:= EAX*T	mul t
	M:= EAX	mov m eax

	EAX:= N	mov eax, n
R := N MOD B	EAX:= EAX÷B EDX:= EAX MOD B	mov edx,0 div b
	R:= EDX	mov r, edx
N:= N÷B	N:= EAX	mov n, eax
	EAX:= R	mov eax, r
R := R*M	EAX:= EAX*M	mul m
	R:= EAX	mov r, eax
S:= S + R	EAX:= S	mov eax, s
	EAX:= EAX + R	add eax, r
	S:= EAX	mov s, eax
	EAX:= M	mov eax, m
M:= M*T	EAX:= EAX*T	mul t
	M:= EAX	mov m eax
	EAX:= N	mov eax, n
R := N MOD B	EAX:=EAX÷B EDX:= EAX MOD B	mov edx,0 div b
	R:= EDX	mov r, edx
N:= N÷B	N:= EAX	mov n, eax
	EAX:= R	mov eax, r
R := R*M	EAX:= EAX*M	mul m
	R:= EAX	mov r, eax
	EAX:= S	mov eax, s
S:= S + R	EAX:= EAX + R	add eax, r
	S:= EAX	mov s, eax

12.1 Conditional Jump Instructions for Signed Order

Exercises:

1. Which of the following are valid. If not indicate why.

a.	**b.**	**c.**	**d.**	**e.**
x dword 456h	cmp eax, x	cmp x, eax	cmp x, 235	cmp 235, x
y dword 44444h				
cmp x,y				

Solution:

a. Is not correct. Cannot use cmp x, y

e. Is not correct. Operand 1 cannot be a numerical value.

The conditional jump instructions for signed order numbers.

Exercises:

Assume al contains the number 5 and n also contains 5. Which of the following incomplete programs will cause a jump:

1.	**2.**	**3.**
cmp al,n	cmp al,n	cmp al,n
je xyz	jne xyz	jnge xyz
xyz:	xyz:	xyz:

4.	**5.**	**6.**
cmp al,n	cmp al,n	cmp al,n
jge xyz.	jle xyz.	jnle al
xyz:	xyz	xyz

7.	**8.**	**9.**
cmp al,n	cmp al,n	cmp al,n
jl xyz	jnl xyz	jg xyz
xyz	xyz:	xyz:

10.
cmp al,n;
jnl xyz:

Solutions:

1. Yes   3. No   5. Yes   7. No   9. No

The unconditional jump instruction

Exercises:

Assume al contains the number 5 and n also contains 5. Which of the following incomplete programs will cause a jump:

1.
```
cmp al,n
jbe xyz
xyz:
```

2.
```
cmp al,n
jnb xyz
xyz:
```

3.
```
cmp al,n
ja xyz
xyz:
```

4.
```
cmp al,n
jnae xyz.
xyz:
```

5.
```
cmp al,n
jae xyz.
xyz
```

6.
```
cmp al,n
je xyz
xyz
```

7.
```
cmp al,n
jb xyz
xyz
```

8.
```
cmp al,n
jnb xyz
xyz:
```

9.
```
cmp al,n
jnbe xyz
xyz:
```

Solution:

1. True . A jump occurs   3. No. A jump does not occur.

5. True A jump occurs   7. No. A jump does not occur.

9. No. A jump does not occur.

12.2 Converting the While-Conditional Statements to Assembly Language

Exercises:

1. Rewrite the above program in a AL pseudo-code where only registers (not variables) are used.

Solution:

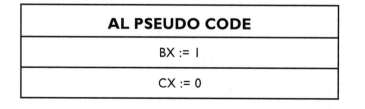

AL PSEUDO CODE
BX := 1
CX := 0

WHILE BX <= 6
BEGIN
EAX := CX
EAX:= EAX + BX
CX :=EAX
EAX := BX
EAX := EAX + 1
BX:= EAX
END

3. Modify the above program by writing an assembly language algorithm that would allow the user to sum arbitrary numbers 1 + 2 + 3 + ...+ m.

Solution:

ASSEMBLY CODE
mov n, 1
mov total, 0
while: cmp n, m
ja end
mov eax, total
add eax, n
mov total, eax
mov eax, n
add eax, 1
mov n, eax
jmp while end:

5. Write an assembly language pseudo code algorithm to compute
$1^2 + 2^2 + 3^2 + ... + M^2$

Solution:

AL PSEUDO CODE
N := I
EAX:= 0
WHILE N <=M
BEGIN
EBX :=N
SQN:= EBX*N
EAX:= EAX + SQN
N:= N + I
END
SUM := EAX

12.3 If-Then Statements

Exercises:

1. From Chapter 5, we have the following algorithm.

PSEUDO - INSTRUCTIONS	EXPLANATION
LARGEST := XI	**We start by assuming XI is the largest**

IF X2 > LARGEST THEN
BEGIN
LARGEST := X2
END
	If the contents of X2 is larger than the contents of LARGEST replace LARGEST with the contents of X2

IF X3 > LARGEST THEN
BEGIN
LARGEST := X3
END
	If the contents of X3 is larger than the contents of LARGEST replace LARGEST with the contents of X3

Write the assembly language code to replicate the pseudo-code:

Solution:

PSEUDO - INSTRUCTIONS	ASSEMBLY LANGUAGE
LARGEST := X1	**mov eax, x1** **mov largest, eax**

IF X2 > LARGEST THEN
BEGIN
LARGEST := X2
END
	cmp x2, largest
	begin: jbe end
	mov largest, x2
	end

IF X3 > LARGEST THEN
BEGIN
LARGEST := X3
END
	cmp x3, largest
	begin: jbe end
	mov largest, x3
	end

3. Write the assembly language algorithm to replicate the pseudo-code:

IF x = a or x = b THEN

BEGIN

::::::::::::::::

END

Solution:

PSEUDO - INSTRUCTIONS	ASSEMBLY LANGUAGE

IF X = A THEN
BEGIN
::::::::::::::::
END
	mov eax, x
	cmp x, a
	begin: jne end
	::::::::::::::::
	end

IF X = B THEN
BEGIN
::::::::::::::::
END
	cmp x,b
	begin: jne end
	::::::::::::::::
	end

12.4 If-Then - Else Statements

Exercise:

1. Assume n is a non-negative integer. We define n factorial as: $n! = n(n-1)$
    $(n-2)...(2)(1)$ for

    $n > 0$ and $0! = 1$. Write an assembly language psuedo code program that will compute the value $10!$.

Solution:

AS PSEUDO CODE
N:= 10
EAX := 1
WHILE N > 1 THEN
BEGIN
EAX := EAX*N
EBX:= N
EBX : = EBX – 1
N:= EBX
END
FACTORIAL := EAX
END:

Application: Assume we have N distinct objects and r of these objects are randomly selected.

3. The number of ways that this can be done, where order is important is

    $_NP_r = N!/(N-r)!$.

Write an assembly language algorithm that will perform the following tasks:

Task1: Assign the integer N and r.

Task2: compute $_NP_r = N!/(N-r)!$.

Solution:

AS PSEUDO CODE
EAX := 1
WHILE N > 1 THEN
BEGIN
EAX := EAX*N
EBX:= N
EBX := EBX − 1
N:= EBX
END
NFACTORIAL := EAX
Q:= N − R
IF Q = 0 THEN
BEGIN
Q:= 1
END
EAX:= 1
WHILE Q > 1 THEN
BEGIN

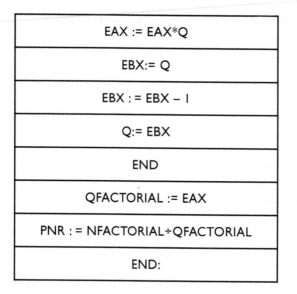

EAX := EAX*Q
EBX:= Q
EBX : = EBX – I
Q:= EBX
END
QFACTORIAL := EAX
PNR : = NFACTORIAL÷QFACTORIAL
END:

5. Write an assembly language psuedo code algorithm that will compute the absolute value of

$$|x - y|.$$

Solution:

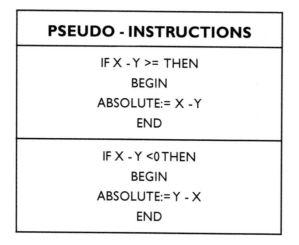

PSEUDO - INSTRUCTIONS

IF X - Y >= THEN
BEGIN
ABSOLUTE:= X - Y
END

IF X - Y < 0 THEN
BEGIN
ABSOLUTE:= Y - X
END

13.1 An Assembly Language Program to Convert a Positive Integer Number In any Base b < 10 to its Corresponding Number in the Base 10.

Exercise:

1. Let $N_{10} = a_0 a_1 a_2 \ldots a_m$. Write an assembly language algorithm that will sum the digits of N.

Solution:

PSEUDO-CODE	AL PSEUDOCODE	ALCODE
EBX:=0	EBX:=0	movebs,0
NUM:=N	NUM:=N	mov num,n
T:=10	T:=10	mov t,10
D:=10^M	D:= 10^M	mov d, 10^m
WHILE NUM <>0	WHILE NUM <>0	while: cmp num,0
		jeend
BEGIN	BEGIN	;begin
A:=NUM÷D	EAX :=NUM	mov eax,nun
	EAX := EAX÷DEDX := EAX MOD D	mov edx,0
		divd
	A :=EAX	mov a,eax
EBX:= EBX +A	EBX:= EBX +A	add ebx,a
NUM:= N MODD	NUM:=EDX	mov num,edx
D:=D÷T	EAX :=D	mov eax,t
	EAX := EAX÷TEDX := EAX MOD T	mov edx,0
		divt
	D :=EAX	mov d,eax
		jmp while
END	END	end:

14.1 Logical Expressions

Logical Statements

Exercise:

1. Complete the following:

PSEUDO - CODE	X	Y	L	Z
X := 2				
Y := 5				
L:= (X + 2*Y > 2)				
Z := .NOT. (L .OR. (.NOT. (X - Y <> 0)))				
Z := (.NOT.(L .AND. (Z .OR. L)) .XOR. Z				

Solution:

PSEUDO - CODE	X	Y	L	Z
X := 2	2			
Y := 5	2	5		
L:= (X + 2*Y > 2)	2	5	**true**	
Z := .NOT. (L .OR. (.NOT. (X - Y <> 0)))	2	5	true	*false*
Z := (.NOT.(L .AND. (Z .OR. L)) .XOR. Z	2	5	true	**false**

Exercises:

1. In the following program, indicate if the following statements are correct or incorrect.

X: = 2

Z := *true*

V := .NOT. (*true* .OR. *false*)

V:= (.NOT.(V .OR.V)) .AND.V

Solution:

all correct

3. Evaluate the following expressions:

Solutions:

   (a) *true*

   (b) *true*

   (c) *true*

   (d) *false*

   (e) *false*

   (f) *true*

14.3 Assigning to Logical Expressions a Logical Value in Assembly Language

Exercises:

1.

Complete the table :

PSEUDO-CODE	AL PSEUDO-CODE	ASSEMBLY LANGUAGE	X	Y	Z	AL
X:= *true*						
Y:= *false*						
Z:= X .AND.Y						

Solution:

PSEUDO-CODE	AL PSEUDO-CODE	ASSEMBLY LANGUAGE	X	Y	Z	AL
X:= true	X:= 1	mov x,1	1			
Y:= false	Y:= 0	mov y,0	1	0		
Z:= X .AND.Y	AL:= X	mov al, x	1	0		1
	AND AL,Y	and al, y	1	0		0
	Z:= AL	mov z, al	1	0	0	0

PSEUDOCODE	AL	X	Y	Z	LOG	EAX	EBX
X:= 5	mov x, 5	**5**					
Y:= 60	mov y, 60	5	**60**				
LOG := (X > 10) .AND. (Y > 10)	mov eax, 0	5	60			**0**	
	mov ebx, 0	5	60			0	**0**
	cmp x, 10	5	60			0	0
	jng L1	5	60			0	0
	mov eax, 1	5	60			0	0
	L1: cmp y, 10	5	60			0	0
	jng L2	5	60			0	0
	mov ebx, 1	5	60			0	1
	L2: and eax, ebx	5	60			**0**	1
	mov log, eax	5	60		**0**	0	1
IF LOG = *true* THEN	cmp log, 1	5	60		0	0	1
BEGIN	begin1: jne end1	5	60		0	0	1
Z:= X + Y	mov eax, x	5	60		0	0	1
	add eax, y	5	60		0	0	1
	mov z, eax	5	60		0	0	1
END	end1:	5	60		0	0	1
ELSE	je end2	5	60		0	0	1
BEGIN	begin2:	5	60		0	0	1
Z:= X*Y	mov eax, x	5	60		5	0	1
	mul y	5	60		5	**300**	1
	mov z, eax	5	60	**300**	5	300	1
END	end2:	5	60	300	0	300	1

Exercise:

1. For the above program, assume x = 20 and y = 30. With these values, change the above program.

Solution:

PSEUDO-CODE	AL	X	Y	Z	EAX	EBX
X:= 20	mov x, 20	**20**				
Y:= 30	mov y, 30	20	**30**			
	mov eax, 0	20	30		**0**	
	mov ebx, 0	20	30		0	**0**
	cmp x, 10	20	30		0	0
	jng L1	20	**30**		0	0
	mov eax, 1	20	30		**1**	0
LOG := (X > 10) .AND. (Y > 10)	L1: cmp y, 10	20	30		1	0
	jng L2	20	30		1	0
	mov ebx, 1	20	**30**		1	**1**
	L2: and eax, ebx	20	30		**0**	1
	mov log, eax	20	30		0	1
IF LOG = *true* THEN	cmp log, 1	20	30		0	1
BEGIN	begin1: jne end1	20	**30**		0	1
	mov eax, x	20	30		0	1
Z:= X + Y	add eax, y	20	30		0	1
	mov z, eax	20	**30**		0	1
END	end1:	20	30		0	1

ELSE	je end2	20	30		0	1
BEGIN	begin2:	20	30		0	1
	mov eax, x	20	**30**		**20**	1
Z:= X*Y	mul y	20	30		**600**	1
	mov z, eax	20	30	**600**	600	1
END	end2:	20	30	600	600	1

14.4 Masks

Exercises:

Assume CX contains an arbitrary number. For the following assembly instructions, explain what changes to CX, if any, result from the following masks:

    1. and cx, cx

Solution:

Since both are the same register, cx will not change.

    3. xor cx, cx

Solution:

Since both are the same register, cx all bits will change to 0.

    5. or cx, (not cx)

Solution:

1 or 0 = 1. Therfore all the bits will be changed to 1.

15.1 Representing One-Dimensional Arrays in Pseudo-Code

Exercises:

1. Write a pseudo- code algorithm that will perform the following tasks:

    Task1: Stores the numbers $2, 2^2, 2^3, ..., 2^n$ in array cells.

    Task2: Add the numbers in the cells.

    Task3: Compute the integer average. (The average without the remainder.)

Solution:

TASK 1:

j = 1

WHILE J≤ n

BEGIN

a(j) := a^j

j := j + 1

END

TASK 2:

sum:= 0

j:= 1

sum:= sum + a(j)

j:= j + 1

END

TASK 3:

integer_average:= sum ÷ n

3. Converting positive decimal integers into binary.

    Write a pseudo- code algorithm that will perform the following tasks:

    Task1: Convert a positive number into binary

    Task 2: Store the binary digits into an array.

Solution:

PSEUDO-CODE
TAKE 1: B= 2
N := BINARY
S:= 0
M:= 1
k:= 1
T:= 10
WHILE N <> 0
BEGIN
R := N MOD B
TEMP(k):= R
N:= N÷B
R := R*M
S:= S + R
M:= M*T
k:= k + 1
END
TASK 2:
d:= k − 1
k:= 1
While 1 ≤ d
A(k):= TEMP(d)
d:=d − 1
k:= k + 1
END

5. A proper divisor of a positive integer N is an integer that is not equal to 1 or N and divides N without a remainder.

For example the proper divisors of 21 are 2, 3, 7 .

Write a pseudo- code algorithm that perform the following tasks:

Task1: Store a positive integer number N.

Task2: Find and store in array all the proper divisors of N.

Solution:

Task 1:

N:= n

Task 2:

k := 2

J := 1

WHILE k ≤ N - 1

BEGIN

R := N MOD k

IF R = 0

  BEGIN

A(J) := k

j := j + 1

  END

k :=k + 1

END

15.2 Creating One Dimensional Integer Arrays In Assembly Language

Exercise:

1. Write a assembly language program that will store the first 50 positive odd numbers.

Solution:

```
x byte ?
mov two,2
mov k, 0
lea ebx, x ; location of array in ebx
while: cmp k,51; k counter
je exit
mov eax ,k;
mul two
add eax, 1; odd number in eax
mov [ebx], al ; store odd number in [ebx]
add ebx,1; moves to next byte
mov ecx, k
add ecx, 1
mov k, ecx; adds one to k and stores it into ecx
jmp while
exit:
```

Storing data in the array without a variable's location

Exercise:

1. Complete the table below.

BYTES

AL INSTRUCTIONS	EAX	EBX	1	2	3	4	5	6	7	8
mov eax, 2										
mov ebx, 7D12Eh										
mov [eax], ebx										
mov eax, 4										
mov ebx, 568923h										
mov [eax], ebx										
mov ebx, 3										
mov [eax], ebx										

Solution:

BYTES

AL INSTRUCTIONS	EAX	EBX	1	2	3	4	5	6	7	8
mov eax, 2h	2									
mov ebx, 7D12Eh	2	0007D12								
mov [eax], ebx	2	0007D12		0 0	0 7	D 1	2 E			
mov eax, 4h	4	0007D12		0 0	0 7	D 1	2 E			
mov ebx, 568923h	4	0056892		0 0	0 7	D 1	2 E			
mov [eax], ebx	4	0056892		0 0	0 7	0 0	5 6	8 9	2 3	
mov ebx, 3h	4	0000000		0 0	0 7	0 0	5 6	8 9	2 3	
mov [eax], ebx	4	0000000		0 0	0 7	0 0	0 0	0 0	0 3	

Retrieving data from an array

Exercise:

1. Extend the following program so that the array data stored can be retrieved to the register ax.

AL CODE	EAX	X		
x dword ? lea ebx,x		dword 1	dword 2	dword 3
mov eax, 13h	00 00 00 13			
mov [ebx], eax	00 00 00 13	00 00 00 13		
add ebx,4	00 00 00 13	00 00 00 13		
mov eax,29h	00 00 00 29	00 00 00 13		

mov [ebx],eax	00 00 00 29	00 00 00 13	**00 00 00 29**	
add ebx,4	00 00 00 29	00 00 00 13	00 00 00 29	
mov eax,25h	**00 00 00 25**	00 00 00 13	00 00 00 29	
mov [ebx],eax	00 00 00 25	00 00 00 13	00 00 00 29	**00 00 00 25**

Solution:

AL CODE	EAX	X		
x dword ? lea ebx,x		dword 1	dword 2	dword 3
mov eax, 13h	**00 00 00 13**			
mov [ebx], eax	00 00 00 13	**00 00 00 13**		
add ebx,4	00 00 00 13	00 00 00 13		
mov eax,29h	**00 00 00 29**	00 00 00 13		
mov [ebx],eax	00 00 00 29	00 00 00 13	**00 00 00 29**	
add ebx,4	00 00 00 29	00 00 00 13	00 00 00 29	
mov eax,25h	00 00 00 25	00 00 00 13	00 00 00 29	
mov [ebx],eax	00 00 00 25	00 00 00 13	00 00 00 29	**00 00 00 25**
sub ebx, 8	00 00 00 25	00 00 00 13	00 00 00 29	00 00 00 25
mov al, [ebx]	00 00 00 13	00 00 00 13	00 00 00 29	00 00 00 25
add ebx, 4	00 00 00 13	00 00 00 13	00 00 00 29	00 00 00 25
mov al, [ebx]	00 00 00 29	00 00 00 13	00 00 00 29	00 00 00 25
add ebx, 4	00 00 00 29	00 00 00 13	00 00 00 29	00 00 00 25
mov al, [ebx]	00 00 00 25	00 00 00 13	00 00 00 29	00 00 00 25

15.3 Reserving Storage for an Array Using the DUP Directive.

Exercise:

Write a program that will perform the following task: store in a dimensioned array the first 100 positive numbers.

Solution:

```
x byte 100        dup (?)
Lea ebx, x
mov al, 1
while: cmp al, 101
je exit
mov [ebx], al
add ebx , 1
add al, 1
jmp while
exit:
```

15.4 Working with Data

Exercise:

1. Complete the following table:

AL INSTRUCTIONS	eax	ebx	9	10	11	12	13	14	15	16	17
mov eax, 2ACD16 h											
mov ebx, 10h											
add ebx, 1h											
mov [ebx], eax											
add [ebx], ebx											
add eax, ebx											

Solution:

AL CODE	eax	ebx	10	11	BYTES 12	13	14	15	16	17	18
mov eax, 2ACD16h	**002ACD16**										
mov ebx, 10h	002ACD16	10									
add ebx, 1h	002ACD16	11									
mov [ebx], eax	002ACD16	11		0	0	2	A	C	D	1	6
add [ebx], ebx	002ACD16	11		0	0	2	A	C	D	2	7
add eax, ebx	**002ACD27**	11		0	0	2	A	C	D	2	7

16.1 Pseudo-code Procedures

Exercises:

1. Write in pseudo-code an algorithm and procedure that will perform the following tasks:

   Task1: Store the following positive integer numbers in an array:

   $n, n + 1, n + 2, n + 3, ..., n + m, \quad m > 0.$

   Task2: Add the numbers stored in the array.

Solution:

PSEUDO-CODE
N:= n
M:= m
CALL ARRAY

```
        PROCEDURE ARRAY
            BEGIN
TASK1: k:= 0
                WHILE k ≤ M
                BEGIN
                X(k)  := n + k
                  k:=k + 1
                  END
TASK2: SUM:= 0
              k:= 0
        WHILE k # M
SUM:= SUM + X(k)

          k:= k + 1
              END
              END
```

16.2 Writing procedures in Assembly Language

Exercises:

1. Write an assembly language algorithm that computes

$$1 + a + a^2 + ... + + a^r + ... + a^N$$

where a > 0 and N > 0.

Solution:

SUM:= 0

J:= 0

R:= 0

WHILE R ≤ N

BEGIN

CALL EXPONENTIAL

SUM:= SUM + P

R:= R + 1

END

PROCEDURE exponential

P := 1

K:= 0

WHILE K ≤ R

BEGIN

P:= A*P

K:= K + 1

END

ret

expontential ENDP

17.1 Definition of Decimal Numbers and Fractions.

1. Which of the following fractions can be reduced to integer numbers:

(a) 1446/558   (b) 12356/2333   (c) 458/3206   (d) 1138/569

Solution:

d

3. Which of the following fractions are proper:

(a) 3/2   (b) 234/567   (c) 1/2

Solution:

b, c

17.2 Representing positive decimal numbers corresponding to proper fractions in expanded form.

1. Expand the following in the form: $0.\overline{a_1 a_2 \ldots a_n} = 0.a_1 a_2 a_3 \ldots a_n a_1 a_2 a_3 \ldots a_n \ldots a_1 a_2 a_3 \ldots a_n$

(a) $0.2\overline{357}$ (b) $0.\overline{0097}$

Solution:

(a) $0.2\overline{357} = 0.235723572357\ldots$ (b) $0.\overline{0097} = 0.009700970097\ldots$

3. Write the following fractions as decimal numbers using the upper bar notation where necessary:

(a) 5/12   (b) −7/8   (c) 5/6   (d) 1/7   (e) −3/7

Solution:

(a) $5/12 = 0.41\overline{6}$ (b) $-7/8 = -0.875$ (c) $5/6 = 0.8\overline{3}$ (d) $1/7 = 0.\overline{142857}$

(e) $-3/7 = -0.\overline{428571}$

17.3 Converting Decimal Numbers to Fractions:

1. Write the decimal numbers as fractions:

(a) 0.0235   (b) 0.1111215   (c) 0.999999

Solution:

    (a) $0.0235 = 235/10000$

    (b) $0.1111215 = 1111215/10000000$

    (c) $0.999999 = 999999/1000000$

1. Write the following decimal numbers as fractions:

    (a) $0.\overline{23}$ (b) $0.\overline{73}$ (c) $0.\overline{8}$ (c) $0.\overline{101}$ (e) $0.\overline{3}$

    (g) 23.468 (h) 2.0078 (i) $0.24\overline{679852}$

Solution:

    (a) $0.\overline{23} = 23/99$ (b) $0.\overline{73} = 73/99$ (c) $0.\overline{8} = 8/9$ (d) $0.\overline{101} = 101/999$

    (e) $0.\overline{3} = 3/9$ (g) $23.468 = 23468/1000$ (h) $2.0078 = 20078/10000$

1. $0.24\overline{679852} = 0.246 + 0.0007985279852... = 246/1000 + 0.7985279852...\ 246/1000$

    $+ 79852/99999 =$

    $[(246)99999]/[(1000)(99999)] + [(79852)(1000)]/[(1000)(99999)] =$

    $[(246)(99999) + (79852)(1000)]/[(1000)(99999)] = [24599754 + 79852000]/99999000 =$

    $104,451,754/99,999,000$

3. Write the following decimal numbers as a decimal number $0.a_1a_2 ... a_n$:

    (a) $0.\overline{7323} + 0.\overline{0083}$ (b) $0.\overline{7323} - 0.\overline{0083}$

Solution:

    (a) $0.\overline{7323} + 0.\overline{0083} = 0.\overline{7406}$

    (b) $0.\overline{7323} - 0.\overline{0083} = 0.\overline{7240}$

17.4 Converting Fractions to Decimal Numbers:

1. Convert the following fractions to decimal: $4/9$

Solution:

Step 1:

    $4/9 = a_1/10 + a_2/10^2 + a_3/10^3 + a_4/10^4 + a_5/10^5 + a_6/10^6 + a_7/10^7 + ...$

    $10(4/9) = 40/9 = (36 + 4)/9 = 4 + 4/9 = a_1 + a_2/10^1 + a_3/10^2 + a_4/10^3 + a_5/10^4 +$

    $a_6/10^5 + a_7/10^6 + ...$

    $a_1 = 4$

Step 2:

$$4/9 = a_2/10^1 + a_3/10^2 + a_4/10^3 + a_5/10^4 + a_6/10^5 + a_7/10^6 + \ldots$$

$$10(4/9) = 40/9 = 4 + 4/9 = a_2 + a_3/10^1 + a_4/10^2 + a_5/10^3 + a_6/10^4 + a_7/10^5 + \ldots$$

$$a_2 = 4$$

$$4/9 = a_3/10^1 + a_4/10^2 + a_5/10^3 + a_6/10^4 + a_7/10^5 + \ldots$$

End of cycle: $4/9 = 0.44444444\ldots = 0.\overline{4}$

3. 67/5

Solution:

$$67/5 = (65 + 2)/5 = 13 + 2/5 = 13.4$$

17.5 Representation of Decimal Numbers

1. Convert the following into integer form:

(a) $281.\overline{9}$ (b) $41256.\overline{9}$

Solutions:

(a) 282   (b) 41257

3. Explain why we cannot convert, using our above algorithm, the following number into a fraction:

0.272772777277772777772...

From your analysis, does such a number exist?

Solutions:

All rational numbers N/M when dividing integer M into N at most can have a finite number of distinct numbers which will repeat over and over again.

0.272772777277772777772...

This number exists but it is not a rational number.

17.6 Definition of Decimal and Fractions

1. Write the following numbers in expanded form:

   (a) 0.231120_4 (b) 0.11111101_2 (c) 0.232323_8 (d) $0.ABC2_{16}$

Solutions

   (a) $0.231120_4 = 2/10_4 + 3/10_4^2 + 1/10_4^3 + 1/10_4^4 + 2/10_4^5 + 0/10^6$

   (b) $0.11111101_2 = 1/10_2 + 1/10_2^2 + 1/10_2^3 + 1/10_2^4 + 1/10_2^5 + 1/10_2^6 + 0/10_2^7 + 1/10_2^8$

   (c) $0.232323_8 = 2/10_8 + 3/10_8^2 + 2/10_8^3 + 3/10_8^4 + 2/10_8^5 + 3/10_8^6$

   (d) $0.ABC2_{16} = A/10_{16} + B/10_{16}^2 + C/10_{16}^3 + 2/10_{16}^4$

17.7 Converting Decimal Numbers Between The base 10 and an Arbitrary Base

1. Convert the following numbers to the base 10:

Solutions:

   (a) $0.231120_4 \mid 2/4 + 3/4^2 + 1/4^3 + 1/4^4 + 2/4^5$

   (b) $0.11111101_2 \mid 1/2 + 1/2^2 + 1/2^3 + 1/2^4 + 1/2^5 + 1/2^6 + 1/2^8$

   (c) $0.232323_8 \mid 2/8 + 3/8^2 + 2/8^3 + 3/8^4 + 2/8^5 + 3/8^6$

   (d) $0.ABC2_{16} \mid 10/16 + 11/16^2 + 12/16^3 + 2/16^4$

Converting infinite decimal numbers in any base b to its corresponding decimal numbers in the base 10:

1. Convert the following numbers to the base 10:

Solutions:

   (a) $0.\overline{6}_8 = 6_8/(108 - 1)_8 \Rightarrow 6_{10}/(8 - 1)_{10} = 6_{10}/7_{10}$

   (b) $0.\overline{01001}_2 = 1001_2/(10^5_2 - 1)_2 \Rightarrow 9_{10}/(2^5_{10} - 1)_{10} = 9_{10}/31_{10}$

   (c) $0.\overline{A5C}_{16} = A5C_2/(10^3_{16} - 1)_{16} \Rightarrow 2652_{10}/(4096_{10} - 1)_{10} = 2652_{10}/4095_{10}$

   (d) $0.\overline{00365}_8 = 365_8/(10^5_8 - 1)_8 \Rightarrow 245_{10}/(8^5 - 1)_{10} = 245_{10}/(32767)_{10}$

Converting finite decimal numbers in the base 10 to its corresponding decimal numbers in any base b:

Checking out computation.

1. Convert 0.6_{10} to the

    (a) base 2   (b) base 4   (c) base 8   (d) base 16

Solutions:

    (a) base 2

$$0.6 = a_1/2 + a_2/2^2 + \ldots$$

$$2(0.6) = 1.2 = a_1 + a_2/2 + a_3/2^2 + \ldots$$

$$a_1 = 1$$

$$0.2 = a_2/2 + a_3/2^2 + a_4/2^3 + \ldots$$

$$2(0.2) = 0.4 = a_2 + a_3/2 + a_4/2^2 + \ldots$$

$$a_2 = 0$$

$$0.4 = a_3/2 + a_4/2^2 + a_5/2^3 + a_6/2^4 + \ldots\ldots$$

$$2(0.4) = 0.8 = a_3 + a_4/2 + a_5/2^2 + a_7/2^3 + \ldots\ldots$$

$$a_3 = 0$$

$$0.8 = a_4/2 + a_5/2^2 + a_6/2^3 + \ldots\ldots$$

$$2(0.8) = 1.6 = a_5 + a_6/2 + a_7/2^2 + \ldots\ldots$$

$$a_5 = 1$$

$$0.6 = + a_6/2 + a_7/2^2 + \ldots\ldots$$

$$0.6 \mid 0.\overline{1100}_2$$

    (b) base 4

$$0.6 = a_1/4 + a_2/4^2 + \ldots$$

$$4(0.6) = 2.4 = a_1 + a_2/4 + a_3/4^2 + \ldots$$

$$2.4 = a_1 + a_2/4 + a_3/4^2 + \ldots$$

$a_1 = 2$

$0.4 = a_2/4 + a_3/4^2 + .$

$4(0.4) = 1.6 = a_2 + a_3/4 + \ldots$

$a_2 = 1$

$0.6 = a_3/4 + \ldots$

$0.6 \Rightarrow 0.\overline{21}_4$

(c) base 8

$0.6 = a_1/8 + a_2/8^2 + \ldots$

$8(0.6) = 4.8 = a_1 + a_2/8 + a_3//8^2 + \ldots$

$a_1 = 4$

$0.8 = + a_2/8 + a_3//8^2 + \ldots$

$8(0.8) = 6.4 = a_2 + a_3/8 + \ldots$

$a_2 = 6$

$8(0.4) = 3.2 = a_3 + a_4/8 \ldots$

$a_3 = 3$

$0.2 = a_4/8 + a_5/8^2 \ldots$

$8(0.2) = 1.6 = a_4 + a_5/8 \ldots$

$0.6 \mid 0.\overline{463}_8$

(d) base 16

$0.6 = a_1/16 + a_2/16^2 + \ldots$

$16(0.6) = 9.6 = a_1 + a_2/16 + a_3/16^2 \ldots$

$a_1 = 9$

$0.6 = a_2/16 + a_3/16^2 \ldots$

$0.6 \mid 0.\overline{9}_{16}$

Converting infinite decimal numbers in the base 10 to its corresponding decimal numbers in any base b:

1. Convert: $0.\overline{1}_{10}$ to base 5

Solution:

base 5

$$0.\overline{1}_{10} = 1/9 = a_1/5 + a_2/5^2 + a_3/5^3 + \ldots$$

$$5(1/9) = 5/9 = a_1 + a_2/5 + a_3/5^2 + a_4/5^3 \ldots$$

$$a_1 = 0$$

$$5/9 = a_2/5 + a_3/5^2 + a_4/5^3 \ldots$$

$$5(5/9) = 25/9 = (18 + 7)/9 = 2 + 7/9 = a_2 + a_3/5 + a_4/5^2 + a_5/5^3 \ldots$$

$$a_2 = 2$$

$$7/9 = a_3/5 + a_4/5^2 + a_5/5^3 \ldots$$

$$5(7/9) = 35/9 = (27 + 8)/9 = 3 + 8/9 = a_3 + a_4/5 + a_5/5^2 \ldots$$

$$a_3 = 3$$

$$8/9 = a_4/5 + a_5/5^2 + a_5/5^3 \ldots$$

$$5(8/9) = 40/9 = (36+4)/9 = 4+4/9 = a_4 + a_5/5 + a_6/5^2 \ldots$$

$$a_4 = 4$$

$$4/9 = a_0/5 + a_6/5^2 + \ldots$$

$$5(4/9) = 20/9 = (18 + 2)/9 = 2 + 2/9 = a_5 + a_6/5^2 \ldots$$

$$a_5 = 2$$

$$2/9 = a_6/5 + a_7/5^2 \ldots$$

$$5(2/9) = 10/9 = 1 + 1/9 = a_6 + a_7/5 \ldots$$

$$a_6 = 1$$

$$1/9 = a_7/5 + \ldots$$

$$0.\overline{1}_{10} => \overline{023421}_5$$

CHECK:

$$0.\overline{023421}_5 = \frac{\overline{23421}_5}{444444_5} => \frac{1736_{10}}{15620_{10}} = 0.\overline{1}_{10}$$

17.8 Converting Decimal Numbers In a Given Base To Fractions In The Same Base

1. Write the decimal numbers as fractions:

(a) 0.0235_8 (b) 0.110111_2 (c) 0.999999_{16}

Solutions:

(a) $0.0235_8 = 235_8/10000_8$

(b) $0.110111_2 = 110111_2/1000000_2$

(c) $0.999999_{16} = 999999_{16}/1000000_{16}$

1. Write the decimal numbers as fractions in the same base:

Solutions:

(a) $0.\overline{0101}_2 = 101_2/(10000_2 - 1) = 101_2/1111_2$

(b) $0.\overline{000723}_8 = 723_8/(1000000_8 - 1) = 723_8/777777_8$

(c) $0235.\overline{7237}_8 = 235 + 7237_8/(10000_8 - 1) = 235 + 7237/777777_8$

(d) $02C5.\overline{7239}_{16} = 2C5_{16} + 7239_{16}/(10000_{16} - 1) = 2C5_{16} + 7239_{16}/FFFF_{16}$

17.9 Converting Numbers Between Different Bases
Converting a finite decimal number less than one

1. Using this quick conversion, convert the following binary numbers to hexadecimal:

(a) 0.011010101_2 (b) 0.000111101_2

Solutions:

(a) $0.0110\ 1010\ 1000_2 \mid 0.6A8_{16}$

(b) $0.0001\ 1111\ 0100_2 \mid 0.114_{16}$

3. In the example above, we converted $0.110111011_2 \mid 0.DEC_{16}$.

Solution:

$0.110111011_2 \Rightarrow 0.3564_{10} \Rightarrow 0.DEC_{16}$.

5. Convert (a) 0.110111011_2 to the base 8. (b) Convert 0.23461_8 to the base 2.

Solutions:

(a) 0.110111011_2 to the base 8. $\Rightarrow 673_8$

(b) Convert 0.23461_8 to the base 2. $\Rightarrow 100111001100001_8$

Converting an infinite decimal number less than one

1. Convert $0.\overline{1011}_2$ to a hexadecimal number. :

Solution:

3. Convert $0.\overline{11011}_2$ to hexadecimal: .

Solution:

$$0.\overline{11011}_2 = 0.1101\ 1110\ 1111\ 0111\ 1011\ .... \Rightarrow 0.\overline{DEFB}_{16}$$

5. Explain why we cannot convert, using our above algorithm, the following number into a fraction:

0.272772777277772777772...

Solution:

It is not a rational number since it is not made up of a finite cycle of digits.

18.1 Representation of Decimal Numbers

1. Write the following in scientific and floating point representation:

0.00234 45.356 - 32

Solutions:

$0.00234 = 234*10^{-5}$

$0.00234 =$ 2.34 E - 3

$45.356 = 45356*10^{-3}$

$45.356 = 4.5356E1$

$- 32 = - 32*10^{0}$

$-32 = -32E0$

18.2 Arithmetic Operations Using Scientific Representation

Multiplication

1. Write the following using scientific representation.

Solutions:

$575.345*0.00234 = (- 575345*10^{-3})*(234*10^{-5}) = (- 575345)*(234)*10^{-8} =$

$= 134630730*10^{-8}$

$678*0.03*2.135 = (678*10^{0})*(3*10^{-2})*(2135*10^{-3}) = (678)*(3)*(2135)*10^{-5} =$

$= 42590*10^{-5}$

$0.0034*0.221 = (34*10^{-4})*(221*10^{-3})$

Addition and Subtraction

1. - 575.345 + 0.00234   678 + 0.03 + 2.135   0.0034 - 0.221

Solutions:

$-575.345 + 0.00234 = -575345 * 10^{-3} + 234 * 10^{-5} = -57534500 * 10^{-5} + 234 * 10^{-5} =$

$= (-57534500 + 234) *10^{-5} = -57534266 * 10^{-5}$

$678 + 0.03 + 2.135 = 678 * 10^{0} + 3 * 10^{-2} + 2135 * 10^{-3} =$

$678000 * 10^{-3} + 30 * 10^{-3} + 2135 * 10^{-3} = (678000 + 30 + 2135) * 10^{-3} = 680165 * 10^{-3}$

$0.0034 - 0.221 = 34 * 10^{-4} - 221 * 10^{-3} = 34 * 10^{-4} - 2210 * 10^{-4} = (34 - 2210) * 10^{-4}$

$= -2176 * 10^{-4}$

Long Division

1. Write the following in a scientific notation form.

   a. 5/7   b. 0.23/0.035

2. Using the above algorithm, convert 1/7 to a 7 place decimal representation.

3. Rewrite the above program in pseudo-code using a while statement. From this program write an assembly language.

18.3 80X86 Floating-Point Architecture

1. What is the largest value (base 10) that can be stored in ST(k)?

Solution:

$2^{80} = 1208925819614629174706175$

Miscellaneous floating point instructions

1. Write an assembly program to compute the sum:

$1^2 + 1/2^2 + 1/3^2 + 1/4^2 + 1/5^2 + 1/6^2.$

Solution:

PSEUDO CODE	FP AL
ONE:= 1.0	one real4 1.0
N:= 1.0	n real4 1.0
K:= 1	k byte 1
Q:= 1.0	q real4 1.0
SUM:= 0	sum real4 0
WHILE K ≤ 6	while: cmp k, 6 jg end
BEGIN	begin
ST:= 1.0	fld n
ST:= 1.0/N	fdiv n
ST:= ST/N	fdiv n
Q:= ST	fst q
ST:= SUM	fld sum
ST:= ST + Q	fadd q
SUM:= ST	fst sum
N:=N + 1.0	fld n fadd one fst n

K:= K + 1	mov eax, k
	add eax, 1
	mov k, eax

END	jmp while end:

Interchanging integer and floating point numbers.

3. It can be shown that $1/4 = 1/3 - 1/3^2 + 1/3^3 - 1/3^4 + ...$

Write an AL algorithm to find for a given n the sum $= 1/3 - 1/3^2 + 1/3^3 - 1/3^4 + ... \pm 1/3^n$

Solution:

PSEUDO CODE	FP AL
SUM:= 2/3	sum real4 0
ONE:= 1.0	one real4 1.0
TWO:= 2.0	two real 2.0
THREE:= 3.0	three real 3.0
MINUSONE:= -1	N byte n
N:= n	k byte 2
K:= 2	minusone real4 -1.0
M- O- D-T:= 0	minusonedivthree real4 0
CE := 0	CE real4 0
ST:= TWO	fld two
ST:= ST /THREE	fdiv three
SUM:= ST	fst sum
ST:= MINUS-ONE	fld minusone
ST:= ST/THREE	fdiv three
M-O-D-T:=ST	fst minusonedivthree
CE:= ST	fst ce
WHILE K ≤ n	while: cmp k , n jg end
ST:= CE	fld ce

ST:= ST*M-O-D-T	fmul minusonedivthree
CE:= ST	fst ce
ST:= SUM	fld sum
8ST:=ST + CE	fadd ce
SUM:= ST EAX:=K	fst sum mov eax, k
EAX:= EAX + I	add eax, I
K:= EAX	mov k, eax
END	jmp while end:

19.1 The control register

Exercise:

1. Write a AL program that will perform the following:

   1. Store in a variable the decimal representation of the number 1/7

   2. Round the number to 10 places of accuracy.

Solution:

PSEUDO-CODE	FP AL
ZERO:= 0	zero word 0
ONE:= 1.0	one real4 1.0
TEN:= 10	Ten word 10
SEVEN:= 7.0	seven real4 7.0
ST:= ONE	fld one
ST:= ST/SEVEN	fidiv seven
ST:= ST*10	fmul ten
Control register:= ZERO	fldew zero
ST:- ST/TEN	fidiv ten

3. It can be shown that $1 + 2 + ... + N = N(N + 1)/2$.

Write an AL algorithm that will compute and store the number: $1.0 + 2.0 + ... + N.0$ and compute, if any, the error $|(1.0 + 2.0 + ... + N.0) - N.0(N.0 + 1.0)/2.0|$.

Solution

PSEUDO CODE	FP AL
ONE: = 1.0	one real4 1.0
N:= n.0	n real4 n.0
K := 1.0	k real4 1.0
WHILE K ≤ n.0	
ST:= ST + K	
END	
ERROR:= |ST - N*(N+ 1)/2|	

20.2 The 80x86 Stack

Exercise:

1. Complete the table. Use only hexadecimal numbers.

AL CODE	AX	STACK											
mov ax, 23deh													
push ax													
mov ax, 3425													
push ax													
mov ax, 7f7ah													
push eax													

Solution:

AL CODE	AX	STACK											
mov ax, 23deh	23dc												
push ax	23dc	23	dc										
mov ax, 3425	0d61	23	dc										
push ax	0d61	0d	61	23	dc								
mov ax, 7f7ah	717a	0d	61	23	dc								
push eax	717a	71	7a	0d	61	23	dc						

The pop instruction

Exercise:

1. Store in a stack the sequence 1,2,...,100.

Solution:

Pseudo - Code	AL
N:= 100	n byte 100
K:= 1	k byte 1
WHILE K ≤ N	while: cmp k,n ja end
EAX:=K	mov eax,k
PUSH EAX	push eax
EAX:= EAX + 1	add eax, 1
K:= EAX	mov k,eax
END	jmp while end:

21.2 Storing Strings

1. Convert the following strings to its ASCII codes:

ASSEMBLY CODE	EAX			
mov eax, '+ YZ'				
mov eax, '/'				
mov eax, '* %'				

Solution:

ASSEMBLY CODE	EAX			
mov eax, '+ YZ'	2B	20	59	5A
mov eax, '/'				2F
mov eax, '* %'		2A	20	25

The string variables:

1. Complete the following tables:

Hamlet BYTE 'Brevity is the soul of wit'

Solution:

Hamlet BYTE 'Brevity is the soul of wit'

42	72	65	76	69	74	79	20	69	73
74	68	65	20	73	6F	75	6C	20	6F
66	20	77	69	74					

21.2

1. Hamlet DWORD 'To be or not to be'

Write a AL program that will move the string in variable Hamlet to the variable Shakespeare DWORD ?

Solution:

ASSEMBLY LANGUAGE PROGRAM
Hamlet dword 5 dup 'To be or not to be'
Shakespeare dword 5 dup ?
lea esi, Hamlet
lea edi, Shakespeare
Movsd
Movsd
Movsd
Movsd
Movsd

The rep instruction

Exercises:

1. Complete the table below:

AL CODE	ECX	Y (DWords in ASCIIsymbols)				X (DWords in ASCIIsymbols)			
x dword 4 dup (?)									
Y dword '123456789abcde'									
mov ecx, 4									

lea esi, y										
lea edi, x										
rep movsd										

Solution:

AL CODE	ECX	Y (DWords in ASCII symbols)	X			
x dword 4 dup (?)						
Y dword '1234'		31323334				
mov ecx, 4	4	31323334				
lea esi, y	4	31323334				
lea edi, x	4	31323334				
rep movsd	0	31323334	31323334	31323334	31323334	31323334

The scas instruction

Exercise:

1. Write a program that will find the position location of "f" in the of the string 'I live in California'

Solution:

```
x dword 20 dup 'I live in California'

mov al, 'f'

lea edi, x

mov ecx, 20

mov eax, ecx

repne scasb

sub eax, ecx
```

22.1 Retrieving strings stored in the variable

Exercises:

1. Write a AL program that will retrieve the string: 'Brevity is the soul of wit' from the variable

SHAKESPEARE word 'Brevity is the soul of wit'

Solution:

```
Shakespeare word 'Brevity is the soul of wit'
lea ebx,Shakespeare
mov ax,[Shakespeare]
add ebx,2
mov ax,[Shakespeare]
add ebx,2
mov ax,[Shakespeare]
add ebx,2
mov ax,[Shakespeare]
add ebx,2
mov ax,[Shakespeare]
add ebx,2
mov ax,[Shakespeare]
add ebx,2
mov ax,[Shakespeare]
add ebx,2
mov ax,[Shakespeare]
add ebx,2
mov ax,[Shakespeare]
add ebx,2
mov ax,[Shakespeare]
add ebx,2
mov ax,[Shakespeare]
add ebx,2
mov ax,[Shakespeare]
add ebx,2
mov ax,[Shakespeare]
```

22.2 Creating and storing a one dimensional string array into the dup(?) directive.

Exercises:

1. Write a AL program that will retrieve the string 'Brevity is the soul of wit' from the variable

   SHAKESPEARE byte 'Brevity is the soul of wit' and copy it into the variable

   HAMLET byte 100 dup(?)

Solution:

Shakespeare word 'Brevity is the soul of wit'
Hamlet word?

lea ebx, Shakespeare
lea ecx, Hamlet

mov ax, [Shakespeare]
add ebx, 2
mov [ecx], ax
add ecx, 2
mov ax, [Shakespeare]
mov [ecx], ax
add ecx, 2
add ebx, 2
mov ax, [Shakespeare]
mov [ecx], ax
add ecx, 2
add ebx, 2
mov ax, [Shakespeare]
mov [ecx], ax
add ecx, 2
add ebx, 2
mov ax, [Shakespeare]
mov [ecx], ax
add ecx, 2
add ebx, 2
mov ax, [Shakespeare]
mov [ecx], ax

```
add ecx, 2
add ebx, 2
mov ax, [Shakespeare]
mov [ecx], ax
add ecx, 2
add ebx, 2
mov ax, [Shakespeare]
mov [ecx], ax
add ecx, 2
add ecx, 2
mov [ecx], ax
add ecx, 2
add ebx, 2
mov ax, [Shakespeare]
mov [ecx], ax
add ecx, 2
add ebx, 2
mov ax, [Shakespeare]
mov [ecx], ax
add ecx, 2
add ebx, 2
mov ax, [Shakespeare]
mov [ecx], ax
add ecx, 2
add ebx, 2
mov ax, [Shakespeare]
mov [ecx], ax
```

INDEX